The Old English *Rune Poe*

MCMASTER OLD ENGLISH STUDIES AND TEXTS 2

Alvin A. Lee (General Editor)

Laurel Braswell

Maureen Halsall

Prudence Tracy (University of Toronto Press)

The Old English *Rune Poem*: a critical edition

MAUREEN HALSALL

UNIVERSITY OF TORONTO PRESS

Toronto Buffalo London

© University of Toronto Press 1981
Toronto Buffalo London

Reprinted in paperback 2016

ISBN 978-0-8020-5477-7 (cloth)
ISBN 978-1-4875-9268-4 (paper)

Canadian Cataloguing in Publication Data

Halsall, Maureen, 1934–
    The Old English rune poem: a critical edition
    (McMaster Old English studies and texts; 2)
    Old English text with parallel English translation.
    Bibliography
    ISBN 978-0-8020-5477-7 (bound)   ISBN 978-1-4875-9268-4 (pbk.)
    1. Old English rune poem – Criticism and inter-
    pretation. 2. Runes. I. Title: The Old English
    rune poem: a critical edition. II. Title: Old
    English rune poem. III. Series.
    PR1749.042H34 1981   829.1   C81-094379-4

TO MY MOTHER

Contents

Preface

Reading the Old English *Rune Poem* offers challenges that only a very thorough critical edition can help the student to meet. To date, no published edition has attempted to deal fully with the poem as literature, far less to supply the runic background necessary for an understanding of the raw materials with which the poet was working. In an effort to remedy these deficiencies, the present edition begins in the first section of the introduction by furnishing the essential runic context for the poem in what amounts to a miniature handbook on the origin, development, and uses of runes, before proceeding to the close examination of text, language, literary sources, style, and themes normal in any critical edition. Following the text and translation of the poem proper, the very full explanatory notes also pay especial attention to the background of each individual rune and rune name, and the appendixes provide analogous material to assist in setting the achievement of the poet into the runic context.

Since many of the sources necessary for an accurate assessment of the Old English *Rune Poem* are written in foreign or dead languages, Modern English translations have been supplied throughout, in order to ensure that this unjustly neglected poem will be accessible, not merely to professional medievalists, but also to undergraduates and to interested members of the general reading public.

I wish to record my gratitude to McMaster University and to the Canada Council for enabling me to take a year's leave in which to complete this edition. Also my thanks are due to the British Library for permission to reproduce the photograph of page 135 from George Hickes' *Thesaurus* which precedes the edited text of the Old English *Rune Poem*. Publication of this book is made possible by a grant from the Canadian Federation for the Humanities, using funds provided by the Social Sciences and Humanities Research Council of Canada, as well as by grants from McMaster University and from the Subsidized Publications fund of the University of Toronto Press.

Introduction

Runes and their Use

The ostensible purpose of the Old English *Rune Poem* was to give
definitions in verse for twenty-nine of the runic symbols known and
used by the Anglo-Saxons. Its author's creative imagination could
not function in total freedom, however, since the order of his stanzas
and the basic core of meaning around which each stanza was built
were dictated by longstanding runic tradition. Like the North Semitic
consonant series (⟨ *aleph* (ox), ⟨ *beth* (house), ⟨ *gimel* (camel),
△*daleth* (door), etc) from which the Old English runes as well as the
Roman letters I am using now are ultimately derived, the so-called
futhorc was characterized both by a fixed sequence of symbols and by
a parallel sequence of meaningful words that were firmly attached to
those symbols and recited to assist in their memorization.[1] In the
same way that the term *alphabet* is based on the Greek versions
(*alpha, beta*) of the mnemonic names for the first two North Semitic
letters, so the term *futhorc* reflects the equally strong traditional
order of the rune sequence, being based on the first six Old English
runic symbols ᚠ · ᚢ · ᚦ · ᚠ · ᚱ · ᚻ and representing the initial sounds
of their mnemonic names: *feoh, ūr, ðorn*, (ie, *thorn*), *ōs, rād, čēn*.
Although some of the twenty-nine runes defined by the poet appear to
have been invented in England after the Anglo-Saxon invasions,[2] the
majority boast a more ancient lineage and can be traced back in
relatively unaltered form to the continental Germanic homeland.[3]
Similarly, many of the names found glossing the runes in the Old
English *Rune Poem* do not appear to be of insular origin, since cognate
names are found in parallel contexts in North Germanic sources.[4] As
might be expected in the course of centuries of transmission, which
included the migration of the Angles, Jutes, and Saxons to a new

country and their conversion to a new religion, some of the rune forms were corrupted[5] and some of the original rune names became obscure or were even replaced.[6] In view of these facts and in order to facilitate a proper understanding of what the author of the Old English *Rune Poem* has made of his raw material, it seems useful to begin by reconstructing briefly in this introduction some of the relevant runic background, which otherwise must be pieced together from widely scattered sources.

THE ORIGIN OF RUNES

Since Germanic society long remained relatively unsophisticated in comparison to the Mediterranean world, it had little need for a business or literary script and seems to have managed without any letters at all until early in the Christian era. The only symbols in use among the tribes of the Germanic north were pictorial: the so-called *hällristningar* (rock-carvings), which obviously had cultic significance. Extant examples of these pre-runic symbols include representations of men and animals, parts of the human body, and various objects, such as axes, arrows, and ships; most prominent of all are the many representations of the sun, including the famous swastika.[7] From the late second century AD, however, a small but increasing number of runic inscriptions began to appear on objects of metal, stone, and bone (and even occasionally on normally perishable wood) found at archaeological sites throughout the Germanic sphere, but mainly among the nations bordering on the Baltic Sea. These inscriptions employ twenty-four hitherto unknown symbols:

ᚠ·ᚢ·ᚦ·ᚨ·ᚱ·ᚲ·ᚷ·ᚹ : ᚺ·ᚾ·ᛁ·ᛃ· ᛇ·ᛈ·ᛉ·ᛊ : ᛏ·ᛒ·ᛖ·ᛗ·ᛚ·ᛜ·ᛞ·ᛟ

representing the sound values *f, u, th, a, r, k, g, w; h, n, i, j, ē* (a sound between *i* and *e*), *p, z* (a sound between *z* and *r*), *s; t, b, e, m, l, ng, d, o* and called, after the values of the first six symbols, the Common Germanic *futhark*.[8]

The angular shape characteristic of runes, both in these early inscriptions and throughout the later development of the *futhark*, betrays the fact that they never were intended for writing as we understand it. Each symbol is composed of straight lines: some vertical, so that they would cut across a grained surface at right angles;

others transverse, running at about a forty-five degree angle to the
verticals and therefore equally distinguishable from any underlying
grain. Clearly, runes are epigraphical rather than cursive forms,
probably designed for carving on objects of wood. Such objects may
have included the slices from a fruit-tree branch on which Tacitus
described first century Germanic augurers as making marks of some
kind for use in lot-casting.[9] Certainly they did include the ashwood
tablets or smoothed sticks on which in the sixth century Venantius
Fortunatus suggested that a delinquent correspondent might contrive to send a runic message in default of more orthodox writing
materials.[10]

The traditional order of the Common Germanic *futhark* is first
recorded in full on a gravestone of the late fourth or early fifth century
found at Kylver on the island of Gotland in Sweden.[11] In mutilated
form it reappears in inscriptions on a number of sixth century objects,
including a silver brooch (or fibula) found at Charnay in France,[12] a
stone pillar found at Breza in Yugoslavia,[13] and a couple of gold
medallions (or bracteates) found at Vadstena[14] and Grumpan[15] in
Sweden. The Swedish bracteates furnish early examples of two long-
lived but puzzling aspects of the Germanic *futhark*: its distinctive
order, which cannot be paralleled in other letter-sequences,[16] and its
frequent division for some unexplained reason into three equal
groups of eight runes;[17] both constitute traditions that must have
been considered significant features of runic lore, since they survived
the linguistic changes which reduced the *futhark*'s later Norse descendant to sixteen runes and expanded its English descendant to as
many as thirty-three runes.

A mere glance would reveal to any novice the fact that the symbols
of the Germanic *futhark* must be modelled on some version of the
alphabet. For indisputable examples of this relationship, compare the
following runic and Roman characters: ᚠ:F, ᚦ:D, ᚱ:R, ᚲ:C, ᚺ:H,
ᛁ:I, ᛋ:S, ᛏ:T, ᛗ:M, and ᛒ:B; and also, when inverted, ᚢ:U and
ᛚ:L. There have been many attempts to identify the exact source of
the *futhark*, with most early runologists opting for either the Greek[18]
or Latin[19] alphabets; but the majority of modern runologists agree
that the best formal parallels are provided by a group of letter-series
based on the Etruscan alphabet that were in use among sub-alpine
tribes in Northern Italy from the fifth century BC until the first century AD, when they were engulfed by the Roman alphabet and became

extinct.[20] In addition to certain letter-forms, runic inscriptions share with their North Italic counterparts a number of distinctive characteristics: variability in the direction of individual letters and even of entire texts, simplification of double consonants, punctuation by means of raised dots or bars, and certain types of content, such as the common maker's formula 'X (Name) made me' or the relatively frequent appearance of the letter-sequence itself, that is, the *futhark* or alphabet alone, without any other message. The agency and route by which North Italic letters were adapted to the needs of Germanic phonology and reached the Baltic are still matters for speculation. Suffice it to say, however, that little doubt now remains regarding the runes' place of origin.[21]

Germanic tradition shows no awareness of any connection between the *futhark* and the alphabet. For the northern imagination, as in the superstitious fears of other illiterate people, letters seem to have possessed mana; thus the *Poetic Edda* reiterates a common attitude in referring to runes as *reginkunnom* (of divine origin).[22] The source of the *futhark* was shrouded in mystery, or even thought to be supernatural, as when the high god of the Æsir, Odin, describes in *Hávamál* the sufferings that he endured upon the world-tree Yggdrasil in bringing the knowledge of runes into the realms of gods and men:

Veit ek at ek hekk   vindga meiði á
  nætr allar nío,
geiri undaðr   ok gefinn Óðni,
  sjálfr sjálfom mér,
á þeim meiði,   er manngi veit
  hvers hann af rótom renn.

Við hleifi mik sældo   né við hornigi;
  nýsta ek niðr:
nam ek upp rúnar,   œpandi nam:
  fell ek aptr þaðan.

(I know that I hung on the windswept tree for nine whole nights, pierced by the spear and given to Odin, myself given to myself, on that tree, whose roots no man can trace. They refreshed me neither with bread nor with drink from the horn; I peered down; I took up runes, howling I took them up; and then fell back.)[23]

THE WORD 'RUNE'

It seems very much in keeping with the attitudes expressed in the quotations from the eddic *Hávamál* above that the term chosen for the *futhark* symbols should be one connoting mystery and secrecy. The root *rūn-* appears throughout the recorded Germanic languages, not merely in words for 'runic character' (such as Old English *rūnstæf*, Danish *rune*, Swedish *runa*, and the Old Norse plural *rúnar*), but also in nouns meaning 'secret, private consultation' (such as Old English *rūn*, Old High German *rûna*, Old Icelandic *rúnar*, and Gothic *garūni*) and in cognate verbs meaning 'to whisper' (such as Old English *rūnian*, Old Saxon *rūnon*, and Old High German *rûnen*). It even appears in words translating μνστήριον and *mysterium*, the Greek and Latin terms for 'divine (ie, Christian) mystery,' in Old English, Gothic, and Old High German religious texts.[24]

USES OF RUNES

In view of the penumbra of mystery surrounding the origin of the *futhark* and the word 'rune,' it is important to know the actual uses to which runes were put, as exemplified both by extant inscriptions and by written accounts of their employment.

Inscriptions in the Common Germanic Futhark

The earliest Germanic inscriptions are very brief, often cryptic, and sometimes even completely untranslatable.[25] Many consist largely or wholly of names: in some cases apparently the name of the owner of an object, in others the name of the maker or of the person who inscribed the runes, in still others a dedicatory or magical name, as on the second century spear-head found in a grave at Øvre Stabu in Norway, which bears the word ᚱ ᚨ ᚢ ᚾ ᛁ ᛃ ᚨ *raunija* (assayer).[26] All or part of the content of a number of early inscriptions is made up of the runes themselves, whether the full *futhark* sequence in traditional order[27] or individual runes divorced from any intelligible context and sometimes repeated in groups, as on the fifth or sixth century amulet found at Lindholm in Sweden, where the rune ᚨ (*a*) occurs eight times in succession and the runes ᚱ and ᛏ and ᛏ (*r* and *n* and *t*) three times in succession.[28] It is difficult to determine what kind of message runes used in this way were intended to convey; certainly they are not employed like Roman letters to spell out words. Possibly the runes in these cryptic inscriptions may have stood for well known rune names, the ancestors of the names by which they were later to be called in Scandinavia and England, or even as abbreviations for other words beginning with the same sounds as those names.[29] It is also not inconceivable that they had some quite different significance, similar to the cult symbolism of pre-runic *hällristningar* with which runes are sometimes found in close association on the same object.[30]

One striking aspect of all the uses of the Germanic *futhark* outlined above is their essentially private character. Unlike Roman inscriptions, which seem designed to inform the world at large about laws enacted, victories won, and the reputations of the eminent dead, early runic inscriptions show astonishingly little concern to instruct the passing reader. Instead, they appear to form part of personally significant acts and to be means of asserting power (as owner, creator, runemaster, weaver of spells, or fulfiller of burial rituals). This impression of privacy is emphasized in the case of certain runic inscriptions which are so far removed from any purpose of public communication as to be buried inside graves, like the *futhark* on the Kylver stone, where only the dead or whatever supernatural beings were thought to visit or inhabit the last resting places of men might peruse the runes and learn their message.[31]

The Reduced Norse Futhạrk

The bulk of extant runic inscriptions are in the later Norse *futhạrk*,[32] a reduced and somewhat modified version of the original Germanic *futhark*, which made its appearance in Denmark about the beginning of the ninth century and, with some variations and simplifications, spread from there to Sweden and Norway and subsequently to all the far-flung places where the Vikings travelled to pillage or to explore and settle.[33] This *futhạrk* consisted of only sixteen symbols:

ᚠ·ᚢ·ᚦ·ᚠ·ᚱ·ᚴ : ᚼ·ᚾ·ᛁ·ᛁ·ᚼ : ᛏ·ᛒ·ᛘ·ᛚ·ᛦ

which, among other related and undifferentiated sounds, represented basically the values: *f, u, th, ạ,* (nasalized *a*), *r, k; h, n, i, a, s; t, b, m, l,* and *R* (a strongly palatalized *r* derived from Germanic *z*).[34] The slight change in the spelling of the name for the rune sequence by the addition of a mark of nasalization under the fourth letter indicates one of many changes in phonology from primitive Germanic to North Germanic of the Viking age which the reduced Norse *futhǫrk* was only very imperfectly equipped to reflect.

An appreciable number of the inscriptions in the reduced Norse *futhǫrk* illustrate uses comparable to those of the parent Germanic *futhark*. Many record the names of owners or makers of objects, or the names of those who carved and coloured[35] the runic inscriptions. Others appear to be charms and spells of various kinds.[36] Some consist wholly or in part of the runic sequence itself.[37] Still others are cryptic[38] or even unintelligible.[39] At least one inscribed stone was found buried from public view in a grave.[40] Runic inscriptions also appear linked with images of ships, men, and animals, similar to those of the pre-runic *hällristningar* mentioned above,[41] as well as in close association with the common serpent motif,[42] and occasionally with figures out of pagan Germanic religion and legend, such as the god Thor and the archetypal Germanic hero Sigurd.[43]

The latter usage of runes in cultic contexts as letters of power is stressed in northern literary sources, such as the eddic *Hávamál*, where runes are termed 'mjök stóra stafi, mjök stinna stafi' (the very great letters, the very powerful letters)[44] and Odin describes them as agents for raising the dead:

þat kann ek it tólpta: ef ek sé á tré uppi
    váfna virgilná,
sva ek ríst ok í rúnom fák,
    at sá gengr gumi
    ok mælir við mik.

(I know a twelfth (spell): when I see up on a tree a corpse swinging from a rope, then I cut and paint runes, so that the man walks and speaks with me.)[45]

Another famous literary episode, found in slightly different versions in both the eddic *Sigrdrífumál*[46] and the *Vǫlsungasaga*,[47] recounts how the valkyrie Sigrdrifa, whom Odin has put into a charmed sleep, is awakened by the hero Sigurd and in return teaches him wisdom. An important part of this preternatural wisdom turns out to be the lore of charms and spells, including the use of various runes: *malrúnar* (speech runes), *hugrúnar* (memory runes), *sigrúnar* (victory runes), ǫlrúnar (ale runes), *bjärgrúnar* (help runes), *brimrúnar* (surf runes), and *limrúnar* (twig runes). Although the first two kinds of rune listed might be interpreted as having some connection with the normal purposes of written characters, the remaining five obviously involve the invocation of superhuman agencies, since they are intended for carving on various objects, respectively to bring success in battle, to prevent poisoning, to ease childbirth, to ensure safe passage, and to cure the sick. We also see supposedly historical figures represented in the sagas as using runes in a magical way; note, for example, how Egill Skallagrimsson carves runes on an ale-horn in a successful attempt to protect himself against poisoning[48] or intervenes to alter an incorrect runic inscription that has been injuring the health of a young girl.[49]

A number of extra-literary inscriptions contemporary with the literary evidence attest to the currency of similar magical usage of runes in the real world, despite modern arguments that such usage was essentially a literary rather than an actual historical phenomenon by the time the North Germanic world was Christianized.[50] Notable among these inscriptions is the runic charm carved on a wooden message stick found at Bergen in Norway, which begins:

Ríst ek bótrúnar,
ríst ek bjärgrúnar:
einfalt við álfum,
tvífalt við trollum,
þrífalt við þursum.

(I carve the bettering runes, I carve the helping runes: once against the elves, twice against the trolls, thrice against the giants.)[51]

The overwhelming majority of Norse inscriptions from the Viking age and later centuries seem purely secular and utilitarian, however, showing no connection with pagan Germanic beliefs or the secret crafts of magic. For example, there are literally thousands of stone monuments to the dead, placed at much frequented spots such as roadsides and bridges,[52] some of which actually invite the passer-by to read the runes and understand their message;[53] it has been argued quite plausibly that these public monuments were in some way associated with the legal inheritance of property.[54] In addition to burial-stones, there are numerous smaller inscribed objects which demonstrate the increasing use of runes for all aspects of recording and communication.[55]

Of special interest among the small runic objects are the rarely found *rúnakefli* (wooden rune-sticks), which often may have served as kindling after performing their primary function and which in any case were bound to perish except in certain soil conditions. Northern literature contains frequent references to carved messages, for instance, the warning carved and sent by Gudrun to her brothers in *Átlamál*,[56] or the announcement of his triumph carved by the Icelandic outlaw-hero Grettir and left at the door of the priest who had deserted him during his combat with the troll.[57] For lack of surviving physical evidence, it was often assumed that the common use of *rúnakefli* belonged more to literature than to life, until the 1955 fire which destroyed much of the old quarter of the city of Bergen in Norway made possible archaeological explorations that unearthed, not only the charm-bearing wooden message-stick quoted earlier, but also hundreds of other *rúnakefli*.[58] These bear inscriptions ranging all the way from records of business transactions, to official communications from royalty, to letters between merchants on conditions of trade, to such very personal messages as the summons from a wife to her husband: 'gya: sæhir: atþu: kak hæim' (Gytha says to go home), or the versified appeal of a lover to his mistress:

Unn þu mer;
ann ek þer.
Gunnhildr, kyss mik!
Kann ek þik.

(You love me; I love you. Gunnhild, kiss me! I know you well.)

What the numerous and varied Bergen inscriptions reveal is a people who were literate in the *futhqrk* and who used it as other nations had come to use the alphabet. Any sense of runes as somehow special characters (what I have termed earlier 'letters of power') appears only in a very limited number of examples which are swamped in the vast quantities of purely utilitarian inscriptions.

Clearly, the large majority of inscriptions in the Norse *futhqrk* were not associated with pagan religion but secular in purpose. There are even a significant number of examples where runes, far from serving pagan ends, were drawn into Christian service.[59] Despite these facts, however, it is interesting to note that, at least in certain parts of the Germanic North, runic symbols never completely severed their connection with pre-Christian beliefs and practices. The continued survival of magical uses of the *futhqrk* is manifest as late as the seventeenth century in Iceland, where people were burned as witches because runic inscriptions were found in their possession and where an official prohibition of the use of runes was thought necessary in 1639.[60]

The Expanded English Futhorc

Runic inscriptions are scarce in England[61] and literary references to runes are even more infrequent. No doubt this was a result of the early conversion of the Anglo-Saxons, which from the beginning of the seventh century onward made the Roman alphabet widely available for secular as well as for religious uses. Despite the relative paucity of the evidence, however, it is not impossible to identify the major functions performed by runes among the Anglo-Saxons and to compare these with the usage of the twenty-four rune Common Germanic *futhark* and its reduced sixteen rune Norse descendant.

The symbol sequence employed by the Anglo-Saxons in England was an expanded version of the original Germanic *futhark*, modified in a number of ways so as to represent with considerable accuracy the nuances of Old English phonology.[62] In its most widely disseminated form this new sequence numbered twenty-eight runes:[63]

ᚠᚢᚦ·ᚠᚱᚻᚷᚹ: ᚺᚾᛁᛄᛂᛈᚳᚷᛋ ᛏᛒᛖᛗᛚᛝᛞᛟ᛬ᚪᚫᚣᛠ

usually transliterated by modern runologists as: f, u, *þ*, (ie, th), o, r, c, g, w; h, n, i, j, ʒ (an arbitrary symbol for a variable sound), p, x, s; t, b, e, m, l, ng, d, œ; a, æ, y, êa.[64] In recognition of the changed sound values of the fourth and sixth symbols, the Old English rune sequence has been given a somewhat altered name: *futhorc* instead of *futhark*. Supplementing the twenty-eight symbols listed above was ᛇ, a variant of the twelfth rune, which appears instead of that symbol in manuscript versions of the *futhorc* such as the Old English *Rune Poem* itself, where the normal epigraphical form of the twelfth rune is displaced and reinserted later immediately before the final rune, making a total sequence of twenty-nine runes.[65] In addition to the symbols described above, there were several other runes with more restricted usage that also came to be recorded in manuscripts and, in fact, are found appended (though without accompanying stanzas) to our only extant version of the Old English *Rune Poem*.[66]

Runic tradition in England can be divided into two separate streams: the primary epigraphical usage, represented by stone monuments and small portable objects and occasionally referred to in literary and other written accounts; and also the secondary manuscript usage, represented by *futhorc* lists, cryptographic treatises, and instances where, for varying reasons, runes are used along with and in place of alphabet letters. Since the latter usage is highly specialized and also probably the immediate source of the material in the Old English *Rune Poem*, it will be examined separately in this introduction under the heading 'Manuscript Uses of the *Futhorc*' (pp 17–19). Epigraphical usage is in any case chronologically prior and therefore warrants examination first.

Pre-Christian runic inscriptions in England do not seem radically different from those on the continent. Mainly they appear on portable objects of metal or bone that often are found at early grave-sites, the texts ranging from names,[67] to a single instance of the *futhorc* sequence itself,[68] to various usually unintelligible formulas, a number of which have been identified as charms.[69] For uses comparable to those of the Norse *rúnakefli* there is no surviving physical evidence, only the literary testimony of a single poem, the so-called *Husband's Message*, where a wooden message-stick summons a lady to cross the sea and rejoin her beloved, summarizing its appeal in the following cryptic passage:

Genyre ic ætsomne ·ᚻ·ᚱ· geador
·ᛠ·ᚹ· ond ·ᛗ· āþe benemnan
þæt he þā wǣre ond þa winetrēowe
be him lifgendum lǣstan wolde
þe git on ǣrdagum oft gesprǣconn.

(In a small space I crowd the runes *sigel*, *rād* together, *ēar*, *wyn*, and *man* (or possibly *dæg*) to assure you with an oath that he was there and that he would perform, while he lived, the true faith of which you two often spoke in earlier days.)[70]

Written accounts which can be interpreted as revealing knowledge of the pagan Germanic use of runes in magic are extremely rare; even the collections of primitive herbal cures, which often contain charms, make no unambiguous references to the efficacy of the *futhorc*.[71] The most convincing example of rune magic is furnished by Bede's well-known story of how the bonds of a young Northumbrian captive called Imma kept falling off whenever his abbot brother, who believed him slain in battle, sang masses for the delivery of his soul. In the original Latin version, Imma's puzzled captors were unable to account for this mysterious phenomenon except by assuming sorcery and therefore asked him whether he had concealed on his person *litteras solutorias* (releasing letters).[72] In the Old English translation of Bede's Latin account, the word *rūne* makes its appearance; Imma is asked 'hwæðer he þā alȳsendlecan rūne cuðe, and þā stafas mid him awritene hæfde, be swylcum men lēas spel secgað and spreocað' (whether he knew the loosening *rūne*, and had written down in his possession those characters, concerning which men talk and tell lying stories).[73] As has been pointed out by others,[74] the normal Old English term for 'runic symbol' is not the simplex *rūn*, but the compound *rūnstæf*, and therefore the accusative form here (*rūne*) could easily be a singular, meaning 'secret' (ie, charm or spell); likewise the word *stafas* could refer to alphabet letters rather than to runes. In refutation of these objections, however, it is significant to note that, when the homilist Ælfric came to retell Bede's story about the end of the tenth century, he readily made a connection between magic and the *futhorc* by representing Imma's captors as asking 'hwæðer he ðurh drȳcræft oððe ðurh rūnstafum his bendas tōbræce' (whether he shattered his bonds by sorcery or by runic letters).[75]

Inscriptions employing runes for secular or magical purposes form a very small proportion of the total corpus of Old English runic texts. The two-pronged conversion of the Anglo-Saxons, by Roman missionaries from the east and south and by Irish missionaries from the west and north, ensured that, long before their continental cousins, the Germanic tribes of England all came into close contact with the bookish, alphabet-based Latin culture of the Christian monasteries. Most extant Old English runic inscriptions postdate the Christianization, as revealed by their style and context, as well as by their literal content. Unlike Norse inscriptions, which may run from right to left,

boustrophedon (in alternating directions, as a field is ploughed),
backwards, or even in serpentine forms,[76] Old English runic texts
show the influence of Roman epigraphy and Latin manuscripts by
normally running from left to right. Sometimes, as on the so-called
Falstone 'hogback,' the same text will occur twice: the Old English
version inscribed in runes, the Latin one in Roman characters;[77] more
often an object has several inscriptions, some in runic, some in
Roman;[78] or *futhorc* symbols actually may be used to inscribe texts
that are not in the vernacular but in Latin.[79] In many instances,
especially on coins, the two forms are mixed and runic symbols are
used indiscriminately along with Roman capitals in spelling out a
single word.[80] Some aspects of the content of Christian era inscriptions may appear to have North Germanic parallels (note, for example, the persistent care to name the person who has raised a gravestone in addition to naming the person commemorated by it, a practice reminiscent of the inheritance-certifying *futhqrk* stones described above); however the appeals to pray for the souls of the
persons named make it obvious that the purpose of these inscriptions
is not secular, but religious.[81]

It is clear that what happened to the *futhorc* when the Christian
missionaries converted the Anglo-Saxons was very different from the
fate of the *futhark* on the continent and in Iceland.[82] Instead of
suppressing the runic characters or relegating them to fringe uses by
the rural illiterate and by opponents of the Church, the English
monasteries adopted the *futhorc*, developed it, and expanded its uses.
One significant reflection of this acceptance of the *futhorc* is the
survival of the ancient Germanic verbs for cutting and interpreting
runes as the standard Modern English verbs for our dealings with any
kind of letters: *wrītan* becoming 'to write' and *rēðan* becoming 'to
read;' no other Germanic language applied the same specialized verbs
to any characters other than runes.[83]

Bede tells us in his *Ecclesiastical History* that, when the Roman
mission was struggling to establish itself in Kent at the end of the
sixth century, Pope Gregory the Great sent a wise letter of advice to
Abbot Mellitus on how to go about effecting conversions. Instead of
alienating the Anglo-Saxons by repudiating all their previous ceremonies and practices, the missionary should win people's hearts by
retaining, but redirecting formerly pagan customs:

Cum ergo Deus omnipotens uos ad reuerentissimum uirum fratrem nostrum
Augustinum episcopum perduxerit, dicite ei quid diu mecum de causa
Anglorum cogitans tractaui; uidelicet quia fana idolorum destrui in eadem
gente minime debeant, sed ipsa quae in eis sunt idola destruantur, aqua
benedicta fiat, in eisdem fanis aspergatur, altaria construantur, reliquae
ponantur ... dum gens ipsa eadem fans sua non videt destrui, de corde errorem
deponat, et Deum verum cognoscens ac adorans, ad loca quae consueuit
familiarius concurrat. Et quia boues solent in sacrificio daemonum multos
occidere, debet eis etiam hac de re aliqua sollemnitas immutari ... Nam duris
mentibus simul omnis abscidere impossibile esse non dubium est, quia et is,
qui summum locum ascendere nititur, gradibus uel passibus, non autem
saltibus eleuatur.

(However, when Almighty God has brought you to our most reverend brother
Bishop Augustine, tell him what I have decided after long deliberation about
the English people, namely that the idol temples of that race should by no
means be destroyed, but only the idols in them. Take holy water and sprinkle
it in these shrines, build altars and place relics in them ... When these people
see that their shrines are not destroyed, they will be able to banish error from
their hearts and be more ready to come to the places they are familiar with,
but now recognizing and worshipping the true God. And because they are in
the habit of slaughtering much cattle as sacrifices to devils, some solemnity
ought to be given them in exchange for this ... It is doubtless impossible to cut
out everything at once from their stubborn minds; just as the man who is
attempting to climb to the highest place, rises by steps and degrees and not by
leaps.)[84]

There is little evidence to show whether or not this programme was
applied to rune lore in the south of England; but in the northern areas
that were Christianized by Celtic missionaries the Church displayed
great willingness to embrace whatever aspects of Germanic culture
could be rendered innocuous through adaptation.

This tolerant attitude resulted in an impressive fusion of different
heritages. For example, in the great standing cross at Ruthwell in
Dumfriesshire it produced a monument typically Celtic in form, but
with Latin inscriptions and Mediterranean style figure sculpture on
the wide north and south faces, supplemented by portions of an Old
English poem on internalizing Christ's crucifixion inscribed in runes
on the narrower east and west sides.[85] An even more striking attempt

to integrate cultures is evidenced by the scenes and inscriptions on a Northumbrian whalebone casket found at Auzon and bequeathed to the British Museum by Sir A.W. Franks.[86] Except for one brief passage where the carver has slipped into Roman characters for a Latin sentence, all the inscriptions are carved in runes: these range from what appears to be a versified description of the source of the material from which the casket was made to a variety of captions describing the scenes depicted on its lid and four sides. The scene on the back of the casket is a warlike representation of the fall of the holy city of Jerusalem; on the left side is shown the classical legend of how Romulus and Remus, the founders of Rome, were suckled by a she-wolf; on the right side appear what are usually interpreted as scenes from the legend of the Germanic hero Sigurd (surrounded by three lines of extremely opaque alliterative verse);[87] on the lid an un-identified bowman defends a building against attackers; and on the front, in the closest juxtaposition of all, are two scenes: the first panel to the left depicting an episode from the Germanic legend of Vǫlundr (Welund the Smith) and immediately to its right a second panel depicting the Adoration of the Magi. No one as yet has explained satisfactorily by what species of adaptation and allegorization the imagination of Christian Northumbria contrived to reconcile this varied inheritance.

Manuscript Uses of the Futhorc

The same welcoming attitude to Germanic culture demonstrated in the epigraphic examples cited above led the Christian monasteries of England to introduce the *futhorc* into the new environment of books, thus establishing a tradition that was to make Old English runes part of the minor scholarly apparatus of all the European monasteries that either directly or indirectly came in contact with English scholarship.[88] Scribes copied down the traditional *futhorc* sequence in manuscripts, recorded for the first time the names by which the individual runes were known and memorized, and also set Latin alphabet equivalents against each runic symbol.[89] This last practice frequently led to the rearrangement of the runes into alphabetic order for readier comparison with Latin, Greek, Hebrew, and other alphabets.[90] In the far from easy process of comparing the two phonologically different sequences of Roman and runic characters, no doubt there emerged very clearly the greater accuracy and simplicity of the two runes Þ and ᚹ for conveying respectively the Old English voiced and voiceless dental spirants (*th*) and the Old English semi-vowel w (first represented in vernacular texts by a clumsy double u borrowed from Latin texts); for by the beginning of the ninth century both these runic symbols had acquired rounded minuscule forms and passed into normal insular bookhand, where they appear to have been completely assimilated with alphabet letters and probably were no longer consciously recognized as runes.[91]

The alphabetized epigraphical forms of the runic characters found a number of other uses in the monasteries of England and Europe: as reference marks, for quire numbering, for scribal signatures, and especially as ornamental capitals to make individual letters stand out on a page.[92] Rather more interesting than these varied, but utilitarian functions of alphabetized runes, is the considerable body of evidence that the Old English *futhorc*, in its traditional order and complete with its ancient division into three groups of runes, became the object of study and of use for cryptographic purposes, where secret Latin messages were conveyed by a runic code based on specifying which of the three traditional groups the rune symbol belongs to and its place within that group.[93]

Of course the testimony of surviving insular manuscripts is more significant in helping us to assess the kind and amount of runic knowledge that the author of the Old English *Rune Poem* may have possessed than any of the continental manuscripts, however important many of those may be in the history of rune forms, rune names, runic cryptography, and the spread of rune lore. Passing over as less relevant the insular examples of runes listed in alphabetic order and focussing instead on known examples of *futhorc* lists in Old English manuscripts, we find considerable evidence for a lively interest in the traditional runes lasting until as late as the end of the eleventh century in England. In addition to the *futhorc* represented by the manuscript of the Old English *Rune Poem*, there is one *futhorc*, divided into the ancient three groups and complete with rune names, in Cotton ms Domitian A.ix, folio 11v.[94] Also there are two *futhorcs*, one with names and one with values only, in Oxford, St John's College ms 17, folio 5v.[95] Finally, according to the evidence of a runic table in the Icelandic Grammar that forms part of George Hickes' *Linguarum Veterum Septentrionalium Thesaurus*, there must have been at least two further *futhorcs*, one with names and one with values only, in the lost Cotton ms Galba A.ii, which was severely damaged by fire in 1731 and completely destroyed by a second fire at the bindery in 1865.[96]

The Old English Rune Names

The insular manuscript evidence most relevant to the present edition is supplied by the numerous Old English texts which illustrate an active vernacular use of runes as symbols for the names by which they were traditionally known. Sometimes this identification of rune and name served as nothing more than a convenient scribal abbreviation, as in the various scattered instances where the words *ǣðel* (or *ēþel*) (home), *wynn* (joy), *mann* (man), and *dæg* (day) are replaced by the symbols ᛟ, ᚹ, ᛗ, and ᛞ.[97] In other cases, authors creatively exploit the identification in order to set the reader's or listener's mind to work at discovering important information concealed in the text. This is the method used in several of the versified riddles of *The Exeter Book*, where runes often function in two ways: both as separate words that carry metrical stress and alliteration and as letters which, taken together, spell out the words of the solution.[98] Similarly, it is the method used in the runic signatures of the poet Cynewulf.

Unlike the anonymous authors of most extant Old English poetry, Cynewulf seems to have felt a special need to be remembered in the prayers of his own and future generations. Accordingly, he devised elaborate verse passages on the sobering theme of the inevitability of death and judgement, where he spelled out the letters of his name in runes that served a double function as significant words in the surrounding poetic text. Since this poet was trusting the well-being of his immortal soul to the existence of an audience capable of deciphering his runic message, the four Cynewulfian signatures would appear to furnish unimpeachable evidence for the widespread knowledge of runes and rune names in Anglo-Saxon England.[99]

Summary: What Rune Lore Did the Author of the Old English Rune Poem Possess?

The evidence outlined above suggests that the author of the Old English *Rune Poem* could have known a number of things about the *futhorc*. Of course there is no doubt regarding his awareness of its long-established order, its forms, and the names traditionally associated with the individual runes: comparison with other Old English manuscript *futhorcs*, both insular and continental, demonstrates that he made use of fairly reliable sources in ordering his stanzas, shaping his runes, and interpreting the meaningful names attached to the runic symbols.[100] It is less certain whether the poet was aware of the traditional division of the rune sequence into three groups, although at least one extant English manuscript divides the *futhorc* in this way[101] and, as suggested later in this introduction, the peculiarities of the poem's stanzaic structure seem to point to the likelihood of some such awareness.[102] It is also unclear whether the poet felt that the order of the final group of three runes defined in his poem was unfixed and the correct nomenclature unsure. Certainly there must have been widespread hesitancy about these three relatively new insular inventions, as shown by the confusion of order, the omission of names, and even the total omission of one or more of the three symbols characteristic of many manuscript *futhorcs*.[103]

Similar problems cloud the vital issue of how much the author of the Old English *Rune Poem* knew about the pagan Germanic background of the *futhorc* and the extent to which runic nomenclature might involve subjects and concepts that were taboo for an orthodox Christian. It is always conceivable that for him the *futhorc* was no more than another alphabet, but one whose unusual order and meaningful mnemonic names made it a far more interesting basis for a poetic exercise than its Roman counterpart.[104] On the other hand, the very word *rūnstæf* (runic symbol) must still have conveyed to any Anglo-Saxon some of the basic connotations of secrecy associated with the Old English simplex *rūn*. Like Ælfric, the poet probably was aware that runes once were used for magical purposes. Furthermore, even supposing that the poet knew runic symbols only from books, throughout their manuscript usage runes remained in some sense special characters, standing out clearly from any surrounding text and potentially cryptic in nature, a circumstance of which he cannot have been unconscious.

Additional discussion of the extent of the poet's rune lore will be found in a number of different contexts later in this introduction as well as in the explanatory notes following the text of the poem.

The Textual Background of
the *Rune Poem*

Normally this section of the edition of an Old English poem would
open with a careful description of the manuscript or manuscripts in
which the poem appears, particularly of the calligraphic style, in an
effort to establish provenance and date. The task of providing such a
description poses some difficulties for any editor of the Old English
Rune Poem, however, because no medieval copy of the poem survives
to be subjected to examination. In 1731, while the Cottonian Library
was reposited in Ashburnham House, that building was devastated by
fire and Cotton ms Otho B.X, which contained the unique version of
the poem, was almost completely destroyed.[1] Fortunately a copy of
the *Rune Poem* had been made about the beginning of the eighteenth
century and, although this handwritten copy has not survived, it
formed the basis for the first printed edition and sole authoritative
text of the poem, which will be described under the next heading in
this introduction. In the absence of the original manuscript, our only
information about it, outside the printed poem, must be garnered
from two catalogue descriptions written very near to the date of the
first edition, plus a couple of catalogue annotations that also appear
to have some relevance.

At the time of the fire, Cotton ms Otho B.X consisted mainly of an
early eleventh century volume of Old English saints' lives, written in
several different hands and amounting to about 170 leaves (all except
fifty-four of which were destroyed in 1731); this collection of hagio-
graphy had been divided into two parts by the insertion of other Old
English material so as to occupy folios 1–142 and 166–94. Between the
two separated parts of the original manuscript were several shorter
items: a couple of homilies in a mid-eleventh century hand, consist-

ing of twelve leaves (ten of which were destroyed) and occupying
folios 143–54; a set of confessional and penitential texts consisting of
twelve leaves (all of which were destroyed) and occupying folios
155–64; and a single leaf containing the Old English *Rune Poem*
(which was totally destroyed) and occupying folio 165. At the end of
the original manuscript was added a life of St Margaret (which was
totally destroyed) occupying folio 195 and perhaps further folios.[2]

The first detailed description of Cotton ms Otho B.x appeared in
Thomas Smith's *Catalogus Librorum Manuscriptorum Bibliothecae
Cottonianae*, pp 70ff. Smith's only reference to folio 165 was confined
to the verso of that leaf, where he noted: 'Characteres Alphabeti
peregrini, numero tantum decem. Aliqui ex his videntur esse literis
Runicis similes.' (Strange alphabet characters, in number as many as
ten. Some of these seem to be like runic letters.)[3] The next
cataloguist, Humphrey Wanley, found this description inadequate,
as shown by the handwritten annotation on his personal copy of
Smith's *Catalogus*,[4] where Wanley noted: 'Litterae antiquae Runicae
numero plane viginti et novem cum observatt. Saxonicis.' (Ancient
runic letters, clearly twenty-nine in number, along with Old English
comments.) When Wanley came to publish his own account of the
manuscript in *Librorum Veterum Septentrionalium ... Catalogus
Historico Criticus*, pp 190ff, he described folio 165 as follows: 'Folium
quod olim ad alium quendam librum pertinuit, nunc hujus pars, in
quo continetur Alphabetum Runicum cum explicatione Poetica,
Saxonice, quod non ita pridem descripsi rogatu Cl. D. Hickesii, qui in
Gram. Anglo-Saxonicae, cap. 22. *de Dialecto Normanno-Saxonica*. p.
135. illud typis evulgavit.' (A leaf that once belonged to some other
volume, now part of this, wherein is contained a Runic Alphabet with
a verse explanation in Old English, which not very long ago I copied
at the request of the most renowned Dr Hickes, who published it in
print in his Anglo-Saxon Grammar, in chapter 22, 'On the Norse-
Saxon Dialect,' p 135.)

Provided that Wanley's experienced and discriminating eye did not
fail him in this instance, folio 165 never really belonged in Cotton ms
Otho B.x and therefore cannot be dated by analogy with the few
scorched and damaged leaves of that manuscript which were sal-
vaged from the 1731 fire. Unfortunately, Wanley's description does
not include any estimate of the date of the script in which the Old

English *Rune Poem* was written, or any speculation as to what manuscript the leaf might have been taken from, or how it came to be
bound up with the manuscript in which he discovered it. In his
Catalogue of Manuscripts Containing Anglo-Saxon, Neil Ker made a
suggestion that could throw a little light on this last issue: citing a
note in the handwriting of Sir Robert Cotton that records the loan of
'A Saxon book of diuers saints liues and the Alphabett of the Old
Danish letter amonghs Mr Gocelins' as well as several other
confirmatory notes, Ker maintained that Cotton ms Otho B.x was at
one time the property of the sixteenth century collector, John Josce-
lyn, and that his may have been the agency responsible for inserting
folio 165 amidst the strikingly different devotional material of that
manuscript.[5]

Although the handwritten comments by Cotton and Wanley,
coupled with the two printed catalogue descriptions quoted above,
constitute our only available references to the original manuscript
version of the Old English *Rune Poem*, there was once an even more
important piece of evidence about folio 165, that is, the lost copy of
the poem which Wanley tells us he transcribed for Hickes and which
served as the basis of the 1705 edition. As Kenneth Sisam made clear in
his useful account of the career and contributions of Humphrey
Wanley,[6] the cataloguist was an extraordinarily skilled palaeog-
rapher with the regular habit of making, not merely copies, but what
amounted to hand-drawn facsimiles of Old English texts. Hence there
is a high degree of probability that the copy which Hickes received
was just such a facsimile, carefully reproducing all the significant
aspects of the original, including its format, punctuation, word-
spacing, marginal notes, and even the very ductus of individual
letters. In fact, Hickes' printer may have been placed in the position
of setting up his type on the basis of what for all intents and purposes
was the Old English manuscript page itself.

THE PRINTED EDITION OF 1705

The Old English *Rune Poem* was first published on page 135 of volume I
of George Hickes' *Linguarum Veterum Septentrionalium Thesaurus*,
a truly monumental scholarly work of which Humphrey Wanley's
Catalogus cited above formed the second enormous volume.

Apparently Hickes had requested Wanley to keep an eye open for any runes encountered in the manuscripts being catalogued and to copy them out for him. As a result, Wanley forwarded for Hickes' collection a considerable amount of runic material, including that found in Cotton ms Galba A.ii, which later was completely destroyed by fire in 1865; as Wanley states in his description of this lost manuscript, it contained: 'Alphabeta Runica diversa, quae cum aliis ex hujusce Bibliothecae Codd. MSS. descripta D. Hickesio imprimenda dedi' (different runic alphabets, a copy of which, along with others from the manuscript volumes of this library, I gave to Dr Hickes for printing.)[7] No doubt the Old English *Rune Poem* from Cotton ms Otho B.X, as well as the important thirty-three rune *futhorc* from Cotton ms Domitian A.ix which appears on page 136 of Hickes' *Thesaurus*, were among the runic material that Wanley spotted and copied in order to assist Hickes in his linguistic research.

George Hickes considered that the Old English *futhorcs* supplied by Wanley constituted evidence of Norse influence on Anglo-Saxon culture in the eleventh century. Thus, in the twenty-second chapter of his *Thesaurus*, entitled 'De dialecto *Normanno-Saxonica* sive *Anglo-Normannica*; & de dialecto *Semi-Saxonica*,' he chose to include the entire text of the Old English *Rune Poem* as an example of the attempts made by Anglo-Saxon clerics and nobles to impress King Canute with their eagerness to study the Danish language:

Hoc ut credam faciunt *runarum Danicarum*, tam simplicium, quam duplicium, descriptio quaedam poetica, *Anglo-Saxonice*, explicata: quae in bibliotheca *Cott.* extat, *Otho B.* 10. p. 165. quamque vix antea & ne vix observatam, nedum publici juris factam, plane quasi ab omnibus doctis spectatu dignam, hic cum *runis* aere incisis, operae & sumptus pretium exhibere judicamus, *Latinis* additis ex adverso elementis, ad ostendendam *runarum* potestatem, una cum iis nominibus quibus appellantur ipsae *runa*.

(I am caused to believe this by a certain verse description of the Danish runes, both single and double, expounding them in Anglo-Saxon, which still exists in the Cottonian library on page 165 of Otho B.X and which, although previously barely noted at all, much less brought into the public jurisdiction, we deem it, as deserving of examination by all learned men, to be worth the trouble and expense of setting forth here in full, along with the runes cut in a copper plate, Latin letters having been added beside them to show the force of the runes, together with those names by which the same runes are called.)[8]

As the most cursory comparison with the Norse *futhǫrk* must reveal,
Hickes made a serious mistake in terming the runes of the Old English
Rune Poem 'Danish.' It seems ungrateful to cavil about this error,
however, since, without the first editor's misplaced enthusiasm for
runes as examples of linguistic hybridism, the poem might never have
been copied by Wanley and hence would have been incinerated for all
time in the 1731 fire at Ashburnham House.

In examining the version of the *Rune Poem* that Hickes gives on
page 135 of his *Thesaurus* (and which is reproduced preceding the
edited text on p 84 in this edition), the reader can distinguish three
separate parts. The main body of the page, consisting of all the words
in the poem, was printed from a font of Old English type cast in
Amsterdam before 1655 for Franciscus Junius and later donated by
him to Oxford.[9] To the left of the poem proper, the runes from ᚠ to ᛏ
(along with their names and phonetic values), followed by q ᚹ
cweorð and the solitary rune ᚪ, were printed from a vertical copper
plate measuring about ten and a half by one and a quarter inches; the
first twenty-nine of these runes were so arranged that each stands
approximately opposite and about three-quarters of an inch away
from the stanza describing it. Beneath the poem were printed, from a
horizontal copper plate measuring about seven-tenths of an inch by
five inches, the two runes ᚺ and ᛇ with their names and values,
followed by a vertical dividing line and then this note: 'Hos characteres ᚠ ᚱ ᚺ ᚹ ᛏ ᚣ ᚠ ᚠ ᚷ ad alia sestinans [for festinans] studioso
lectori interpretanda relinquo.' (These characters O L D W N X F O G,
hastening on to other matters, I leave for the studious reader to
interpret.)

One important aspect of the appearance of page 135 is the obtrusive
presence of the insular alphabet equivalents which, together with the
rune names, have been added beside the vertical row of runes. Hickes'
account, quoted above, states that these are additions, but does not
indicate when or by whom they were added. Any sensitive reader,
observing the riddling nature of the poem, must feel considerable
doubt that either the rune names or the sound values formed part of
the text when the Old English *Rune Poem* was first composed and
recorded; certainly the earliest manuscripts of the Norwegian *Rune
Poem* and the Icelandic *Rune Poem* do not spoil the intellectual game
between poet and audience in such a way.[10] Long ago George Hempl[11]
demonstrated that all the sound values, plus the four extra runes

without corresponding stanzas that are tacked on at the bottom of the poem and a number of variant rune forms and rune names that clutter the vertical columns, were borrowed from the *futhorc* list appearing in another Cotton manuscript, Domitian A.ix, which Hickes printed on page 136 of his *Thesaurus* immediately following the poem, as a second example of Danish influence on Anglo-Saxon culture.[12] In the face of Hempl's evidence, the only logical conclusion to be drawn is that either George Hickes or Humphrey Wanley (in an effort to make Hickes' task of comparison easier) inserted all this linguistic apparatus. Hickes' reference to 'double' runes quoted above suggests that at least the variant rune forms were in the copy he received from Wanley.

In his important article on Hickes' additions just cited, George Hempl made a statement that has teased the scholarly world for many decades: 'The way that Hickes writes the names makes it appear that putting them in was an afterthought with him; indeed, I believe I can trace them to their source, but I refrain from saying more until the necessary material is in my hands.' Unlike Hempl, I cannot pretend to trace the rune names in question to their source. The same list of names is not to be found associated with any extant English *futhorc*. Although in one curious aspect, the abnormal spelling of the eighth rune name as *wen*, the Old English *Rune Poem* possibly could have borrowed from the *futhorc* in Cotton ms Domitian A.ix, seven of its other rune names differ and three more are absent altogether from that manuscript. Those who would prefer to attribute the rune names printed by Hickes to the original scribe of Cotton ms Otho B.X, folio 165, must take a further significant point into consideration: the fact that the spelling of the eighth rune name does not fit the orthographic tradition of the poem proper, where the same word is spelled *wyn* a total of five times.[13] My best guess is that neither Hickes nor Wanley was responsible for adding the rune names to the Old English *Rune Poem*, but that some earlier reader, perhaps as far back as Anglo-Saxon times, had access to an Old English *futhorc* with names that was no longer extant by the time Sir Robert Cotton formed his library, and used this lost *futhorc* to gloss the runes and answer the riddles posed by the twenty-nine stanzas of the poem.

George Hickes appears to have made no attempt, as the first editor of the Old English *Rune Poem*, to perform any of the usual editorial tasks: to set up the alliterative lines in a format recognizable to modern eyes as verse, to emend obvious errors in the text, to regu-

larize word division and spelling, or to supply modern punctuation.
Except for segregating the runes in a separate column with explanatory sound values and rune names, and indicating the beginning of
each new stanza by means of hanging indention, it seems doubtful
that Hickes or his printer interfered very much with the copy of the
poem received from Wanley. In all likelihood any other changes
made by them were accidental, the result of misreading Wanley's
facsimile of insular script.[14] Probably Hickes' printed version repro-
duces many of the peculiarities of the manuscript. As one example of
this kind of direct imitation, note how the 1705 edition sets out the
Old English *Rune Poem* as prose (just as Old English poetry codices
were accustomed to do with verse), but nonetheless indicates that
the various stanzas are separate entities by beginning each on a new
line with a rune replacing what would otherwise be the first word of
the stanza. The assumption that this method of indicating the discrete nature of the individual stanzas goes back to the original manuscript is supported by the use in Hickes' printed text of a closing
punctuation mark normally reserved by Anglo-Saxon scribes for the
end of a heading, a paragraph, or a completely separate entry, situa-
tions where a run-on would confuse intentionally distinct items.[15]

The nine runic characters that Hickes lists at the bottom of page 135
in his *Thesaurus* and leaves for the reader to interpret all can be found
among the twenty-nine runes described in the poem; probably they
constitute nothing more than meaningless scribbling or a *probatio
pennae* by some later reader. Since a letter count of the poem suggests
that the original text covered more than one side of folio 165 in the
manuscript,[16] it is possible that these nine runes were scribbled on a
blank space at the end and that they may have been the ones which
caught the eye of Thomas Smith and caused him to insert a separate
entry for folio 165 in his description of Cotton Otho B.X. Otherwise,
these characters are of no significance whatsoever in any discussion
of the Old English *Rune Poem*.

DATING AND LOCALIZING THE TEXT

Language

The language reproduced on page 135 of Hickes' *Thesaurus* should be
divided into two distinct parts for separate examination: that is, the
forms of the Old English rune names listed in the column of runic

information to the left of the text, as opposed to the language of the poem proper. Individual peculiarities of both will be discussed separately in the explanatory notes on particular words following the text of the poem. What will be presented here is a summary of such characteristics as may assist in establishing provenance and date.

If, as suggested earlier in this introduction, the rune names were added to the poem by some later hand than that of the original scribe, there can have been no compelling reason for linguistic harmony between them and the main body of the text. It is interesting to note, therefore, that, although there is nothing identifiably non-West Saxon about the bulk of the forms, rune name XIX *eh* (horse) is abnormal, possibly an example of Anglian smoothing (see Campbell's *Old English Grammar* #227),[17] and rune name VIII *wen* (joy) does not coincide with the spelling of the same word in the usual West Saxon form *wyn(n)* as many as five times in the poem proper (that is, in lines 37, 55, 85, 89, and 94). Since *y* was unrounded and lowered to *e* in Kent by the tenth century (see Campbell #288), it seems likely that *wen* may be a Kentish form; in support of this theory, Charles Wrenn's stimulating article on late Old English rune names[18] offers some manuscript substantiation that this variant may have been a distinguishing feature of runic tradition in the south-east of England. Less certain evidence of Kentish influence on the rune nomenclature is furnished by rune name XXVIII *īar* (corrected to *īor*) whose meaning remains doubtful; one possible explanation of the curious alternation here may be that it is an indicator of the spelling confusion about the four diphthongs *ĕo*, *ĕa*, *ĭo*, *ĭa* which arose from the ninth century tendency in Kent to raise *ĕo* to *ĭo* and then unround *ĭo* to *ĭa* (see Campbell #280, 297). The remainder of the rune names show normal West Saxon or even late West Saxon forms; note, for example, the unsmoothed diphthongs in rune names I *feoh* (wealth), XIII *ēoh* (yew), XV *eolhx* (elk?), and XVIII *beorc* (birch) (as opposed to rune name XIX *eh* (horse) cited above); the West Saxon monophthongization of *īe* to *ȳ* in rune names VII *ġyfu* (gift) and X *nȳd* (need) (see Campbell #300, 301); and the late West Saxon smoothing of *ēa* to *ē* in rune name XII *ġēr* (year) (see Campbell #312). So much dialectical and chronological variety in a list of only twenty-nine words suggests a long and chequered history of transmission for the rune names that appeared on page 135 of Hickes' *Thesaurus*.

Almost all the language in the main text of the Old English *Rune*

Poem is unquestionably West Saxon, with the exception of three possibly Kentish forms that show the raising of *ǣ* to *ē* in *sēmannum* (line 45) and *beþ* (line 46) and the unrounding and lowering of *ȳ* to *ē* in *brēneð* (line 43) (for which features see Campbell # 288); it is noteworthy that these three forms occur within two adjoining stanzas. The remaining deviations from standard West Saxon are readily explicable as evidence of a late tenth century date for Cotton ms Otho B.x, folio 165.

There are several such indicators in the treatment of stressed vowels. For instance, the text shows an obvious falling together of spellings with *y* and *i*: as in the late West Saxon rounding of *i* to *y* in the neighbourhood of a labial, represented by the almost universal spelling of earlier *biþ* as *byþ* (see Campbell #318); or in the opposite tendency for *y* to unround and appear as *i* before *h*, represented by *hiht(e)* (lines 32 and 45), *tōhiht* (lines 12 and 75), *Drihtne* and *Drihtnes* in lines 3 and 74, as opposed to the normal form *Dryhten* in line 61 (see Campbell #316); or in various inverted spellings with *y* for *i* where there is nothing to cause rounding, as in *unstyllum* (line 58), *gerysena* (line 72), and *wyle* (line 61), as opposed to the normal form *wile* in line 3 (see Campbell #317). Similarly, we find the late West Saxon monophthongization of *ĭe* as *y̆* in *byrneþ* (line 17), *hwyrft* (line 25), and *trȳwa* (line 48) (see Campbell #299–301). Also *syllan* (line 33) represents a late West Saxon change common to the *sel-* group (see Campbell #325). *Hlehter* (line 38) and *wexeð* (line 42) are examples of the late West Saxon smoothing of *ea* to *e* (see Campbell # 312). If the form *ēst* is correct in line 68 and not merely a scribal error for *eft*, it may represent the late West Saxon monophthongization of diphthongs (see Campbell #329.2). The presence of two different parasitic vowels in *wætere* (line 26) and *wature* (line 42) reinforces the interchange of *æ* and *a* to demonstrate the falling together in the pronunciation of front and back *a* which appears in name elements from AD 950 (see Campbell #363–7 and 329.3, fn 2).

Other examples typical of late West Saxon occur in the treatment of unstressed vowels. For instance, the falling together of unstressed vowels to an undifferentiated *schwa* (see Campbell #49 and 369–87) results in an understandable scribal confusion of spellings: as in *frōfur* (lines 1, 11, and 58) for standard *frōfor*; *oftust* (lines 17 and 41) and *gelīcust* (line 30) as opposed to *oftast* (line 73); *herenys* (line 19) for standard *herenes*; *underwreþyd* (line 37) for *underwreþod*; *wynan* (line 37) and *māgan* (line 59) for *wynnum* and *māgum; fǣrylde* (line 49) as opposed to *fǣrelde* (line 86); *tūdder* (line 52) for standard *tūddor; nēþun* (line 64) for *nēþan*; and *staþule* (line 82) for *staþole*. The text also shows typical loss of medial vowels after both long and short syllables in *brīdles* (line 66), *fōdres* (line 88), and *wǣtre* (line 89) (see Campbell #388–92) as well as the loss of vowels in contracted verb endings, such as *hæfþ* (lines 23 and 41), *hwyrft* (line 25), and *hylt* (line 82) (see Campbell #732). The uncontracted verb forms *healdeð* (line 48) and *hafaþ* (line 88) are not necessarily evidence of a non-West Saxon origin for the poem, however, since other examples do appear in West Saxon texts (see Campbell #734 and 762).

Consonant forms support the suggestion of late West Saxon provenance. In a number of places throughout the poem *n* appears for *m* in final unstressed syllables (see Campbell #378). Note *miclun, ungemetun, gehwylcun, breostan, wyrtrumun, wynan, secgun,* and *gehwylcun* (in lines 2, 8, 9, 27, 37, 37, 68, and 90 respectively) in comparison to the many instances where the dative plural endings are well preserved. There is also evidence of late West Saxon metathesis of [sk] to [ks] in the spelling *fixa* (line 87) as opposed to *fisces* (line 46) (see Campbell #440). The assimilation and simplification of verbal consonant endings appears only in *hwyrft* (line 25) and *hylt* (line 82); both probably are evidence of southern origin (see Campbell #732–5 and compare Sievers[19]).

In summary, despite the frequent assumption by scholars in the past that the Old English *Rune Poem* must go back to an eighth or ninth century and probably Anglian original,[20] there is no linguistic evidence for this provenance and date in the existing text, which shows only southern and basically late West Saxon forms.

Punctuation

The version of the Old English *Rune Poem* reproduced in Hickes' *Thesaurus* shows typical Old English punctuation by means of a single dot; normally this dot would be placed on a level with the middle of the letters where in poetry manuscripts it served the metrical purpose of marking the end of each half-line of verse.[21] From time to time this verse punctuation is omitted in Hickes' text, totally in the case of stanzas VI, VIII, X, XII, and XVI, and sporadically in a number of other stanzas; it is also misplaced five times: in lines 3, 5 (twice), 38, and 72. There are, however, many lines and several complete stanzas where the single dot is used with perfect metrical regularity. It is noteworthy that there is not a single appearance of the semicolon, which came into common use before the beginning of the eleventh century for ending sentences.[22]

The verse punctuation by single dot is reinforced at the end of stanzas by the invariable appearance of a closing ornamental mark consisting of a triangle of dots resembling a colon followed by a medial dot. Such usage of an ornamental triangle of dots is characteristic of the mid-tenth century Winchester hand which Neil Ker identifies in the *Parker Chronicle* annals for 925–55 in Corpus Christi College Cambridge ms 173, folios 26–27,[23] as well as in the fragments of Bede's *Ecclesiastical History* in Cotton ms Otho B. xi, folios 1–34, 37–8, and Otho B.x, folios 55, 58, 62,[24] and most fully exemplified in the three collections of medical recipes and charms known as *Bald's Leech Book* in British Library Royal ms 12 D.xvii.[25] A careful examination of these manuscripts reveals that the triangle of dots was used only at the ending of discrete entries, where no further material was added to fill out the line and where the next entry began a new line of its own (as, for example, at the end of *The Battle of Brunanburh* in the *Parker Chronicle*, folio 27r; or at the end of sections of Bede's *History* on folios 16, 18, and 21; or at the end of each item in the *Leech Book*'s table of contents, folios 1–6). If the scribe of Cotton ms Otho B.x, folio 165 followed the Winchester scribe's practice of placing his triangle of dots at the righthand margin of the page, the individual stanzas of the Old English *Rune Poem* must have stood out very prominently as puzzles for separate solution.

All aspects of the marking, including not only punctuation but also the use of a hyphen to indicate a runover word (as in *anfen-gys*, line 8),[26] point to a late tenth century date for the manuscript version of the *Rune Poem*.

Regularity of Metre

It is often argued that the Old English *Rune Poem* must be a fairly early composition. Partly this argument is based on the unsafe assumption that the runic content necessitates an early date; but also it is based on the frequently noted correctness of the verse. As E.V.K. Dobbie put it in his introduction to the poem: 'the regularity of the meter, together with the poet's general adherence to the style and diction of the older poetry, places a pre-Alfredian date of composition almost beyond question.[27]

Indeed, there can be no question but that the metre of the Old English *Rune Poem* is notably regular: with the exception of line 39, where there is a lacuna in the text, the lines scan easily according to the accepted verse types and alliterate after the best models.[28] In many ways this hyper-correctness reminds the reader of that paean of West Saxon martial triumph we have entitled *The Battle of Brunanburh*, which cannot possibly antedate the battle itself, fought in 937. Both poets seem to take similar delight in their technical virtuosity in handling the traditional metre and diction. Since heroic verse of such regularity as *The Battle of Brunanburh* could still be composed at or near Winchester in the middle of the tenth century, there would appear to be no inherent impossibility in assigning the composition of the Old English *Rune Poem* to the same West Saxon milieu at a time close to the date of the manuscript text copied by Humphrey Wanley for Hickes' *Thesaurus*, that is, a date indicated by the linguistic evidence to be some time in the latter half of the tenth century.

Sources and Genre of the *Rune Poem*

The Old English *Rune Poem* was not the only versified treatment of the runic symbols. Three other poems of varying provenance and date also either list and name or list and define the runes known to their authors; the modern titles of these poems are: the *Abecedarium Nordmannicum*, the Norwegian *Rune Poem*, and the Icelandic *Rune Poem*.[1] Unfortunately, all three are based, not on the Old English *futhorc*, but on the reduced Norse *futhqrk* and therefore provide information on only sixteen runes; nonetheless, their data are invaluable in attesting to the meanings of the traditional rune names, as demonstrated by the many references made to them in the explanatory notes to this edition.

The existence of so many rune poems has caused scholars to speculate that all may be descended from one original Germanic ur-poem which was in widespread use among the early Teutonic tribes for mnemonic purposes, that is, to aid both in identifying the name of each rune unmistakably and in preserving the fixed sequence of the Common Germanic *futhark*. This view has percolated even into general literary histories, such as Albert C. Baugh's *A Literary History of England*, where Kemp Malone confidently states: 'It seems altogether likely that the runes from the first were learned by means of a poem in which each rune began a section, though in the original poem the sections may have been quite brief – possibly no more than a short verse each. From this original poem the three runic poems were presumably descended.'[2] Some of the more daring scholars have ventured to assume that the hypothetical ur-poem represented and perpetuated concepts of great cultic significance, both through the individual rune names and through their traditional order. This assumption has resulted in elaborate attempts to reconstruct the important elements of pagan Germanic religion on the basis of the extant poems.[3] Such misplaced enthusiasm for reconstructing the primitive ancestor of the Old English *Rune Poem* has induced at least one scholar to emend the extant Old English text so as to reveal its supposed original more clearly.[4]

In assessing the possibility that the Old English *Rune Poem* may be descended from an oral Germanic ur-poem, it is helpful to outline briefly here the nature and content of the other three rune poems and of the manuscripts in which they were found. The full texts of the three poems, along with Modern English translations, are printed for the reader's convenience in Appendix B.

The Abecedarium Nordmannicum

This much discussed bit of ninth century doggerel occurs on page 321 of St Gall, Stiftsbibliothek, ms 878, a manuscript which Bernhard Bischoff attributed to the hand of Walahfrid Strabo (c 808–49), who studied in his youth under Hrabanus Maurus at Fulda.[5] The poem is found in a grammatical context, being appended to a series of extracts from Isidore of Seville's *Etymologiae* which end with 'De litteris' (that is, 'On the Alphabets' of the three sacred languages: Hebrew, Greek, and Latin), and immediately follows a good early example of the Old English *futhorc*. The basic sequence of rune symbols is that of the Danish *futhqrk*, but several of them have been glossed with Old English runes taken from the *futhorc* above. Each rune symbol is accompanied by its mnemonic rune name; and the resultant set of symbols and names is introduced in correct order by means of crude alliterative half-lines that describe exactly where each fits in the traditional sequence and, in the case of the last two groups of five runes, even where each fits in terms of the tripartite division of the *futhqrk*.[6] The scanty linguistic evidence afforded by the poem reveals a strange mixture of Old Norse rune names embedded in a text consisting of both Low and High German forms.[7]

It is difficult to determine how the *Abecedarium Nordmannicum* ever came to be composed or what purpose it was intended to serve. Georg Baesecke has suggested that it may have had its origin at Fulda, being adapted from a Danish original for use in the school there as part of the ninth century missionary effort directed towards Scandinavia.[8] Certainly the poem as it stands gives no indication of any esoteric background of pagan cults or magic. Still less does it have any intrinsic poetic merit. Instead, it reads very much like something a none too gifted teacher might concoct to help dull students with their memorization. There is no significant resemblance between this inept alliterative jingle and any of the other three rune poems.

The Norwegian Rune Poem

This interesting verse description of the Norse *futhqrk* is known only from copies made in the seventeenth century, since the unique medieval version, which once formed part of a law manuscript in the collection of the University Library at Copenhagen, was destroyed by fire in 1728. Textual examination indicates that the author of the poem was Norwegian and that the manuscript from which it was copied cannot have been earlier than the thirteenth century.[9]

The Norwegian *Rune Poem* is much more extensive than the *Abecedarium Nordmannicum*, consisting of as many as thirty-two long lines arranged into sixteen stanzas, each on a different Norse rune. The first line of every stanza alliterates internally; the second does not, but picks up the alliteration of the preceding line in its initial word and is also linked to the first line by end-rhyme so as to form a couplet. The pattern of alliteration normally ignores the opening sound of the rune name involved, a possible explanation being that, since only the rune itself (with no rune name glossing it) stood at the beginning of each stanza,[10] it may have been thought too easy to give away the first letter of the rune name by means of an alliterative clue.

Each stanza opens with a statement, paraphrasing the rune name, which occupies the whole of the first line. This is followed in the second line by a gnomic comment that often appears to be only tenuously, if at all, related to the opening statement. There are several clear allusions to figures out of Norse mythology and legend, notably to Regin (line 10), Frothi (line 20), Tyr (line 23), and Loki (line 26). Also there is one unambiguous reference to Christ (line 14). The bulk of the content, however, is naturalistic, consisting of gnomic statements about life in this world. Despite occasional opaque comments (for example, in lines 5 and 28), the language is relatively straightforward and simple.

In a number of ways the language and content of the Norwegian *Rune Poem* resemble that of the Old English *Rune Poem*. Note, for example, the similar interest in gnomic truth as well as the almost formulaic similarity of concepts revealed by comparing such phrases as the Norwegian poet's 'Hagall er kaldastr korna' (Hail is the coldest of grains) and 'Ár er gumna góðe' (Harvest is a boon to men) with the English poet's 'Hægl byþ hwītust corna' (Hail is the whitest of grains) and 'Gēr byþ gumena hiht' (Harvest is the joy of men). However, unlike its Old English counterpart, the Norwegian *Rune Poem* has no discernible thematic structure: considered as a whole, it seems little more than a series of separate couplets on a variety of subjects, linked only by the use of the same stanzaic form throughout and held in their present order only by the artificial device of the traditional *futhqrk* sequence.

The Icelandic Rune Poem

This highly skilled poetic treatment of the Norse *futhqrk* is known from four manuscripts, of which the oldest, Copenhagen, Arnamagnaean Library ms 687, goes back only as far as the fifteenth century.[11] The poem consists of sixteen stanzas of three short lines each; the first two lines of each stanza are linked by alliteration, while the third has its own internal alliteration. As in the case of the Norwegian *Rune Poem*, the oldest manuscript of the Icelandic *Rune Poem* gives only the runes (without rune name glosses)[12] at the beginning of the stanzas and the initial letter of the rune name normally is left out of the alliterative pattern.

In a variety of instances, the language of the Icelandic *Rune Poem* echoes that of its Norwegian predecessor. For example, note the similarity in the descriptions of *fé* (wealth) as *frænda róg* (discord among kinsmen), Norwegian *frænda róge*; *þurs* (giant or demon) as *kvenna kvöl* (sickness of women), Norwegian *kvenna kvillu*; *kaun* (ulcer) as *barna böl* (fatal to children), Norwegian *barna bǫlvan*; *hagall* (hail) as *kaldakorn* (cold grain), Norwegian *kaldastr korna*; *nauð* (necessity) in terms of *kostr* (choice), Norwegian *koste*; *ár* (harvest) as *gumna góði* (a boon to men), Norwegian *gumna góðe*; *Tyr* as *einhendr áss* (the one-handed god), Norwegian *œinendr ása*; *bjarkan* (birch) as *laufgat lim* (leafy branch), Norwegian *laufgrønstr líma*; and *maðr* (man) as *moldar auki* (augmentation of dust),

Norwegian *moldar auki*. The two poems diverge sharply, however, in fundamental ways. For instance, their definitions of *úr* and *óss* show a quite different understanding of the meaning of both rune names.

More important than similarities and dissimilarities of detail, is the far greater sophistication of the Icelandic poet, as demonstrated in both the style and the content of his lines. The definitions of the runes offered in the Icelandic *Rune Poem* are much less simple and much less naturalistic than those in its Norwegian counterpart. They reveal an author adept in the lore of the skalds, who constructs many of his lines out of established poetic metaphors or *kenningar*, such as *kletta búi* (cliff-dweller, for giant).[13] He delights in using kennings to ring changes in the imagery of his definitions, as when *fé* (wealth), first defined in a fairly straightforward way as 'a source of discord among kinsmen,' is varied in succession to 'fire of the sea' and 'path of the grave-fish' (ie, serpent or dragon). The poet was very learned in Norse mythological and legendary lore, as shown by the epithets he uses; compare, for example, the terms used to describe Odin in stanza four or Tyr in stanza twelve. One most significant indicator of the author's sense of poetic propriety is the complete absence of any reference to God or Christ or the saints, as if he would no more mix his pantheons than his metaphors. At the end of each stanza in the earliest extant manuscript is appended a sort of scholarly apparatus that underlines the difference in erudition between the Icelandic *Rune Poem* and its Norwegian counterpart: first a Latin synonym of the rune name described is provided; then this is supplemented by an Icelandic poetic term for 'king' or 'prince,' whose initial sound alliterates with the absent rune name, thus furnishing a second learned clue to the solution of the runic riddle.

Despite all the learned and poetic refinements outlined above, the Icelandic *Rune Poem* remains very like its Norwegian predecessor in one important respect: its lack of overall structure and direction. The sixteen stanzas, although fascinating in themselves and even homogeneous in their approach to the task of definition, read like a series of separate exercises on a variety of different topics.

Summary

Anyone in search of traces of an oral Germanic ur-poem in the four extant rune poems, the *Abecedarium Nordmannicum*, the Old

English *Rune Poem*, the Norwegian *Rune Poem*, and the Icelandic *Rune Poem*, must be puzzled as to its form and content. Assuming that this hypothetical ur-poem was chanted in some kind of alliterative verse, were the lines long, like those in the tenth century English and thirteenth century Norwegian poems, or short, like those in the ninth century *Abecedarium* and the fifteenth century Icelandic poem? And how many such verses were used in describing each rune? Even more important, what can have been the core content of the original lines, since the bulk of the descriptive statements in the later poems show quite different treatments of their common rune names?

Careful comparison of the four extant rune poems reveals not only an enormous range in chronology, but even greater disparities in content, style, and purpose. The earliest, the *Abecedarium*, really ought to be dismissed from this comparative analysis altogether, since it does not deserve the term 'poem.' As for the remaining three, it is difficult to perceive any closer connection among them than is readily explicable by ordinary rune lore on the one hand (that is, the names of the runes in traditional sequence) and by the shared word-hoard of alliterative formulas on the other, a word-hoard which was the common property of the Germanic-speaking world and which manifests itself in many other poetic contexts outside the rune poems.[14]

In summary, if there was an oral Germanic ur-poem, it can have contributed little beyond the surviving notion of composing verse about the rune sequence to the authors of the four written poems under discussion here. However, as the following sections of this introduction will endeavour to demonstrate, it is not necessary to assume the existence of such an ur-poem in order to account for the composition of the Old English *Rune Poem*.

LINKS WITH LITERATURE OF KNOWLEDGE AND WISDOM

Gnomic Utterance

From ancient times and among many peoples, knowledge has been transmitted by means of brief, pithy statements, often in verse form. Note, for example, the Old Testament proverbs.[15] The masters of classical rhetoric knew, understood, and promoted this practice: Aristotle discusses it in his *Rhetoric*;[16] and Quintilian terms such

gnomic utterances *sententiae* (judgements).[17] We find individual
sententious sayings scattered throughout Old English poetry; for instance in *Beowulf*, where they often are placed in the mouth of
Beowulf himself in order to stress the unusual way in which great
wisdom and great strength are coupled in that archetypal hero king.[18]
In order to ensure their preservation for posterity, gnomic utterances
also were assembled into oral and written collections. As Ernst
Curtius commented, 'Such lines are "mnemonic verses." They are
learned by heart; they are collected; they are arranged in alphabetical order that they may be ready at hand.'[19] Among Latin collections
of this kind familiar to the Anglo-Saxons were the *Distichs of Cato*,
which appear both in the original and in translation in various Old
English manuscripts; these verses were particularly admired and imitated by vernacular poets, as shown in the free compositions in the
same style which often follow the *Distichs* in extant manuscripts.[20]

The Anglo-Saxons preserved and presented all manner of knowledge in such collections: from the ancient and probably oral *thulas*
(lists of Germanic kings, tribes, and heroes) which make up the bulk
of the poem on the life and repertoire of an imaginary *scop* (oral poet)
called Widsith (far-traveller),[21] to the moralizing catalogues of
human careers and modes of dying known as *The Gifts of Men*[22] and
The Fortunes of Men,[23] or the groups of versified maxims found in *The
Exeter Book*[24] and in Cotton ms Tiberius B.i, folio 115.

Like the stanzas of the Old English *Rune Poem*, the first of the
Cotton manuscript maxims are primarily *biþ*-gnomes (pithy statements using the verb *biþ* (is)); for example:

Cyning sceal rīce healdan.   Ceastra beoð feorran gesȳne,
orðanc enta geweorc   þā þe on þisse eorðe syndon,
wrǣtlīc weallstāna geweorc.   Wind byþ on lyfte swiftust;
þunar byð þrāgum hlūdast.   þrymmas syndan Crīstes myccle.
Wyrd byð swīðost.   Winter byð cealdost,
lencten hrīmigost –   hē byð lengest ceald;
sumor sunwlitegost –   swegel byð hātost,
hærfest hrēðēadegost: hæleðum bringeð
gēares wæstmas   þā þe him God sendeð.
Sōð bið switolost.   Sinc bið dēorost,
gold gumena gehwām;   and gomel snoterost,
fyrngēarum frōd,   se þe ǣr feala gebīdeð.
Wēa bið wundrum clibbor.   Wolcnu scrīðað.[25]

(A king must rule a realm. [Roman] cities are visible from afar, cunning works of giants which remain upon the face of this earth, wondrous fortresses of wall-stones. In the sky the wind is swiftest; thunder is loudest in its seasons. The glories of Christ are great. Fate is strongest. Winter is coldest, spring frostiest – it is chilly longest. Summer is most beautifully bright – the sun is hottest, harvest most glorious: it brings to men the fruits of the year which God sends them. Truth is most clear. Treasure is most precious, gold to every man; and the old man wisest, experienced from bygone years, who formerly endured many things. Woe is wondrously clinging. The clouds sail along.)

Bith-gnomes consist mainly of brief summary statements, not of one man's private perceptions, but of community experience over centuries; they trace patterns observed in the animate and inanimate world as well as in the course of human life under God and *wyrd* (fate). Many different kinds of observation are mixed together; for there were then no rigidly isolated categories of knowledge, such as we insist on now in this scientific age – no water-tight compartments separating the subjects of astronomy, meteorology, geology, botany, zoology, political science, social science, theology, literature, and the fine arts. Hence there could be no unconnected or meaningless fact, but each observation had bearing on the others as part of the universal plan (note, for example, the juxtaposition of human woe with weatherclouds; experience and truth with gold). The *bith*-gnomes attempt to recognize and record stable realities in the mysterious flux of life. Surprise has little part in this kind of utterance; the reader feels only the shock of recognition, a sense of familiar truth, of certainty, inevitability, and everlastingness in the way things are. Unquestionably, such gnomic statements epitomized the Anglo-Saxons' understanding of themselves and of their world; and thus they enjoyed a long and vigorous history. As future discussions in this introduction and in the explanatory notes will show, the Old English *Rune Poem* partakes in numerous respects of the lively Old English gnomic tradition.

Riddles

A slightly more indirect approach to the transmission of knowledge and wisdom was by means of verbal puzzles or riddles, which put the mind of the listener or reader to work at identifying the subject described. Like gnomic utterance, this method also had a venerable lineage: compare in the Hebrew tradition Samson's riddle to the Philistines[26] or in the Greek tradition the riddle of the Sphinx which Oedipus finally answered, a very famous riddle about the ages of man that has reappeared in various periods and among many peoples: 'What goes on four legs in the morning, two legs in the afternoon, and three legs in the evening?'[27] Verse riddles in Latin were a favourite pastime for Anglo-Saxon clerics, as exemplified by the series of *aenigmata* by Hwætberht (Eusebius, abbot of Wearmouth), including four on letters of the alphabet;[28] by the riddle collection of Tatwine, archbishop of Canterbury;[29] and, most influential of all, by the century of Latin riddles composed by Aldhelm, abbot of Malmesbury and bishop of Sherborne, to glorify God's creation.[30]

Latin *aenigmata* were much admired and imitated by Old English vernacular poets, as demonstrated by the verse translations of Aldhelm's *De Creatione* (On Creation)[31] and *De Lorica* (On a Chainmail Coat)[32] which form part of the collection of Old English riddles preserved in *The Exeter Book*. Indeed, it is well to be reminded at this point that the bulk of extant Old English poetry was composed by clerics, who must have been as intimately acquainted with Latin verse as with their native songs and who, like the famous Aldhelm, may even have been equally adept at composing both.[33] The vernacular poets were not slavishly imitative, however. For example, in addition to the verbal clues furnished by the main text of their riddles, they often added a distinctively Germanic touch in the form of runic clues, as in Exeter riddle 19 whose subject is 'a man going hawking on horseback':

Ic on sīþe seah ᛫ ᛋ ᚱ ᚠ
ᚻ᛫ hygewloncne hēafodbeorhtne,
swiftne ofer sǣlwong swīþe þrægan.
Hæfde him on hrycge hildeþryþe
᛫ᚾ ᚠᛗ᛫ nægled ne rād
᛫ᚠᚷᛗᛈ᛫ Wīdlāst ferede
rynestrong on rāde rōfne ᛫ ᚻ ᚠ
ᚠ ᚠ ᚠ ᚾ ᛫ Fōr wæs þӯ beorhtre
swylcra sīþfæt. Saga hwæt ic hātte.

(On a journey I saw a *sigel rād ōs hægl*, proud, with a shining head, run very swiftly over the plain.

On its back it bore a brave
nȳd ōs man; he did not ride in riveted mail upon the
āc gyfu eh wynn. Ranging far he journeyed;
strong in running, on his way he carried a bold *ċēn ōs*
feoh ōs āc hægl. The passage was by that much the finer,
the journey of these. Say what I am called).[34]

Here the individual runes represent their names, which fit into the
alliterative metre of the poem; but also, taken in groups as letters and
read backwards, they spell out the four words that make up the
riddle's solution: *hors* (horse), *mon* (man), *wega* (ways), and
haofoc (hawk).

    As the detailed discussion of the techniques and themes of the Old
English *Rune Poem* later in this introduction will show, the poem has
a great deal in common with vernacular verse riddles, not least being
its author's delight in verbal ingenuity and his habit of using runic
symbols both to disguise and at the same time to reveal sought after
knowledge.

PARALLELS WITH ALPHABETIC POEMS

The notion that letters can be something more than a script for direct
communication is as ancient as the first recorded riddles and gnomic
utterances. A vast body of poetry from as early as the Sibylline Books[35]
used the acrostic device to convey messages additional to those of the
main text. This kind of intellectual game of making alphabet letters
perform a double function was widespread in the Christian Latin
literature of the Middle Ages, and is reflected, as we have seen, in the
methods of the Old English riddles described above as well as in the
way Cynewulf employs runes, both as an integral part of his description of man's ineluctable death and judgement and as a way of
spelling out his own signature for posterity.

    The acrostic technique most relevant to the Old English *Rune Poem*
is the use of the traditional alphabet sequence as an ordering device
for the verses of a poem. This usage can be traced back as far as the
alphabetic psalms of the Old Testament, where each verse begins
with one of the letters of the Hebrew alphabet.[36] The structural use of
the alphabet was adopted by Christian poets from the early days of
the Church: beginning with Commodian,[37] it appears in the verse of
such influential Latin poets as Hilary of Poitiers,[38] St Augustine of

Hippo,[39] Venantius Fortunatus[40] and Sedulius.[41] The greatest of the
Church Fathers and founder of theology, St Augustine, tells us that
his contemporaries called such *psalmos* (hymns) *abecedarios*;[42] and
no doubt his own alphabetical *Psalmus contra partem Donati* both
reflected and encouraged the popularity of the form. The fifth century
poet, Sedulius, also must have had considerable impact upon
would-be Latin versifiers among the Anglo-Saxons, as evinced by the
fact that one of his alphabetical hymns is quoted by Bede in *De Arte
Metrica*[43] as well as appearing in a number of Old English manuscripts.[44] Furthermore, it is interesting to note that the teachers to
whom the Anglo-Saxons were most deeply indebted for their mastery
of Latin style, that is the Irish monks, manifested an early and continuing interest in *abecedaria*: the oldest Irish Latin verse is an alphabetical hymn on Saint Patrick by Sechnall (Secundus);[45] and the
sixth and seventh centuries boast at least half a dozen more examples, including St Columba's *Altus Prosator*.[46] As a result of these
combined influences in England, we encounter the use of the alphabet as an ordering device for Latin verse from early Northumbrian
compositions such as Bede's alphabetic hymn in honour of St Ethel-
dreda[47] to the alphabetic hymns of Wulfstan in the last century of
Anglo-Saxon rule.[48]

More important than these *abecedaria*, which merely use the alphabet in order to treat other subjects, are two Latin poems that take
the alphabet itself for their topic. The first, *De Letteris Monosyllabis
Graecis ac Latinis*,[49] is by Ausonius, a poet whose work probably was
known in Anglo-Saxon England;[50] however, this poem is not itself
acrostic in form and could have supplied no more than the idea that
the alphabet might be described in verse. The second example offers a
number of closer parallels to the Old English *Rune Poem*. Of unknown
authorship, this Carolingian poem is known by the title *Versus
Cuiusdam Scoti de Alphabeto* (Verses on the Alphabet by a Certain
Irishman); it is found in the eleventh century Cambridge University
Library ms Gg.5.35 and the tenth century British Library ms Royal
12.c.xxiii, as well as in various continental manuscripts. The following few stanzas from the beginning of the poem will give some idea of
its structure, style, and content.

A Principium vocis ueterumque inventio mira
  Nomen habens domini sum felix uoce pelasga;
  Exsecrantis item dira interiectio dicor.

B Principium libri, mutis caput, alter in ordo,
   tertia felicis uere sum syllaba semper;
   Si me graece legas, uiridi tum nascor in horto.

C Principium caeli, primis et luna figuris;
   Et me clerus amat, legeris si graece, latinus;
   Littera sum terrae pedibus perscripta quaternis.

D Ablati casus nox sum et pars septima linguae,
   Omnipotentis habens nomen, cum 'us' bannita iuncta;
   Sum medium mille et ueterum mala nota deorum.

A First of the voiced sounds (ie, first vowel [or perhaps a baby's first cry?])
and marvellous invention of antiquity, having the name of the Lord (see Rev.
22:13 'I am *alpha*') I am blessed in the Pelasgan tongue (ie, Greek); also I am
uttered as a dire interjection in cursing (ie, 'Ah!').

B First of the word 'book' (*biblos*), foremost among the voiceless sounds (ie,
consonants), second in alphabetical sequence, truly I am always the opening
sound of the trisyllabic word 'blessed' (*beatus*); if you read me in Greek (ie,
the letter *beta*, homonym of the plant name *beta*), then I grow in a green
garden.

C First of the word 'heaven' (*caelum*) and shaped like the new moon; and
clerics love me, whether read in Greek (the letter *kappa*) or Latin (*cappa*,
cape); I am a letter inscribed in the earth by fourlegged feet (ie, the C-shaped
marks made by horseshoes).

D (As a preposition *de*) I govern the ablative case and am the seventh part of
speech, having the name of the Omnipotent when joined with the syllable *-us*
(ie, *Deus*); I am half of one thousand (in Roman numberals) and of old an
evil sign of the pagan gods (before the god's name, D signified *deus*).[51]

   In all, the poem gives enigmatic descriptions of twenty alphabet
letters, presented in sequence from *A* to *V* and handled in a manner
both playful and learned. It would be foolhardy to suggest that
this particular Latin poem was familiar to the author of the Old English *Rune Poem*, especially since there is at least one other example
of the composition of Latin verses on alphabet letters, emanating
from Northumbria as early as the eighth century,[52] to show that the

Versus Cuiusdam Scoti de Alphabeto by no means constituted a unique insular phenomenon. What is significant about the parallel drawn here, however, is that, no matter how different the descriptions of the meaningless letters of the alphabet given above may be from the descriptions of the meaningful names of the runes in the Old English *Rune Poem*, both poets devote a stanza to describing each letter, their stanzas are modelled on riddles and normally three lines in length, and each of the sets of stanzas is arranged according to the traditional sequence of the letters described.

SUMMARY

The preceding discussion of possible sources and relevant genres demonstrates clearly that the environment in which The Old English *Rune Poem* came into being was rich in influences that could have assisted in suggesting the underlying concept of the poem and determining the literary shape it was to take. The Germanic runes may, indeed, have been memorized with the aid of verses, although it is obvious that these mnemonic verses must have been very short if they were to facilitate rather than impede the process of oral memorization and transmission. Whether the author of the *Rune Poem* was aware of this hypothetical practice is impossible to assess; more than likely he knew of the *futhorc* order only from the manuscript tradition. However, the manuscripts he knew undoubtedly also included acrostic poems, where the verses were arranged in the order of the Latin alphabet, and may even have included poems whose subject matter was the alphabet itself. It would require no great leap of the poet's imagination to recognize the superior possibilities of the *futhorc* for a verse exercise of this kind.

Once determined on such an exercise, the poet would be constrained by the intractability of the traditional rune names into defining a set of words which, for the most part, had current meanings in the Old English vocabulary: the names of various animals, plants and trees, and other objects and concepts of specifically human value. This kind of subject matter would lead him almost inevitably to the sort of utterance characteristic of the well-loved maxims and riddles. The somewhat mysterious quality of the runic symbols would confirm his choice of the riddle form. Where the poet went from that point is properly the topic of the next section of this introduction.

Style and Themes of
the Old English *Rune Poem*

Alliterative Metre

It is doubtful whether the Old English *Rune Poem* was intended for
singing aloud. Despite Kenneth Sisam's belief that voiced rune names
would be instantly recognizable as such by Anglo-Saxon audiences,[1]
it is obvious that much of the effect of any Old English poem containing runes depends upon the distinctive appearance of the rune symbols in contrast to the ordinary insular script on a manuscript page.[2]
Also, the riddling effect of the twenty-nine stanzas of the *Rune Poem*
surely would be wasted if the rune names, which are the subjects of
their enigmatic descriptions, were uttered aloud, as they inevitably
must be in any oral recitation of the poem in order to complete the
alliterative stress pattern of the first line of each stanza. The probable
fact that the poem was and remained literary or 'bookish' in character
does not imply that it participated any less fully in the conventions
inherited from oral Germanic poetry, however. As Larry Benson has
shown, poems redolent of monastic scholarship, such as the Old
English translation of the *Meters of Boethius*, show just as much ease
in handling the traditional diction as do the possibly earlier and at
least apparently more secular poems, such as *Widsith* and *Beowulf*.[3]

Whichever of the two major methods of scansion currently in use
(the isochronous method or the non-isochronous method) is applied
to the *Rune Poem*, it quickly emerges that the 'rules' of Germanic
versification as outlined by Eduard Sievers[4] have been meticulously
observed. Alliteration is both correct and ample. The alliterative
pattern of the first line of the poem is set by the initial sound of the
rune name described in stanza I; this same practice obtains in the

remaining twenty-eight stanzas. Line 1 is also typical in another respect: like the bulk of the lines in the *Rune Poem*, it has three alliterative stresses, that is, on the rune name *feoh* (wealth) and the noun *frōfur* (benefit) in the first half-line or 'a-verse' and on the noun *fīra* (men) in the second half-line or 'b-verse.' Where the poet deviates from this pattern of triple or 'full' alliteration, it is either because he has introduced even heavier alliteration (as in the hypermetric lines of the ninth stanza and in the transverse alliteration of lines 27, 36, 37, 40, and 92), or because a verse is what A.J. Bliss terms 'light'[5] – a condition that John C. Pope explains as occurring when the primary stress introducing the line has been replaced by an initial harp-stroke or rest[6] (as in lines 12, 18, 40, 44, 47, 49, 50, 58, 61, 62, 65, 66, 70, 79, 80, 83, and 91), or by a lightly stressed conjunction (for example, *gif* (if) in lines 3, 64, and 72 and *ðon* (when) in line 46),[7] or else because the primary stress has been made to fall on the thematically significant verb *sceal* (must.). The only exceptions to these general principles are: line 9, where the formulaic phrase *manna gehwylcum* (for all men) precludes two alliterative stresses; line 22, where the shift from the opening formula '*byþ* plus noun' has broken the pattern; and lines 38 and 39, which form part of the singularly opaque and textually corrupted *peorð* stanza and are therefore poor examples of the poet's metrical techniques.

Most of the lines in the *Rune Poem*, as well as many of the half-lines, are almost separable entities. This should not be unexpected in a poem consisting essentially of brief descriptive vignettes, where the normally great structural importance of nouns and adjectives in creating alliterative verses is further emphasized by the content. Where enjambement does occur (as between lines 14–15, 20–1, 23–4, 27–8, 33–4, 39–40, 48–9, 49–50, 51–2, 61–2, 67–8, 68–9, 72–3, 78–9, 79–80, 84–5, 87–8, 91–2), usually it is the result of the appearance of a verb to complicate the appositional structure and vary the monotony of the rhythm. A notable exception is the enjambement between lines 13–14, which is the product of a deliberate design to throw the adjective *sēfte* (easy) into high relief by placing it in a position of primary stress at the beginning of line 14, where it alliterates with its opposite *swīþhwæt* (strenuous). In many of the other instances of enjambement cited above, it is worth noting that the runover statement begins with a 'light' half-line where, according to Pope's system of scansion, the initial pause or harp-stroke opening the b-verse serves to bunch up the syllables in the fourth measure of the line; the consequent rapid pronunciation of several syllables at the end of the first line makes the fully stressed initial words of the next line stand out prominently in contrast, as in lines 14b–15a where the metrical emphasis is made to fall on the important phrase *mēare mægenhear-dum*.

There may have been a number of reasons for the poet's use of the unmistakably heavy hypermetric couplets in stanzas ix and x, one of which will be discussed in the next section of this introduction under the heading of 'Stanza Structure.' As yet no one has succeeded in explaining the functional principles for the occasional expansion to hypermetric lines in Old English poetry. In this poem, nonetheless, whatever the general principle involved, the immediate effect is clear: it produces in the listener a sense of rapid motion and change, an impression particularly suited to the content of stanza ix, the *hægl* stanza. Perhaps in a figurative sense, the crowded, active hypermetric lines are equally suitable to the poet's statement in stanza x that even the oppressive grip of *nȳd* (need, hardship) can be transmuted like *hægl* (hail) into something quite different and beneficial (a possible parallel reinforced by the repetition of the final verb of the *hægl* stanza: *weorþeþ* (changes)).

Most of the poet's metrical pyrotechnics are displayed to striking effect in the concluding stanza of the *Rune Poem*. In the first line, the triple alliteration involves and gives a useful clue to the rune name *ēar* (earth, meaning grave). The hurried effect of line 91, caused by the lightness of its a-verse, puts the first word of the following line: *hrāw* (dead body) into a position of prominence, which is emphasized by its isolation as the only syllable in the first foot or measure of verse 92a. The horror of the inevitable action taking place in line 92 is stressed both by the transverse alliteration and by the rhyming of the two infinitive endings in *hrāw cōlian, hrūsan cēosan* (the dead body to grow cold, to choose the earth). By separating the adjective *blāc* (pallid) from its noun *hrāw* (dead body), placing the adjective at the beginning of a new line and coupling it, through alliteration as well as through imagery and syntax, with *gebeddan* (bedfellow or spouse), the poet compounds the horror and repulsiveness of mortality. Finally, through the last three parallel clauses, with their compound use of triple rhyme in the a-endings of the nouns *blēda* (fruits), *wynna* (joys), *wēra* (human covenants), and the *ge*-prefixes and *aþ*-endings of the verbs *gedrēosaþ* (fall), *gewītaþ* (depart), and *geswīcaþ* (betray or fail), the poet uses all his mastery to hammer home his message and bring the Old English *Rune Poem* to an emphatic close. His technique here is strongly reminiscent of the brilliant closing passage of *Beowulf* (lines 3180–2), where the eulogy of the virtues of that archetypal hero-king reaches its climax in a string of rhyming superlatives.

Stanza Structure

The bulk of Old English poetry is not organized into stanzas, but consists of a kind of alliterative blank verse.[8] It is somewhat surprising, therefore, to note the way in which the Old English *Rune Poem* is divided up into sets of lines, mainly three in number, as recognized by the triple dot end-punctuation discussed on page 31. Although the poet's decision to create a succession of riddling descriptions for all the symbols of the *futhorc* made the production of discrete sets of lines almost inevitable, nonetheless the reader who begins to work through the first couple of dozen lines of the finished poem is struck by the regularity of their division into eight equal sets, which inevitably are identified as eight three-line stanzas. There can be little question of such a regular format being the product of accident; furthermore, it is strongly reminiscent of the three-line stanzas of two of the letter-poems described above: the Icelandic *Rune Poem* and the *Versus Cuiusdam Scoti de Alphabeto*, where both authors also confined their various descriptions of the symbols involved to passages of equivalent length.

The construction of each individual stanza in the Old English *Rune Poem* follows a relatively simple pattern. The stanza opens with a strong primary stress on the first word of the first line, resulting from the fact that the rune name, which is invariably the initial word of the stanza describing it, always sets the alliteration for the first line. Normally the gnomic verb *byþ* (is) comes next, followed by a fairly detailed description of what the rune name denotes or connotes. Unlike the difficult allusive kennings of its Icelandic counterpart, most of the descriptions in this poem are quite direct: all three lines usually are devoted to presenting a single vignette of the person, creature, object, or phenomenon involved. For examples of this straightforward approach among the first eight stanzas, see numbers

II: *ūr* (aurochs), III: ðorn (thorn), IV: *ōs* (mouth), VI: *čēn* (torch), and VIII: *wyn* (joy). In a few instances, the stanza is effectively divided in half because the poet has chosen to present the subject from two different points of view, as (apparently for comic purpose) in stanza V: *rād* (riding) and (clearly for moral purpose) in stanzas I: *feoh* (wealth) and VII: *ġyfu* (generosity); but obviously even here the basic attempt is to present a coherent descriptive statement that will jog the reader's memory and assist in identifying the rune name. There is no need for the poet to use the essentially alien technique of rhyme or to carry the alliteration over from one line to the next in order to link the stanza into a unity. In fact, one of the problems in reading the poem is that the stanzas are almost too nugget-like and therefore in danger of resembling twenty-nine separate poems.

Upon examination of the order in which the stanzas are placed, their essentially discrete nature emerges still more clearly. Except for the common alliterative metre and the shared opening formula (*A* (rune name) *byþ B* (definition)), there are few overt connections between one stanza and the next: no enjambement, no references to a previous statement, no anticipation of what is to come in a later stanza. Indeed, there seems to be no thematic significance for most aspects of the stanza order; for example, no compelling reason why the *ūr* stanza could not follow the ðorn stanza instead of preceding it. It is evident that, just as the poet accepted and composed his vignettes on the basis of the heterogeneous conglomeration of animal, vegetable, human, celestial, and elemental rune names found in contemporary *futhorc* lists, so (with the possible exception of the final two runes) he adopted and worked within the traditional order of the runes in those same lists; only in his refusal to attempt to create an emphatic close for his poem on the unpromising basis of the rune name *īor* (some kind of fish) do we find any evidence that he may have chafed at the restraints imposed by the *futhorc* order.[9]

It comes as something of a shock to discover the apparently unnecessary irregularity of stanza length which marks the last twenty-one stanzas of the *Rune Poem*, especially after an expectation of uniform patterning in structure as well as in content has been so firmly established in the first eight stanzas that it has come to serve as one of the poet's most effective methods of linkage. The reader wonders why a poet capable of writing eight consecutive uniform three-line stanzas on a variety of different subjects should suddenly switch

to two-line hypermetric stanzas for numbers IX and X, back to the
earlier three-line norm for four more stanzas, and then to four-line
stanzas (interspersed with three-line stanzas) for numbers XV,
XVIII–XXII, and XXV, culminating in a five-line stanza for number
XXIX. Certainly the subject matter does not necessitate this kind of
stanzaic diversity. Of course the poet may not have been greatly
concerned about regularity of stanza length or of metrical line, but
this seems unlikely in such an otherwise careful stylist. Also it is
always possible that the poet considered an unbroken succession of
end-stopped three-line vignettes potentially boring and attempted to
vary the monotony. If so, his choice of stanzas to present in hypermetric lines or to extend by one or more lines could have been completely
haphazard. It is interesting to note, however, that these irregularities
occur in patterns that follow the boundaries of the ancient tripartite
groupings of the Germanic *futhark* and of both its Old English and
Norse descendants.

It would be ludicrous to pretend here that the author of the Old
English *Rune Poem* knew any more than we do today about the cultic
significance of the *futhark* order and its three distinct groups among
his early Germanic ancestors who dwelt around the Baltic at least five
hundred years before this poem was written. On the other hand, there
is a high degree of probability that he was aware of the contemporary
division of the Old English *futhorc* into three groups of runes for
purposes of cryptic communication, surviving evidence of which
includes the divided *futhorc* on folio11v of Cotton ms Domitian A.ix,[10]
as well as the secret runic code-writing of the Hackness Cross inscriptions.[11] Hence it may not be a useless exercise to examine carefully
and in detail the correspondences between the traditional *futhorc*
divisions and the shifts in stanza length peculiar to the *Rune Poem*.

First comes the initial group of eight stanzas from *feoh* (wealth) to
wyn (joy), corresponding to the first tripartite division of the Common Germanic *futhark* (what seventeeth century Icelandic scholars,
referring to their own reduced Norse *futhqrk*, were to call *Freys ætt*
(the family, or the group of eight, belonging to the god Frey));[12] all
these stanzas are three lines in length and they establish the norm of
expectation for the rest of the poem. Then the opening of the second
group of stanzas, which includes the eight runes from *haegl* (hail) to
sigel (sun), called *Hagals ætt* (the family of the god Hagal),[13] is
marked unmistakably as a new beginning by the crowded hyper-

metric lines of stanzas IX and X. After this, the poet returns to his previous three-line norm for the middle four stanzas of the group, Next he breaks the sequence with a single four-line stanza, to be followed after two more stanzas by a run of five four-line stanzas; the two intervening three-line stanzas thrust into prominence in this way deal with the final rune of the second group, *sigel* (sun), and the first rune of the third group, *tīr* (the name of a star).

After the *tīr*-stanza, the bulk of the remainder of the third traditional group, called *Týrs ætt* (the family of the god Tyr),[14] consists, as previously noted, of five four-line stanzas. When the stanza length reverts to three lines again, the effect is to emphasize by contrast the two final runes of the original Germanic *futhark*. It should be noted that these two symbols often interchanged position, so that it remains somewhat unclear which properly was the last rune in the ancient *futhark*; evidence of this uncertainty about the traditional order appears as early as the *futhark* on the sixth century Swedish Vadstena[15] bracteate and is reflected in late Anglo-Saxon times by the conflicting order of the English *futhorc* in Cotton ms Domitian A.ix[16] as opposed to the order of the stanzas in the *Rune Poem*. When embarking on the final five runes, which represent the Anglo-Saxon expansion of the original *futhark*, the poet signals the first rune, *āc* (oak), as a new beginning by means of a four-line stanza. Then he continues with three normal three-line stanzas. Finally in the last stanza, which is intended to summarize the poet's message and bring his poem to an emphatic conclusion, the number of lines is expanded to the maximum stanza length in the entire poem, five full and complexly constructed lines.

While the scheme of varying stanza lengths described above results in a poem that lacks stanzaic symmetry, it seems quite likely that it is the result of deliberate planning. The author of the Old English *Rune Poem* appears to have seized upon the traditional divisions of the *futhorc* as cues for appropriate places to create metrical effects that would jolt readers into continued alertness, thus maintaining our interest in both the form and the content of his twenty-nine riddling definitions of the runes.

POETIC DICTION

When the probably monkish author of the *Rune Poem* chose vernacular alliterative verse (rather than, for example, Latin hexameters) as his medium of expression, this choice involved more than an abstract and empty rhythmical pattern to be filled with any words he might select to use; it entailed the employment of a large body of traditional verbal formulas designed to meet the needs of metrical composition by means of ready-made alliterating half-lines. The same formulas and formulaic phrases are found in examples as disparate as the martial poetry of the heroic epic *Beowulf* and the triumphant *Battle of Brunanburh* as opposed to specifically Christian saints' legends and allegories like *Andreas* and the Physiologus poems *Panther, Whale, and Partridge*. These metrical formulas have been subjected to concerted study since Francis P. Magoun, Jr focussed scholarly attention upon them in the context of Caedmon's hymn;[17] one fact which has emerged clearly from such investigations is that the use of these traditional aids was not limited to that semi-legendary figure, the Germanic oral *scop* (poet or maker), but is evident even in translations from Latin texts, where what are obviously the products of learned labours in the monastery take on a curiously heroic flavour.[18]

It is not surprising, therefore, to encounter well-known heroic vocabulary, including familiar half-line formulas, in the *Rune Poem*. Note, for example, the words used for 'man.' There are six instances of the word *man* itself scattered throughout the poem, including the rune name in line 59; the simplex *man* four times in lines 2, 9, 71, and 74; and the compound *sēmannum* once in line 45. But what a thesaurus of convenient alliterative synonyms from *æ* to *w* the poetic word-hoard has furnished to vary that prosaic term, including *æþeling* (in lines 18, 49, 55, and 84), *beorn* (in lines 34 and 43), *eorl* (in lines 12, 55, 84, and 90), *guma* (in lines 19 and 32), *hæle* (in line 70), *hæleþ* (in line 56), *lēod* (in line 63), *rinc* (in line 13), *ðegn* (in line 7), *wiga* (in line 39), plus the plural nouns *elde* (in lines 77 and 81), *firas* (in lines 1 and 83), and *niþþas* (in line 27). The generalized reference of these synonyms is obvious in the way many are used to form part of half-line universalizing formulas, such as: *fira gehwylcum* (line 1), *ðegna gehwylcum* (line 7), and *rinca gehwylcum* (line 13), which clearly are no more than alliterative variants of *manna gehwylcun* (for every man) (line 9); or the phrase *beorna gehwylcne* (every man) (line 43); or the two phrases meaning 'for the sons of men:' *niþa bearnum* (line 27) and *elda bearnum* (line 77).

In a few instances, the poet also employs the kind of specifically poetic terminology known as the 'kenning,' where a simple concept like *sǣ* (sea) appears in the guise of *fisces beþ* (fishes bath) (line 46) or *ganotes bæþ* (gannet's bath) (line 79), or the inanimate ship metaphorically becomes a *brimhengest* (sea-horse).[19] Such terminology was the common property of all alliterative poets, serving elsewhere as it does here both to fill out their rhythmic measures and to dignify their verse.

Much of the stately, ornamental, almost lapidary effect of Old English poetry results from the use of variation, by means of appositional half-line phrases. Such variation is used liberally in the Old English *Rune Poem* in order to amplify and reinforce its twenty-nine verse definitions. Note for example, how stanza II emphasizes the ferocity of *ūr* (the aurochs) by the use of the appositional noun phrase *felafrēcne dēor* (a very fierce beast) and also by the further variant of a formulaic epithet well known to readers of *Beowulf*: *mǣre mōrstapa* (a notorious moor-stalker).[20] Similarly the glory and bounty of the light-giving God are stressed by the appositional phrases for rune XXIV *dæg* (day): *Drihtnes sond* (God's sending) and *mǣre Metodes lēoht* (the glorious light of the Creator).

Appositional half-lines may be noun phrases, consisting of a single qualified noun, as in the examples above; they also may be based on adjectives, as in the series describing the dangerous *ðorn* (thorn) by means of the adjectives *scearp* (sharp) (line 7a), *yfel* (painful) (line 8a), and *rēþe* (fierce) (line 7b). Often the half-lines contain compound epithets, that is, two nouns or two adjectives joined by 'and.' Such compounds either can be correlative, as in *sāres and sorge* (pain and sorrow) (line 23, varying *wēana* (woes) in the preceding line), or can be contrastive, as in *ēadgum and earmum* (the haves and the have-nots) (line 76, amplifying the meaning of the less specific *mannum* (mankind) two lines before). In all cases however, the purpose is clear: to construct a picture of the subject described by piling up complementary details about its nature. Sometimes there is no verb at all in the stanza, except for the 'equals-sign' of the copula verb *byþ*; and then the massed noun and adjective blocks begin to rival the static quality of sculpture (examine, for example, the description of *ēoh* (yew-tree) in stanza XIII).

The normal use of half-line appositional formulas as a descriptive technique in narrative poetry is to produce set-pieces of amplification designed to identify unmistakably and underline the significance of the type of person, setting, deed, or object involved at that point in the action. No doubt contemporary audiences relished such pauses in the narrative, where the poet displayed his skill in the art of varia-

tion.[21] In the *Rune Poem*, however, which is of necessity a collection
of such set-pieces of amplification without any intervening action,
there is danger of a superfluity of descriptive riches as well as of a
certain monotony and choppiness resulting from the lack of a narrative line. The poet does his best to avoid this effect by attempting to
humanize and put as much action as possible into his descriptions:
there are, for example, people sharing the wealth in stanza I, grasping
or lying down among the thorns in stanza III, bestriding the powerful
horse in stanza V, sitting in the torch-lit hall in stanza VI, giving and
accepting gifts in stanza VII, playing games in stanza XIV, voyaging in
stanza XVI, riding out their restlessness in stanza XIX, tossing about
terrified in stanza XXI, travelling east over the water in stanza XXII,
enjoying the delights of home in stanza XXIV, and being buried in
stanza XXIX. Even the vegetable world takes on anthropomorphic
activity and apparent volition in the stanzas on ðorn (thorn), *eolhx*
(elk[-sedge]), *āc* (oak), and *æsc* (ash). The illusion of activity and
change is fostered also by the effort to vary the metre and stanza
length described earlier, as well as by the deliberate reversal of a
stanza's initial direction in the middle or pivotal line—usually from a
carnal to a spiritual end, as the next section of this introduction will
demonstrate.

THEMES AND PURPOSE

The Old English *Rune Poem* has never enjoyed a very high reputation
as literature. With almost the single exception of F.G. Jones' valiant
effort to demonstrate the poem's worth,[22] most commentators have
regarded it as a mediocre curiosity, of more interest to runologists
than to literary critics. See, for example, Lucien Musset's brief dismis-
sal of the poem:

> La valeur du texte n'est pas considérable; ses images manquent singulière-
> ment de variété et d'originalité. À des clichés empruntés au repertoire le plus
> banal de la poésie héroïque s'ajoutent des allusions chrétiennes sans aucun
> élan. Il est vrai que le programme était ingrat et que l'intention de l'auteur
> anonyme était surtout de faire preuve de dextérité et d'érudition.[23]

(The literary value of the text is not very great; its images are singularly
lacking in variety and originality. To commonplaces borrowed from the most
shop-worn word-hoard of heroic poetry are added Christian allusions totally

lacking in vitality. The truth is that the scheme was unrewarding and that the anonymous author's purpose above all else was to offer a proof of his ingenuity and learning.)

As parts of the previous discussion in this introduction have demonstrated, the task which the author of the *Rune Poem* set himself was indeed a difficult one, requiring all his ingenuity and learning to accomplish well; but to ignore his real purpose and hence damn the product of his efforts as arbitrarily as Musset and others have done constitutes a disservice to the poet and to the reading public alike.

It is my contention that the author of the *Rune Poem* recognized in the *futhorc* an opportunity to compose a poem about the temporal world in which he lived and its relationship to the eternal world in which he hoped and believed. The poet must have been well aware of the fact that his proposed task would prove very demanding. The rune names, as he knew them, were both heterogeneous and uncompromisingly secular in meaning, perhaps even still tinged by the pagan past; and their traditional order imposed rigorous constraints on his freedom to develop his theme. Yet the poet was prepared to take up the challenge of forging all this mass of inherited rune lore into a Christian unity; and in my view he had considerable success.

To summarize the nature of his raw material in greater detail, the author of the *Rune Poem* was faced with a set of twenty-nine rune names, many of which involved natural phenomena. There were three examples of animal life: one a wild animal, *ūr* (aurochs); one a tame animal, *eh* (horse); and one a fish, *īor* (some unidentified kind of fish). There were six examples of plant life, including four much admired large trees: *ēoh* (yew), *beorc* (birch), *āc* (oak), and *æsc* (ash); plus two smaller and decidedly less pleasant plants: *ðorn* (thorn) and *eolhxsecg* (elk-sedge). There were two different aspects of the earth: as fruitful provider of edible crops, *ġēr* (harvest), and as ultimate burial place, *ēar* (grave). There were three manifestations of water: liquid as *lagu* (sea), solid as *īs* (ice), and melting as *hægl* (hail). There were three celestial phenomena: one of the night, *tīr* (a planet, star, or constellation), and two of the day, including *dæg* (day) itself and the closely related *sigel* (sun). In addition, the rune names involved ten references to man, one going back as far into the past as the legendary Germanic culture hero Ing, but most referring to various aspects of contemporary human life, from strenuous riding in

the outdoors (*rād*) or profiting from hardship (*nȳd*), to sitting com-
fortably in a torch-lit hall (*čēn*), speaking wisdom (*ōs*), sharing
treasure (*feoh* and *ʒyfu*), living in bliss (*wyn*), playing games
(*peorð*), delighting in the company of other men (*man*), enjoying the
possession of land and home (*ēþel*), and ultimately relinquishing all
these things in death (*ēar* and also *man*).

Many of the rune names were relatively intractable, lending themselves with difficulty, if at all, to an apposite Christian message.
What religious comment can one make about an aurochs or a birch
tree without venturing into overt allegory, which is something this
poet chose never to do? Other rune names, however, facilitated the
formation of Christian associations. For example, *feoh* (wealth)
must inevitably be exposed by any cleric as only a transitory good.
Similarly, *ʒyfu* (gift or giving) lent itself to interpretation as charity;
and *nȳd* (hardship) was traditionally understood by Christians as
God's testing of man. *Ġēr* (harvest) remained a time for thanksgiving
to God even after the Christianization. Also *man* (man) could hardly
be defined without a reference to the curse of mortality consequent
upon Original Sin. *Dæg* (day) was an ancient symbol of the God who
separated light from the primordial darkness. In Christian symbolism, *laʒu* (sea) was widely used to represent the instability of this
world and the insistent need to seek a firmer dwelling-place in
Paradise.[24] Finally, *ēar* (earth) would almost inevitably recall the
return of man's body to its constituent clay at the time of burial. This
list of rune names obviously susceptible to Christian reinterpretation
numbers no more than eight out of a total expanded *futhorc* of
twenty-nine runes. How did the author of the *Rune Poem* contrive to
assimilate the entire body of disparate *futhorc* material to the same
didactic purpose?

First of all, the poet did not make the mistake some moralists do of
undervaluing the potential human worth of any of the subjects in-
voked by the rune names. Most of his stanzas are miniature celebra-
tions of the good things of this world—a world that, after all, was
thought to be the creation of a loving God.

Thus wealth in stanza I is declared to be a universal benefit, albeit a
transitory one. The aurochs in stanza II may be a dangerous beast,
perhaps, but is also shown as a model of courage. The thorn in stanza
III becomes almost a respected adversary. Man's delight in listening
to wise conversation is echoed in stanza IV. The strenuous aspect of

horseback riding receives jocular treatment in stanza v. The brilliance of the torch in stanza vi is a characteristic delightful to the very highest classes. Gift-giving honours both parties involved in stanza vii. Stanza viii assures us that man can experience joy in this world. Hail is no scourge in stanza ix, but a continuing wonder to behold, as it falls from heaven and goes through its sudden whirling movements and final mysterious transformation to fresh water. Even hardship in stanza x turns out well in the end. Ice in stanza xi is both a miracle and also extremely beautiful, a natural jewel gracing the winter world. Harvest in stanza xii is a boon to all. The yew tree, described in detail in stanza xiii, is admirable, useful, and a pleasure to have on one's land. Men laugh companionably as they play games in the mead-hall in stanza xiv. Elk-sedge in stanza xv, like the thorn in stanza iii, is revealed as a warrior worthy of respect in the defence of its home. The sun in stanza xvi is a continuing symbol of deliverance for seafarers. The planet (or star or constellation) Tir in stanza xvii, like all heavenly bodies above the fickle moon, is an emblem of trustworthiness in the darkness of night. The birch in stanza xviii is tall and beautiful and also a reproductive marvel. The horse in stanza xix is a splendid animal for nobles to take pride in as well as a source of recreation to its owner. Family life is treasured in stanza xx. The rough sea in stanza xxv may be terrifying, but it also has an aura of exhilarating challenge. Heroic legends, like that of Ing in stanza xxii, can be suggestive topics to recall and ponder. Home in stanza xxiii is where we enjoy ourselves best and feel most secure. Day is deservedly beloved by all in stanza xxiv. The oak in stanza xxv is useful to man in at least two different ways: as a source of nutriment for the boar's flesh he relishes and as timber for the ships in which he adventures. The ash tree in stanza xxvi is tall and highly prized, especially for making stout spears. The bow in stanza xxvii is both decorative and useful. The unidentifiable fish in stanza xxviii lives its own strange watery life in constant delight. Only the grave in stanza xxix has no mitigating human pleasure associated with it.

Modern readers must be careful always to remember that even the most ascetic medieval monk could not repudiate the created world as evil in itself: the Church taught that the postlapsarian world still consisted of a shower of good gifts poured upon thankless man by a beneficent God. Only human perversity in valuing the gifts more than their giver and failing to recognize the transience of all physical things (including man's own body) could transform our earthly dwelling-place into a potential source of evil. Such excessive love of the world was a sign of spiritual blindness, the inability to see the greater eternal good shadowed forth by the transitory images of the divine book of creation for even the illiterate to read.[25] Hence the author of the *Rune Poem* was in no way unorthodox when he created delightful vignettes descriptive of each of the rune names in stanzas far too long to be of any mnemonic value for the utilitarian transmission of *futhorc* lore. His obvious intention in composing these stanzas was to transmit some of his own pleasure and interest in the created universe to the reader, who would exercise his mind in deciphering the individual enigma posed by each successive stanza and feel again and again the agreeable shock of recognition which belongs alike to the tradition of gnomic statement and to the riddle form.

Yet, from the beginning to the end of the poem, the author takes care to put the good things of the world into proper perspective. In the very first stanza he seizes the opportunity to transform the ᚠ rune, *feoh* (wealth), which always represented an important human value, into the subject for a little homily on how to handle worldly goods. This note of warning sounds again at various points throughout the poem; for example, in stanza VII on *gyfu* (giving), in stanza X on *nȳd* (hardship), and even, less directly, in apparently secular verses, such as stanza XXII on the mysterious arrival and inevitable departure of Ing. The warning receives its fullest statement only in the final stanza, where the poet gathers up the various strands of the poem and weaves them into an unmistakable pattern, epitomizing all that he has attempted to show before. The disruption in the *futhorc* sequence by his reversal of the normal positions of ᛡ *īor* (a fish) and ᛠ *ēar* (the earth) furnishes striking evidence that only the image of the grave would serve his thematic purpose in the closing stanza. In line 90, the sense of joy which has underlain all the previous stanzas turns to unmitigated terror ('ēar byþ egle eorla gehwylcun' (earth is loathsome to every man)) and a truly frightening passage ensues where the physical world, in which poet and reader have shared their instinctive delight, is reduced to an image of the wretched flesh, the pale, cold human body, contacting the earth it has loved too dearly in an ineluctable and lasting embrace. Then, in an inexorable trio of parallel rhyming phrases, the poet strips away all the comforts that will depart from man when his body enters its final resting place, just as they also will depart from the whole created world at the Apocalypse:[26] 'blēda gedreosaþ, wynna gewītaþ, wēra geswīcaþ' (the fruits of the earth will fail, joys will depart, and all man-made covenants will be broken).

The ancient Common Germanic *futhark* began with *feχu (cattle) and ended with *ōþil (land); its twenty-four runes have often been seen as encapsulating the entire world view of a primitive agricultural people.[27] The *futhark*'s expanded Anglo-Saxon descendant, the Old English *futhorc*, has been carefully manipulated by the author of the Old English *Rune Poem* so as to serve a similar function, to epitomize the more sophisticated vision of creation which pervaded the mind of Christian Europe in the Middle Ages.

The Literary Achievement
of the *Rune Poem*

As the previous sections of this introduction clearly demonstrate, any critical evaluation of the Old English *Rune Poem* must assess its literary achievement in the context of the anonymous poet's difficult runic raw materials, his skill in handling the inherited conventions of alliterative verse, and his overriding purpose of shaping the twenty-nine verse definitions of the Anglo-Saxon *futhorc* symbols into an imitation of the concise and cryptic wisdom literature so popular among his contemporaries – all in an attempt to recreate in micro-cosm a world he saw as declaring the glory of God and showing His handiwork in its every part. The result of the poet's endeavours lies at the literary polar extreme from most modern verse, particularly from those nineteenth and twentieth century poems which attempt to present themselves as the product of what Wordsworth termed 'the spontaneous overflow of powerful feelings.'[1] It is a carefully crafted didactic poem, designed to convey moral and spiritual instruction along with and by means of poetic pleasure, very much as Horace advised so many centuries before in his much quoted *Ars Poetica*, lines 343–4:

Omne tulit punctum qui miscuit utile dulci,
Lectorem delectando pariterque monendo.

(He has gained every vote who has mingled profit with pleasure by delighting the reader at once and instructing him.)[2]

At the same time, the *Rune Poem* imitates what the most influential of the early Church Fathers, St Augustine of Hippo, identified as the method of the Holy Scriptures, by requiring considerable intellectual effort on the part of the reader, first in discovering the correct rune name described by each stanza and then in perceiving how illuminatingly that name has been incorporated into the poet's overall Christian vision. No doubt the author hoped to increase the esteem in which his verses were held in direct proportion to the difficulties placed in his reader's path, on the grounds that, as the revered Augustine himself assures us in *De Doctrina Christiana* II, vi, 8,: 'cum aliqua difficultate quaesita multo gratius inveniri' (what is sought with difficulty is discovered with more pleasure).[3]

It is self-evident that, in order to understand any Old English poem properly, eventually we must make some attempt to 'medievalize' ourselves: to try to see poetry neither as the product of emotional reactions nor as primarily designed to elicit them, but as the result of a rigorous intellectual exercise intended to furnish similar mental activity as well as spiritual edification for the committed reader. In the case of the *Rune Poem*, this necessity manifests itself unambiguously from the outset; there is very little basis for a romantic reading of its ninety-four lines. The poet's concern to teach, to make human moral application, precludes any serious attempt at lyrical descriptive passages; only the occasional description of one of the numerous natural objects, such as stanza XI on *īs* (ice) or stanza XVIII on *beorc* (birch), affords a rare and almost accidental glimpse of what his imagination might have given us, had his purpose been different. Similarly, the necessary discontinuity of subject from stanza to stanza precludes the development of the kind of sustained meditation on a single theme found in elegiac poems of equivalent length, such as the haunting *Wanderer* and *Seafarer*, or the vigorous narrative effects found in heroic poems of equivalent length, such as the stirring *Battle of Maldon* and *Battle of Brunanburh*. Yet stanza II on *ūr* (aurochs) provides convincing evidence that the poet was by no means incapable of composing in the heroic vein, and stanza XXIX on *ēar* (the earth as grave) is as powerful an evocation of human loss as any five-line passage in the better known elegiac poems. As demonstrated in the full discussion of the poem's style and themes earlier in this introduction as well as in the explanatory notes to the text, the reader who wishes to appreciate the literary achievement of the *Rune Poem* must begin with both a greater sensitivity to individual detail and a greater readiness to perceive loose and subtle structuring methods than most of us find necessary for an immediately positive response to the first surface attractions of the elegiac and heroic poems named for comparison above.

The initial demands presented by the *Rune Poem*, coupled with its unambiguously Christian outlook, probably account for the low esteem in which it has been held by many modern critics, particularly by the now almost extinct species of critic who saw its sole redeeming value in the pagan vestiges thought indivisible from rune lore.[4] General critical opinion in this century, where it pronounces on this poem at all, has contributed little more than a variously phrased reiteration of Bruce Dickins' discouraging statement in the introduction to his edition that the poem is 'exactly parallel ... to the old nursery rhyme:

"A was an Archer who shot at a frog;
 B was a Butcher who had a big dog."'[5]

Note, for example, how even a critic with the sensitivity of Stanley B. Greenfield dismisses the literary pretensions of the *Rune Poem* in half a sentence: 'As poetry the verse needs little comment ...' Yet there can be no doubt that both the techniques and the content of this poem would have been extremely congenial to contemporary Anglo-Saxon readers. They would have rejoiced, not only in the overt didacticism encountered so frequently in its twenty-nine stanzas, but also in the pervasive riddling qualities, the deliberate ambiguities, shifts in perspective, significant juxtapositions, antithesis, and play on words – all of which would have been welcomed as opportunities to stretch the reader's mind and thereby enable him to understand a little more of the book of divine revelation presented by the created world in which he lived and which this poem was designed to mirror.

Thus, paradoxically, the Old English *Rune Poem* serves more effectively than many other far more frequently anthologized and applauded examples to introduce the student to the very centre of medieval poetic and intellectual interests. In so doing, it furnishes in its own ninety-four lines an excellent instance of that true eloquence which the poet praises in stanza IV on ōs (mouth, speech) as the support of wisdom, a comfort to wise men and the joy and delight of every noble.

Notes

1 For the history of the North Semitic consonant series through its various descendants (Phoenician, Greek, Etruscan, Roman, and runic) see David Diringer, *The Alphabet*.

2 For details on the new Anglo-Saxon runes see the explanatory notes on stanzas IV, XXV, XXVII, XXVIII, and XXIX, as well as the discussion beginning on page 12.

3 Compare the Common Germanic *futhark* given on page 4 with the Old English *futhorc* given on page 12. Except for the sixth, twelfth, and twenty-second runes, which were lengthened from half-size to normal height, there are very few differences between the twenty-four original runes as represented by both.

4 Compare the bulk of the rune names in the Old English *Rune Poem* with the rune names listed or defined in the *Abecedarium Nordmannicum*, the Norwegian *Rune Poem*, and the Icelandic *Rune Poem* printed in Appendix B; and also examine the rune name etymologies introducing the discussion of each stanza of the Old English *Rune Poem* in the explanatory notes.

5 For an example of a corrupted rune form see the explanatory note on stanza XIV.

6 For examples of rune names that had little or no currency in Old English, see the explanatory notes on stanzas II, IV, VI, XIV, and XV; for names that appear to be replacements of some kind see the explanatory notes on stanzas III and XXVI.

7 See L. Balzer, *Hällristningar fran Bohuslän* and H. Shetelig and H. Falk, *Scandinavian Archaeology*, chapter 10.

8 The Common Germanic *futhark* shown in this introduction is a normalized version based on a number of variant early inscriptions. For the authoritative study of these inscriptions see Wolfgang Krause, *Die Runeninschriften im älteren Futhark* (cited hereafter as Krause) and its

1966 revision with the assistance of H. Jankuhn. See also Helmut Arntz and Hans Zeiss, *Die einheimischen Runendenkmäler des Festlandes*. A selected anthology of inscriptions in the twenty-four rune Common Germanic *futhark*, as well as in both the reduced sixteen rune Norse *futhǫrk* and the expanded twenty-eight to thirty-three rune Old English *futhorc*, forms the second part of Lucien Musset's invaluable handbook, *Introduction à la Runologie* (cited hereafter as Musset). For a brief English summary of the early Germanic *futhark* inscriptions see Ralph Elliott's *Runes, an Introduction* (cited hereafter as Elliott, *Runes*).

9 Tacitus, *Germania*, chapter 10. For the full text of this reference see the explanatory note on stanza 1. It is interesting to observe that Tacitus' famous passage describes Germanic augurers as picking up three marked slips of wood; possibly the specific number could have some connection with the traditional tripartite division of the *futhark* (see footnote 17 below for this persistent division).

10 Venantius Fortunatus, *Carmina* VII.18, lines 18–19, edited by F. Leo, *Monumenta Germaniae Historica*, IV, i, p 173:

Barbara fraxineis pinguatur rhuna tabellis
Quodque papyrus agit, virgula plana valet.

(Let the barbarous rune be painted on ash-wood tablets
And what papyrus can do, a smoothed stick is also good for.)

11 See the photograph of the Kylver stone in Elliott, *Runes*, plate II, fig 3.
12 See the photograph of the Charnay fibula in Elliott, *Runes*, plate III, fig 6.
13 See the photograph of the Breza pillar in Musset, plate I, figs 1 and 2.
14 See the photograph of the Vadstena bracteate in Elliott, *Runes*, plate II, fig 4.
15 See the photograph of the Grumpan bracteate in Elliott, *Runes*, plate II, fig 5.
16 Attempts to account for the order of the *futhark* symbols span a considerable time-period and involve widely divergent theories. They include W.W. Skeat's wildly ahistorical attempt to associate the order with the initial letters of the Lord's Prayer: 'fæder ure, thu onheofonum ... thin rice cume,' etc, in 'The Order of Letters in the Runic Futhork.' More worthy of serious consideration are several attempts to find its source in the order of the alphabet, including those of George Hempl in 'The Origin of the Runes,' and G. Baesecke in *Vorgeschichte des deutschen Schrifttums*, pp 94–125. Other runologists have been confident that they discerned content-groupings, such as the antithetical pairs seen by F. von der Leyen in 'Die germanische Runenreihe und ihre Namen,' or the groupings by topic (eg, weather and seasons) seen by W. Jungandreas in 'Die germanische Runenreihe une ihre Bedeutung.' More adventurous than these

are the various attempts to trace cultic or magical significance in the
futhark order: one such is Sigurd Agrell's *Runornas talmystik och dess
antika förebild* (an approach vigorously repudiated by A. Baeksted in his
important *Målrunar og Troldrunar, Runemagiske Studier*); another is
Karl Schneider's ingenious study, *Die Germanischen Runennamen* (cited
hereafter as Schneider, *Runennamen*), especially the complex charts and
diagrams of interrelationship in the Tafeln at the end of the book. Lucien
Musset gives a brief but well-balanced evaluation of the actual *futhark*
evidence in his *Introduction* #49–53.

17 For a discussion of the practice of dividing the *futhark* into three groups,
especially in relation to the common use of these divisions in runic
cryptography, see René Derolez' indispensable *Runica Manuscripta*
(cited hereafter as Derolez), pp 89–169, but especially pp 137ff.

18 The most influential exponent of this theory was Otto von Friesen, whose
attribution of runes to a Greek-Gothic source was at one time promul-
gated by the *Encyclopaedia Britannica*; for a full exposition of his hypothesis with supporting evidence see 'Om runskriftens härkömst.'

19 For a detailed exposition of the Latin theory of origin see Ludvig Wimmer's
monumental *Die Runenschrift*. (F. Holthausen's German translation
rather than the original Danish will be cited hereafter as Wimmer).

20 For a persuasive enunciation of the theory of North Italic origin see
Magnus Hammarström's 'Om runskriftens härkömst.'

21 For a concise summary of the various theories of origin and a judicious
evaluation of the merits of the North Italic theory as opposed to other
theories see Musset #13–20.

22 *Hávamál*, verse 80, from the edition by D.E.M. Clarke, which is the source
of all future quotations from the peom. Compare also the inscription on
the late fifth century Swedish stone found at Noleby: 'runo fahi
raginakudo' (I paint the runes which come from the gods), photographically reproduced in Elliott, *Runes*, plate xi, fig 28, and the similar inscription on the eighth century Sparlösa stone, for which see Ivar Lindquist,
Religiösa runtexter. II: Sparlösa-stenen.

23 *Hávamál*, verses 138–9.

24 See the excellent article by T.H. Wilbur on 'The Word "rune."'

25 For examples of *futhark* inscriptions see the collections cited in note 8
above, especially that of Wolfgang Krause whose inscriptions often will
be cited by number in this portion of the discussion.

26 See Krause no 11 and also the somewhat unclear photograph of the Øvre
Stabu spearhead in Elliott, *Runes*, plate iv, fig 8.

27 See the inscribed *futharks* cited in notes 11–15 above.

28 See Krause no 38 and the photograph of the Lindholm amulet in Elliott,
Runes, plate vi, fig 19.

29 Note the repetition: ᚷ ᚨ ᚷ ᚨ on the fifth century spearshaft found at Kragehul in Denmark, which has been interpreted as an abbreviation for the prayer: 'g(ibu) a(uja), g(ibu) a(uja)' (give luck, give luck). See Krause no 39.

30 Observe the close association of runes with sun and ship symbols on the fifth century stone found at Kårstad in Norway (Krause no 44 and Musset, plate III, fig 6). Compare the similar association of runes with pre-runic type symbols on the third century Kowel and Dahmsdorf spearheads (Krause nos 8 and 9).

31 For inscribed stones buried from public view in graves, note, in addition to the Kylver stone (cited in note 11 above), the six other stones cited among Anders Baeksted's statistics in 'Begravede Runestene.' These include the important sixth century Noleby stone (Krause no 52) cited in note 22 above.

32 For the texts of extant inscriptions in the later Norse *futhqrk* and its various local and chronological modifications see: Lis Jacobsen and Erik Moltke, *Danmarks Runeindskrifter*; Magnus Olsen, *Norges Innskrifter med de yngre Runer* and 'Runic Inscriptions in Great Britain, Ireland and the Isle of Man;' Anders Baeksted, *Islands Runeindskrifter*; and Sven Söderberg, Erik Brate, Elias Wessén, and others, *Sveriges Runinskrifter* I–XIII. Musset also includes a selection in the 'Anthologie Runique' which forms the second part of his *Introduction*.

33 Musset gives a helpful outline of the development and spread of the later (or *yngre* (younger)) Norse *futhqrk* in chapter IV of his *Introduction*, pp 213ff. See also the brief English account in Elliott, *Runes*, pp 21ff.

34 For the sequence of the later Norse *futhqrk* see the ninth century Danish Gørlev stone (Jacobsen and Moltke no 239); and compare the ninth century version presented in the *Abecedarium Nordmannicum*, reproduced in facsimile in Derolez, p 78 and also printed in Appendix B to this edition, where its rune forms can be compared with the later variants found in the thirteenth century Norwegian *Rune Poem* and the fifteenth century Icelandic *Rune Poem*.

35 On the practice of colouring incised runes with black, white, and red paint for greater legibility see Musset #147. Hence the word *faihian (to paint), later *stæina* (to stain), appears from the fifth century in runic inscriptions with the meaning 'to carve runes,' even on metal bracteates where no paint could have been involved (see Jacobsen and Moltke, bracteates 66 and 74). Compare also Fortunatus' use of the word *pinguatur* in note 10.

36 For examples of charms inscribed in the Norse *futhqrk* see the runic amulets of the Viking age listed in Jacobsen and Moltke, col 82, fn2.

37 See the Gørlev stone cited above in note 34.

38 Notable among cryptic inscriptions is the famous Swedish stone found at Rök. See Otto von Friesen, *Rökstenen*; Elias Wessén, *Runstenen vid Röks kyrka*; Lis Jacobsen, 'Rökstudier;' the photograph in Musset, plate XIV, fig 18; and the description of the various cryptic systems used on the Rök stone in Derolez, pp 143ff.

39 For examples of unintelligible inscriptions in the Norse *futhąrk* see Elias Wessén and Sven B.F. Jansson, *Upplands Runinskrifter*, nos 427, 466, 468, 483, 487, 522, 529, 811, 888, 902, 1000, 1170, 1175, 1178–80.

40 The Danish stone found at Nørre Brarup was so buried (see Jacobsen and Moltke no 9).

41 For examples of these pictorial motifs see the stones found at Jelling, Århus, Tullstorp, and Hunnestad (Jacobsen and Moltke nos 42, 66, 271, and 285), and also at Lyrestad and N. Åsarp, shown in E. Svärdström, *Västergötlands runinskrifter*, nos 14 and 181. Compare the references in note 7.

42 For examples of the runic serpent (*runslangen*) see Musset, plates XV–XX.

43 Note the representations of Thor fishing on the Swedish stone found at Altuna and on the Gosforth Cross in Cumberland, England (for which see Johannes Brøndsted, 'Thors fiskeri.') Note also the representations of the Sigurd legend on the rock inscriptions of Ramsundsberget and Gök (for which see E. Brate and E. Wessén, *Södermanlands runinskrifter*, nos 101 and 327).

44 *Hávamál*, verse 142.

45 *Hávamál*, verse 157.

46 *Sigrdrífumál*, verses 6–13, from the third edition of the *Edda* by G. Neckel and H. Kuhn (cited hereafter simply as *Edda*).

47 See the edition of the *Vǫlsungasaga* by R.G. Finch, *The Saga of the Volsungs*, pp 35–7.

48 *Egils saga Skalla-grimmssonar*, chapter 44.

49 *Egils saga*, chapter 72.

50 See Baeksted's excessively sweeping repudiation of the evidence for rune magic cited in note 16 above.

51 See Aslak Liestøl, 'Jeg rister bodruner, jeg rister bjærgruner.'

52 See the discussion of the positioning and inscriptional content of these stone monuments in Musset, pp 239ff, noting especially the numerical chart by geographical location on p 241.

53 For invitations to *raþu* (interpret, Modern English read) in Norse *futhąrk* inscriptions see the Swedish stones at Hillersjö and Ågersta in Wessén and Jansson, nos 29 and 729.

54 For inscribed stones which clearly are intended to establish inheritance rights see the Swedish stones found at Nora and Hillersjö in Wessén and Jansson, nos 130 and 729.

55 Examples of smaller inscribed objects include wooden message-sticks (*rúnakefli*), weapons, jewels, toilet articles, utensils, coins, etc. For runic coinage see Jacobsen and Moltke, cols 557–79; Erik Moltke, 'De danske Runemønter og deres Praegere;' and Brita Malmer, 'A Contribution to the Numismatic History of Norway in the Eleventh Century,' especially pp 354–6. For a brief summary of the other uses see Musset, #175.

56 See *Átlamál*, verses 4–12, where Gudrun 'rúnar nam at rísta' (began to carve runes), which later were changed by Attila's messenger so that Hogni's wife, Kostbera, could not interpret the warning message (G. Vigfusson and F.Y. Powell, *Corpus Poeticum Boreale*, vol I, 322–3).

57 *Grettis saga Asmundarsonar*, chapter 66.

58 See Aslak Liestøl, 'Runer frå Bryggen,' pp 35–53; 'Correspondence in Runes,' pp 17–27; and 'The Literate Vikings,' pp 69–78; see also the article cited in note 51 above.

59 Specifically Christian inscriptions included prayers on behalf of the dead, such as 'kuþ hialbi salu hans' (may God help his soul), or appeals to the Virgin Mary or to the Archangel Michael – prayers not dissimilar to those also addressed to Thor. For an indication of the range of the inscriptions invoking supernatural powers see Musset #153 and 189.

60 On the fate of runes in seventeenth century Iceland see the second edition of Helmut Arntz' *Handbuch der Runenkunde* (cited hereafter as Arntz, *Handbuch²*), p 268.

61 The fullest collection of Old English runic inscriptions is still George Stephens, *The Old-Northern Runic Monuments of Scandinavia and England*. For a fairly recent bibliography of these inscriptions see Hertha Marquardt, *Die Runeninschriften der Britischen Inseln*. Musset includes a few English inscriptions in the 'Anthologie Runique' which forms the second part of his *Introduction*. Also, Ralph Elliott presents a selection in *Runes*, chapter 7; and R.I. Page's *An Introduction to English Runes* (cited hereafter as Page, *English Runes*) includes many inscriptions interspersed throughout the text.

62 See Page, *English Runes*, chapter 3 on the phonology of the expanded *futhorc*. The dates for these changes cannot be fixed with any precision, but probably the process was essentially completed by the eighth century: see Wolfgang Keller, 'Zur Chronologie der altenglischen Runen'; also R.I. Page, 'Language and Dating in Old English Inscriptions.'

63 Compare, for example, the twenty-eight rune *futhorc* sequence on the ninth century Thames sword (or scramasax), photographically reproduced in Elliott, *Runes*, plate III, fig 7.

64 For these commonly accepted transliterations established by Bruce Dickins, see his 'A System of Transliteration for Old English Runic Inscriptions.'

65 See the explanatory note on stanza xxvIII of the edited text of the Old English *Rune Poem* below.

66 For these additional runes see page 25.

67 For example, see the Hamwih bone with the name ᚻᚠᚩᚠ *Catæ* reproduced in Page, *English Runes*, plate 5.

68 Inlaid on the Thames scramasax, cited in note 63.

69 For example, see the amulet rings from Bramham Moor and Kingmoor reproduced in Page, *English Runes*, plates 7 and 8. These and others are also described in Bruce Dickins, 'Runic Rings and Old English Charms,' p 252, as well as in D.M. Wilson, 'A Group of Anglo-Saxon Amulet Rings.'

70 See the photographic facsimile of this runic message in R.W. Chambers, Max Förster, and Robin Flower (eds), *The Exeter Book of Old English Poetry*, folio 123v; for a printed edition see George Philip Krapp and Elliott Van Kirk Dobbie (eds), *The Exeter Book* (cited hereafter as *Exeter Book* or ASPR III), pp 225–7. For an interesting discussion see Ralph Elliott, 'The Runes in *The Husband's Message*.' John C. Pope argues persuasively that the speaker in *The Husband's Message* is indeed a *rúnakefli* in 'Palaeography and poetry,' pp 42–63. On the two most problematical aspects of the runic message, ie, the verb introducing the sequence (*genyre* or *gecyre* or *gehyre*) and the final rune (*man/monn* or *dæg*), see also the recent discussion by Margaret Goldsmith in 'The Enigma of *The Husband's Message*,' especially pp 251ff.

71 G. Storms in *Anglo-Saxon Magic* interprets *The Nine Herbs Charm* as runic. He translates 'þā genām Wōden viiii wuldortānas, slōh ða næddran þæt hēo on viiii tōflēah' as 'For Woden took nine glory-twigs, he smote then the adder that it flew apart into nine parts' (pp 188–9). Then Storms goes on to paraphrase the passage as follows: 'He takes nine glory-twigs, by which are meant nine runes, that is nine twigs with the initial letters in runes of the plants representing the power inherent in them, and using them as weapons he smites the serpent with them. Thanks to their magical power they pierce its skin and cut it into nine pieces' (p 195). Obviously the word *wuldortānas* is open to quite different non-runic interpretations.

72 See B. Colgrave and R.A.B. Mynors, *Bede's Ecclesiastical History of the English People* (cited hereafter as Bede) iv, 22.

73 See Thomas Miller's edition of *The Old English Version of Bede's Ecclesiastical History of the English People*, EETS, OS, XCV. iv. 22.

74 For example, by Page, *English Runes*, pp 112–13.

75 See Benjamin Thorpe, *Homilies of the Anglo-Saxon Church*, II, p 358.

76 On the variable direction of Norse inscriptions see Musset #43, plus the photographs appended to his *Introduction* in plates IV, V, VI, XIV, XV, XVI, and XIX.

77 For the Falstone 'hogback' see Elliott, *Runes*, plate XIII, fig 32, which includes a clarifying drawing.

78 See the reproduction of a fragment of the Hackness Cross in Elliott, *Runes*, plate XIV, fig 33 and his discussion of the inscriptions on pp 83–6; see also the Ruthwell Cross, cited below in note 85, for both runic and Roman inscriptions.

79 For example, see the Latin word ᚠᚹᛁᛏᚠᛏᚠᚱᛗᚻ *afitatores* (for *habitatores* (the inhabitants)) on the back of the Franks Casket (cited in note 86 below) or the Christ symbol ᛁᚻᚱ ᚤᚴᚱ IHS XPS incised on the oak coffin of Saint Cuthbert made at Lindisfarne in AD 698 (reproduced in Page, *English Runes*, fig 35).

80 See the coins of the East Anglian kings Beorna (c.AD 760) and Æthelberht (c.AD 790), reproduced in Elliott, *Runes*, plate V, figs 15 and 16, for this mixture of runic and Roman characters.

81 For example, see the facsimiles of the inscriptions of two stones, one from Great Urswick and the other from Thornhill, in Page, *English Runes*, pp 154 and 155. Respectively, they read in a kind of alliterative verse:

Tunwini settæ æfter Torhtredæ

becun æfter his bæurnæ;   gebiddæs þer saulæ.

(Tunwini set up a monument for his son (lord?) Torhtred;

pray for his soul.)

and

Gilswiþ arærde   æfte Berhtswiþe

becun on bergi;   gebiddaþ þær saule.

(Gilswith raised a monument on a mound (hill?) for Berhtswith;

pray for her soul.)

82 That the connection between runes and pagan practices was strong in the opinion of the continental church is shown by the famous *De inventione litterarum* treatise, where runes are associated with incantations, divinations, and similar 'secret' matters; see Derolez, pp 354ff, for the two variant texts of the *De inventione* and for a brief discussion of both. Note also the banning of runes in Iceland, cited above in note 60.

83 On the specialized nature of the verbs *wrītan (to cut) and *rēðan (to interpret) see Musset #41.

84 Bede, i, 30.

85 See the photographs of the Ruthwell Cross in Elliott, *Runes*, plates XVI and XVII, and his discussion of the figure motifs and inscriptions on pp 90–6, plus Page's discussion in *English Runes*, pp 148–52. For the inscribed poem see Bruce Dickins and A.S.C. Ross, *The Dream of the Rood*, and also Elliott Van Kirk Dobbie, *The Anglo-Saxon Minor Poems* (cited hereafter as Dobbie), pp 114ff.

86 See the photographs of the Franks Casket in Elliott, *Runes*, plates XIX–XXIII and his discussion of the figure motifs and inscriptions on pp 96–108, plus Page's discussion in *English Runes*, pp 174–82. See also Dobbie, pp 204ff for the versified inscriptions.

87 Probably because of its pagan content, the carver has chosen to render this text more difficult by replacing all the vowels with arbitrary runes, a not unknown cryptic device (for which see Derolez, p 138).

88 Copious background material on the widespread use of English runes in the monasteries of the continent is provided by Derolez, *passim*. The interested reader will note that the continental evidence for Old English runes bulks much larger than the insular evidence.

89 It is important to recognize that, with the exception of the Thames scramasax (cited in footnote 63 above), our only *futhorcs* are found in manuscripts. Without the interest taken by English monks in recording the *futhorc* sequence, equating runes with Roman alphabet letters, and setting down their oral mnemonic names, we today would know very little about Old English runes.

90 An excellent illustration of the interest taken in alphabetized runes is furnished by the *De inventione* treatise, cited in footnote 82 above. Note also the photographic reproduction in Derolez, plate VI of a typical series of parallel 'alphabets' found in Munich, Bayerische Staatsbibliothek, Lat. ms 14436, fol 1r.

91 For the dates of the assimilation of these two runes see the explanatory notes on stanzas III and VIII.

92 These varied uses of runes are described in Derolez, pp 385ff.

93 See Derolez, pp 120ff on the *isruna* tract and other cryptic devices based on the *futhorc* which were in use both in England and on the continent.

94 See the photographic reproduction of Cotton ms Domitian A.ix, fol 11v in Derolez, plate I, and his discussion of the manuscript on pp 3–16. In a tradition dating back as far as Humphrey Wanley's *Catalogus Historico Criticus* of 1705, the press-marks for Cotton Domitian manuscripts are shown both with and without the shelf-letter A. Thus Wanley himself uses the shelf-letter for all five of the Domitian manuscripts listed in his prefatory 'Syllabus Bibliothecarum' but omits it in the catalogue entries for 'Domitianus 8' on page 220 and 'Domitianus ix' on page 239. Two of the Keepers of Manuscripts for the British Museum adopted more consistent, but opposite practices: thus, Joseph Planta omitted the shelf-letter from the press-marks of all Cotton Domitian manuscripts in his catalogue published by the British Museum Department of Manuscripts in 1802 entitled *A Catalogue of the Manuscripts in the Cottonian Library deposited in the British Museum*; and more recently, T.C. Skeat has reinserted the shelf-letter in his list of Cotton press-marks on page 10 of the 1962

revised edition of *The Catalogues of the Manuscript Collections* published by the Trustees of the British Museum. Neil Ker's *Catalogue of
Manuscripts Containing Anglo-Saxon* followed Planta's practice in omit-
ting the shelf-letter for the four Domitian manuscripts listed. Since all the
runologists quoted in this edition have included the shelf-letter in their
citations, I shall do likewise in order to avoid confusion for the reader.

95 See the photographic reproduction of Oxford, St John's College ms 17, fol
5v in Derolez, plate III, and his discussion of the manuscript on pp 26ff.

96 See the discussion of Hickes' monumental work on pp 23–7 of this introduction and also Derolez' discussion of the lost Cotton ms Galba A ii on
pp 34–52 of his *Runica Manuscripta*.

97 For further details on these runic grammalogues see Derolez, pp 396ff and
also the explanatory notes on stanzas VIII, XIX, XX, and XXIII.

98 For example, see the riddle quoted on page 41.

99 Examine the texts of the Cynewulfian signatures printed in Appendix A of
this edition. See also the articles by Ralph Elliott, 'Cynewulf's Runes in
Christ II and *Elene*' and 'Cynewulf's Runes in *Juliana* and *Fates of the
Apostles*.'

100 Note that the rune names in the continental manuscript *futhorcs*, which
are used for purposes of etymological comparison in the explanatory
notes, are all a good deal older than those represented by the manuscript
of the Old English *Rune Poem* and probably are of Northumbrian rather
than southern origin. See the general note on pages 95–6 for further
details.

101 See the divided *futhorc* in Cotton ms Domitian A.ix, cited in footnote 94
above.

102 See the discussion of stanza structure on pages 49–52.

103 Note, for example, the lacunae in the manuscripts cited for etymological
comparison in the explanatory notes on stanzas XXVII–XXIX.

104 See the discussion of the comparable Latin alphabetic verse on pages
42–5.

THE TEXTUAL BACKGROUND OF THE *RUNE POEM*

1 For an account of the Cottonian Library and of the Ashburnham House
fire see E.J. Miller, *That Noble Cabinet: a History of the British Museum*,
pp 34–5. Of 958 volumes, 114 were destroyed and 98 badly damaged by the
fire.

2 For an account of the present state of Cotton ms Otho B.x see Neil Ker,
Catalogue of Manuscripts Containing Anglo-Saxon (cited hereafter as
Ker), items 177–9. Ker's description of the destroyed sections of the manu-
script is based on Wanley's *Catalogus*, pp 190–3.

3 Smith's entire description of Cotton ms Otho B.x is reproduced in Derolez, pp 17–18.
4 Wanley's annotated copy of Smith's *Catalogus* is now in the Bodleian Library, Gough London 54.
5 Ker, pp 228–9 and 230.
6 Kenneth Sisam, 'Humphrey Wanley.'
7 Wanley, *Catalogus*, p 231. See also the comment in Smith's *Catalogus*, p 61, regarding: 'Runica quaedam praecipue in fine libri. 101, 127, 129' (Some runic material chiefly at the end of the book [in folios] 101, 127, 129 [of Galba A.ii]).
8 *Thesaurus*, p 134.
9 For an account of the various uses of Junius' font of Old English type see Eleanor Adams, *Old English Scholarship in England from 1566 to 1800*, pp 167–8.
10 Regarding the absence of rune names from the Norwegian *Rune Poem* and the Icelandic *Rune Poem* see pages 35 and 36 of this introduction.
11 George Hempl, 'Hickes's Additions to the Runic Poem.'
12 Hickes introduced this *futhorc* as follows: 'Extat & altera literarum *Dano-runicarum* descriptio, cum explicatione Anglo-Saxonica, in eadem bibliotheca (*Domitianus A.9*) quam in tabella lectori studioso hic infra offero' (There is also another list of Danish runic letters, with an Anglo-Saxon gloss, in the same library (Domitian A.ix) which I present to the studious reader here below in a chart).
13 For *wen/wyn* see the explanatory note on stanza VIII.
14 It is impossible to determine whether the copying errors which I have corrected in the edited text of the poem are attributable to the printer, to Wanley, or to some earlier scribe involved in the transmission of the text during the Anglo-Saxon period.
15 See the discussion of the manuscript punctuation on pages 30–1.
16 On this point my calculations coincide with those in F.G. Jones's thesis, 'The Old English *Rune Poem*' (cited hereafter as Jones), p 5.
17 A. Campbell, *An Old English Grammar*. This popular grammar (cited hereafter as Campbell) will be used in the grammatical references in this edition as the one most readily accessible to English speaking students; future citations will be incorporated directly into the text.
18 Charles Wrenn, 'Late Old English Rune Names.'
19 E. Sievers, 'Zur Rhythmik des germanischen Alliterationverses,' p 474.
20 The scholars responsible for the two major English editions of the Old English *Rune Poem* both have promoted this unsubstantiated belief in an early origin. See Bruce Dickins, *Runic and Heroic Poems of the Old Teutonic Peoples* (cited hereafter as Dickins, *Runic Poems*), p 6; and also see Dobbie, p xlix.

21 Compare the regular use of the single lozenge-shaped dot at the caesural pause and at the end of each line in the Junius manuscript, as shown in the facsimile by Sir Israel Gollancz, entitled *The Caedmon Manuscript*.

22 On the date of the introduction of the semicolon see Ker, p xxxiv.

23 Ker, p 58. See also the facsimile edition by Robin Flower and Hugh Smith, entitled *The Parker Chronicle and Laws*, fol 27r, which clearly shows the marginal triangle of dots.

24 Ker, pp 233–4.

25 Ker, p 333. See also the facsimile edition by C.E. Wright, entitled *Bald's Leech Book*.

26 See the discussion of the introduction of the hyphen in Ker, pp xxxv–xxxvi.

27 Dobbie, introduction, p l.

28 See the discussion of the alliterative metre on pages 46–9 of the introduction.

SOURCES AND GENRE OF THE *RUNE POEM*

1 See the texts of the three Norse rune poems in Appendix B to this edition.

2 Kemp Malone in A.C. Baugh *et al*, *A Literary History of England*, p 34.

3 Notable among these reconstructors of primitive Germanic beliefs are several of the continental scholars cited in footnote 16 on page 65 above, including von der Leyen, Jungandreas, Agrell, and Schneider.

4 Examples of Karl Schneider's emendations of the Old English *Rune Poem* are cited in the explanatory notes on stanzas III, XIII, XVI, XIX, and XX.

5 Consult the discussion of the contents and date of the St Gall manuscript in Derolez, pp 73ff. For its provenance see B. Bischoff, 'Eine Sammelhandschrift Walahfrid Strabos (Cod. Sangall. 878).'

6 The exact nature of the runic information in the *Abecedarium Nordmannicum* can be assessed better from the facsimile in Derolez, p 78, than from the printed version given in Appendix B to this edition.

7 See the concise summary of the mixture of linguistic forms in Musset #61.

8 G. Baesecke, 'Das Abecedarium Nordmannicum.'

9 See the edition with German translation and discussion of provenance and date by Ludvig Wimmer, pp 273–80. See also the edition with English translation and discussion of provenance and date by Bruce Dickins, *Runic Poems*, pp 6–7, 24–7.

10 On this point see Wimmer, p 276: 'Die runennamen im anfang jedes verses werden in der handschrift durch die entsprechenden runen bezeichnet' (The rune names at the beginning of each verse are indicated in the manuscript by means of the corresponding runes).

11 See the edition with German translation and discussion of provenance and date in Wimmer, pp 281–8. See also the edition with English translation and discussion of provenance and date in Dickins, *Runic Poems*, pp 7–8, 28–33.

12 On this point see Wimmer, p 281: 'lässt aber die namen aus' (but it [Copenhagen, Arnamagnaean Library ms 687] omits the names).

13 Compare *bergbúi* (cliff-dweller) in *Hymiskviþa*, verse 5 (Vigfusson and Powell, p 220) and note also the various other kennings cited in Dickins, *Runic Poems*, pp 28–33.

14 For example, note the appearance of the *corn*-formula (which is shared by the Old English, Norwegian, and Icelandic rune poems) in *Seafarer*, lines 32–3: 'Hægl fēol on eorþan, corna caldast' (Hail fell on the earth, that coldest of grains) (*Exeter Book*, p 144). It is significant to note that in *Seafarer*, as throughout Old English poetry, hail is a part of the elegiac motif; only the Old English *Rune Poem* finds hail a natural wonder instead of a source of misery (on which point see pages 57–60 of this introduction for a discussion of the poet's characteristic approach to the created world).

15 For a brief example, taken at random, see Proverbs 20:1–5 below (and compare with the Cotton gnomes cited on page 39 as well as with the *bith*-gnomes that constitute the bulk of the stanzas of the Old English *Rune Poem*):

Wine is a mocker, strong drink is raging:
and whosoever is deceived thereby is not wise.

The fear of the king is as the roaring of a lion:
whoso provoketh him to anger sinneth against his own soul.

It is an honour for a man to cease from strife:
but every fool will be meddling.

The sluggard will not plow by reason of the cold;
therefore shall he beg in harvest, and have nothing.

Counsel in the heart of man is like deep water;
but a man of understanding will draw it out.

16 Aristotle, *Rhetorica* II, 21.

17 Quintilian, *Institutiones Oratiae* VIII, 5.3.

18 For example, see Beowulf's gnomic pronouncements concerning *wyrd* (lines 573–4) and interdynastic marriages (lines 2029–31), and note Hrothgar's observation in lines 1842–4: 'Ne hȳrde ic snotorlīcor on swā geongum fēore guma þingian. þū eart mægenes strang, and on mōde frōd.' (I never heard so young a warrior discourse more wisely. Thou art both strong in might and wise of mind.) This and all future *Beowulf* citations are taken from the third edition of Fr. Klaeber, *Beowulf and the Fight at Finnsburg*.

19 Ernst Curtius, *European Literature and the Latin Middle Ages*, p 58.
20 For examples of the *Distichs* and vernacular imitations see: Cambridge, Trinity College ms R.9,17 (819), fols 1–48; also British Library Cotton mss Julius A.ii, fols 141–4; Vespasian D.vi, fols 73v–6; and Vespasian D.xiv, fols 7–11. For a convenient edition of the vernacular texts, see R.S. Cox, 'The Old English Dicts of Cato.'
21 *Widsiþ*, Exeter Book, pp 149–53.
22 *The Gifts of Men*, Exeter Book, pp 137–40.
23 *The Fortunes of Men*, Exeter Book, pp 154–6.
24 Note the similarity between the concern to acquire and transmit wisdom expressed throughout the Old Testament book of Proverbs, but especially in Chapter 1, verses 1–7, and the sentiments expressed in the introduction to the Exeter *Maxims* (*Exeter Book*, pp 156–7):

Frige me frōdum wordum.   Ne læt þīnne ferð onhælne
dēgol þæt þū dēopest cunne.   Nelle ic þē mīn dyrne gesecgan,
gif þū mē þīnne hygecræft hylest   and þinne heortan geþohtas.
Glēawe men sceolon gieddum wrixlan.   God sceal mon ǣrest hergan,
fægre, fæder ūserne ....

(Question me with wise words. Do not let your heart conceal your deepest knowledge. I shall not be willing to tell you my secrets, if you conceal your wisdom and the thoughts of your heart from me. Wise men should exchange verses. First one must praise God, our Father, joyously ....)
25 *The Cotton Maxims*, Dobbie, pp 55–6.
26 For Samson's riddle see the Old Testament book of Judges, chapter 14, verse 14.
27 For the riddle of the Sphinx see L. Laistner, *Das Rätsel der Sphynx*.
28 For Hwætberht's alphabetical riddles see Erika von Erhardt-Siebold, *Die lateinischen Rätsel der Angelsachsen*, pp 251–6; also H. Hahn, 'Die Rätseldichter Tatwin und Eusebius.'
29 For Tatwine's riddles see Hahn.
30 For Aldhelm's riddles see J.H. Pitman, *The Riddles of Aldhelm*.
31 *Exeter Book*, riddle 40.
32 *Exeter Book*, riddle 35.
33 For Aldhelm's reputation as an oral vernacular poet (*scop*) see William of Malmesbury, *De Gestis Pontificum Anglorum* in the edition by N.E.S.A. Hamilton, v, p 336.
34 See the facsimile of *The Exeter Book* edited by R.W. Chambers *et al*, fol 105r and the printed edition of Krapp and Dobbie, p 189. As Derolez notes (p 398), '... in the Exeter Book: wherever a rune stands for its name, there is a dot before and after it; when a sequence of runes is to be read in the

same way, each pair of runes is also separated by a dot. On the other hand, when several runes are to be read as one word, i.e. only by their sound value, there is a dot before and after the whole group, but none between the runes.' In the case of riddle 19, the rune names must be pronounced in order to fill out the metrical pattern, but only their initial letters supply the clue: the names mean nothing.

35 According to Cicero, *De Divinatione*, II, 111–12, in the edition by A.S. Peace, pp 529–32.

36 See Old Testament Psalm 119, whose one hundred and seventy-six verses are divided into twenty-two eight line stanzas corresponding to the twenty-two letters of the Hebrew alphabet: *aleph, beth, gimel, daleth, he, vau, zain, cheth, teth, jod, caph, lamed, mem, nun, samech, ain, pe, tzaddi, koph, resh, schin,* and *tau.*

37 The eighty poems of Commodian's *Instructiones* are all in acrostic or alphabetical form. For quotation and discussion of the technique see F.J.E. Raby, *A History of Christian-Latin Poetry from the Beginnings to the Close of the Middle Ages* (cited hereafter as Raby, *Christian-Latin Poetry*), p 13.

38 Two of Hilary's extant hymns are alphabetical. See Guido M. Dreves, C. Blume, and H.M. Bannister, *Analecta Hymnica Medii Aevi* (cited hereafter as *Analecta Hymnica*) vol L, pp 4ff.

39 For Augustine's *Psalmos contra partem Donati* see Jacques Paul Migne, *Patrologia Latina* (cited hereafter as PL), vol XLIII, col 23.

40 See Fortunatus' alphabetical song dedicated to Bishop Leontius: *Carmina* I, 16.

41 See Sedulius' alphabetical hymn in *Analecta Hymnica*, vol LI, p 340.

42 See PL, vol XLIII, col 23.

43 Bede, *De Arte Metrica*, 11 and 21 in J.A. Giles, *The Miscellaneous Works of Venerable Bede*, pp 60 and 75.

44 For example, British Library Royal ms 2.A.xx and Harleian ms 3072. Bede names Sedulius as one of Aldhelm's models (*Ecclesiastical History*, v, 18). In brief, as Raby summarizes in *Christian-Latin Poetry*, p 110, Sedulius was 'read as a model of style, and imitated by generations of versifiers.'

45 For Secundus' alphabetical hymn see *Analecta Hymnica*, vol LI, p 340.

46 For *Altus Prosator* see J.H. Bernard and R. Atkinson, *The Irish Liber Hymnorum*, vol i, pp 66ff. See also pp 14, 137, 158 for other examples.

47 *Ecclesiastical History*, iv, 20.

48 For Wulfstan's alphabetical hymns see *Analecta Hymnica* vols XLIX, p 9 and LI, p 164.

49 For Ausonius' alphabetical poem see W. Schulze, *Kleine Schriften*, p 450; the poem is also printed in H.G.E. White (ed), *Ausonius*, p 289.

50 J.D.A. Ogilvy, *Books Known to the English, 597–1066*, discusses Aldhelm's possible debt to Ausonius on pp 96–7.

51 For the full poem by this anonymous Britisher see A. Baehrens, *Poetae Latini Minores*, vol v, pp 375–8. For interesting explanatory notes see Henri Omont, 'Poème anonyme sur les lettres de l'alphabet.'

52 See Hahn and von Erhardt-Siebold for Hwætberht's alphabetical riddles.

STYLE AND THEMES OF THE *RUNE POEM*

1 Kenneth Sisam, 'Cynewulf and His Poetry,' especially pp 20ff.

2 The effect of runic symbols on the page was so distinctive that they even were used in one of the manuscripts of the first of thie *Poetical Dialogues of Solomon and Saturn* (Cambridge, Corpus Christi College ms 422), in addition to the corresponding Roman capitals, in order to make the letters of the *Pater Noster* prayer stand out more clearly. See R.J. Menner's edition, pp 5ff, 80ff; see also his rather romantic discussion of these ornamental letters as 'the last vestiges of an ancient pagan Germanic tradition, according to which the runes themselves possessed magic power' (p 49), an interpretation rightly castigated by Kenneth Sisam in his review of the edition in *Medium Ævum*, 13, pp 28–36.

3 Larry D. Benson, 'The Literary Character of Anglo-Saxon Formulaic Poetry' (cited hereafter as Benson).

4 See chapter II of his *Altgermanische Metrik* for Sievers' exposition of the familiar five verse types.

5 Bliss is the best known modern exponent of the non-isochronous approach to scansion. See his *The Metre of Beowulf*, espcially chapter 10 re 'light' verses.

6 The isochronous or 'musical' approach to scansion is commonly associated with the name of Pope. See his *The Rhythm of Beowulf* for a full exposition.

7 In his plausible simplification of Pope's method of scansion entitled 'A New Approach to the Rhythm of *Beowulf*,' Robert P. Creed suggests a helpful way of dealing with the stresses in lines like these. See especially the amendment to his Rule II on p 32.

8 Although each of the so-called stanzas of *Deor* is introduced by a large capital and terminated by highly ornamental end-punctuation (:- :7), they are only irregular groupings of lines, whose sole excuse for the term 'stanza' lies in the final refrain (see the physical layout of the poem in the Chambers facsimile of the *The Exeter Book*, fol 100r).

9 For the normal position of the *īor* rune see Cotton ms Domitian A.ix, fol 11v in Derolez, plate I.

10 See Derolez, plate I.

11 For the use of the divided *futhorc* on the Hackness Cross see Derolez, pp 140ff; Elliott, *Runes*, plate XIV, fig 33, and his discussion on pp 83ff; also see

Page, *English Runes*, plate 15 and his discussion on pp 64–6. There is some possibility that the *futhorc* used here may have had a fourth division to accommodate the full expansion to thirty-three runes.

12 Derolez deals with the *ættir* at length in *Runica Manuscripta*, pp xix, 89–169 (and especially on pp 139ff and in Appendix II, pp 165ff). For briefer discussions see Elliott, *Runes*, p 14, and Page, *English Runes*, pp 62ff.

13 See the citations in note 12 immediately above.

14 See the citations in note 12 immediately above.

15 For the Vadstena bracteate see Elliott, *Runes*, plate II, fig 4.

16 See Derolez, pp 3–16, and plate I.

17 Francis Peabody Magoun, Jr, 'Bede's Story of Caedmon: the Case-History of an Anglo-Saxon Oral Singer.' See also his 'The Oral Formulaic Character of Anglo-Saxon Narrative Poetry.'

18 See Benson on this curious intermingling of traditions.

19 For sea-kennings see H. Marquardt, *Die altenglischen Kenningar*, pp 164, 226.

20 Compare *mære mearcstapa* (notorious boundary-treader, ie, outlaw), *Beowulf*, line 103.

21 For examples in heroic narrative poetry, compare the piling up of half-line epithets used to introduce King Æthelstan in the opening lines of *The Battle of Brunanburh* or to reflect the impact that the young Beowulf had upon the Danish court when he began to address them (*Beowulf*, lines 399–406).

22 Jones, p 68: 'viewed against the background of a body of poetry with a storehouse of extremely conventional metrics, language, and themes, the poem can emerge as a unified, coherent, and for its length, a forceful poem.'

23 Musset #63.

24 In Old English poetry the obvious examples of this are *Seafarer*, *Christ*, lines 847–66, the turbulent sea-passage in *Andreas*, and the highly significant intrusion of the sea-image into Adam's representation of his willingness to endure extreme earthly tribulation in order to win his way back to Paradise in Genesis B, lines 828–35 (see the explanatory note on stanza XXI for the text of this passage).

25 For the most influential enunciation of this attitude to the created world see Augustine, *De doctrina Christiana*, 1.4(4) in J.P. Migne (ed), *Sancti Aurelii Augustini Opera Omnia*, PL, XXXIV, cols 20–1.

26 For Old English homilies on the Judgement Day see those listed in Ker, pp 527–36. Bede's poem *De die iudicii* (from Cambridge, Corpus Christi College ms 201) is printed in Dobbie, pp 58–67. See also the Exeter Book poem on the Judgement Day, printed in ASPR III, pp 212–15. Two related

poems from the *Vercelli Book* and the *Exeter Book*, both known as *Soul and Body* are printed in ASPR II, pp 54–9 and ASPR III, pp 174–8 respectively. The Cynewulfian signatures printed in Appendix A to this edition provide other instances of the apocalyptic vision of the Anglo-Saxons.

27 See the references in footnote 16 on p 65 above, especially Karl Schneider's *Die Germanischen Runennamen*.

THE LITERARY ACHIEVEMENT OF THE *RUNE POEM*

1 See his Preface to *Lyrical Ballads* in *The Prose Works of William Wordsworth*, W.J.B. Owen and J.W. Smyser (eds) I, p 126.
2 See *Horace's Epistles and Ars Poetica*, F.G. Plaistowe and A.F. Watt (eds).
3 See PL, XXXIV, col 39.
4 For an extreme example of this kind of repudiation of Christian elements see R.C. Boer, 'Wanderer und Seefahrer'; other examples are listed by Nora Kershaw, *Anglo-Saxon and Norse Poems*, pp 16ff.
5 Dickins, *Runic Poems*, p v.
6 *A Critical History of Old English Literature*, p 193.

The Old English *Rune Poem*

E Codice MS. Bibliothecæ Cottonianæ, cujus nota, Otho. B. 10.

býþ ꝼꞃoꝼuꞃ. ꝼiꞃa ᵹehpýlcum. ꞃceal ðeah manna ᵹebpýlc. miclun hýt ðælan.
ᵹiꝼ he pile. ꝼoꞃ bꞃihtne bomeꞃ hleotan.
býþ anmob. ꞇ oꝼeꞃ hýꞃneb. ꝼela ꝼꞃecne. beoꞃ ꝼeohteþ. miþ hoꞃnum. mæꞃe moꞃ ꞃtapa. ꝼ iꞅ mobiᵹ puht.
býþ ðeaple ꞃceaꞃp. ðeᵹna ᵹehpæce. anꝼen-ᵹýꞃ ýꝼýl. unᵹemetun peþe. manna ᵹehpýlcun. ðe him miþ ꞃeꞃteð.
býþ onbꝼꞃuma. ælcpe ꞃpꞃæce. piꞃbomeꞃ ppaþu. anð piꞇena ꝼꞃoꝼuꞃ. anð eopla ᵹehꝼam. eabꞃýꞅ anð to hihꞇ.
býþ onꝼecýbe. pinca ᵹehpýlcum. ꞃeꞃte anð ꞃpiþhꝼæꞇ. ðam ðe ꞃiꞇꞇeþ onuꝼan. meaꞃe mæᵹen heaꞃbum. oꝼeꞃ mil paþaꞃ.
býþ cpicepa ᵹehꝼam cuþ on ꝼýꞃe blac anð beoꞃhꞇlic býꞃneþ. oꝼꞇuꞃꞇ ðæꞃ hi æþelinᵹaꞃ inne ꞃeꞃꞇaþ.
ᵹumena býþ ᵹlenᵹ anð henenýꞃ. ppaþu ꞁ pýpꞃcýpe ꞁ pꞃæcna ᵹehꝼam aꞃ anð æꞇpiꞃꞇ ðe býþ oþna leaꞃ.
ne bꞃuceþ ðe can peꞃna lýꞇ ꞃaꞃeꞃ anð ꞃonᵹe anð him ꞃýlꝼa hæꝼþ blæb ꞁ blýꞃꝼe anð eac býꞃᵹa ᵹeniht.
býþ bpiꞇuꞃꞇ copna. hꞃýꞃꝼꞇ hiꞇ oꝼ heoꝼoneꞃ lýꝼꞇe. pealcaþ hiꞇ piꞇbeꞃ ꞃcuꞃna. peopþeþ hiꞇ to pæꞇeꞃe ꞃýððan.
býþ neapu on bꞃeoꞃꞇan peopþeþ hi ðeah oꝼꞇ niþa beaꞃnum to helpe anð to hæle ᵹe hꝼæþne ᵹiꝼ hi hiꞃ hlýꞃꞇaþ æpoꞃ.
býþ oꝼeꞃ cealbunᵹe metum ꞃliboꞃ ᵹliꞃnaþ ᵹlæꞃ hluꞇꞇuꞃ ᵹimmum ᵹelicuꞃꞇ. ꝼloꞃ ꝼoꞃꞇe ᵹe populiꞇ ꝼæᵹen anꞃýne.
býþ ᵹumena hihꞇ ðon ᵹob læꞇeþ haliᵹ heoꝼoneꞃ cýninᵹ hꞃuꞃan ꞃýllan beoꞃhꞇe bleba beoꞃnum anð ðeaꞃꝼum.
býþ uꞇan unꞃmeþe ꞇꞃeop. heaꞃb hꞃuꞃan ꝼæꞃꞇ hýꞃbe ꝼýꞃeꞃ. pýꞃꞇꝼumun unbeꞃppeþýð pýnan on eþle.
býþ ꞃýmble pleᵹa. anð hlehꞇeꞃ plancum ðæꞃ piᵹan ꞃiꞇꞇaþ on beoꞃ ꞃele bliþe æꞇ ꞃomne.
ꞃeccaþ hæꝼþ oꝼꞇuꞃꞇ on ꝼenne. pexeð on paꞇuꞃe. þunbaþ ᵹꞃimme. blobe bꞃeneð beoꞃna ᵹehpýlcne ðe him æniᵹne onꝼenᵹ ᵹebeð.
ꞃe mannum ꞃýmble biþ on hihꞇe ðonn hi hine ꝼepaþ oꝼeꞃ ꝼiꞃceꞃ beþ oþ hibꞃum henᵹeꞇ bꞃinᵹeþ to lanbe.
biþ ꞇacna ꞃum healbeð ꞇꞃýpa pel. piþ æþelinᵹaꞃ a biþ onꝼæpýlbe. oꝼeꞃ nihꞇa ᵹenipu. næꝼꞃe ꞃpiceþ.
býþ bleba leaꞃ. beneþ eꝼne ꞃpa ðeah ꞇanaꞃ buꞇan ꞇubbeꞃ. biþ on ꞇelᵹum pliꞇiᵹ. þeah on helme hpýꞃꞇeb ꝼæᵹeꞃe. ᵹeloben leaꝼum lýꝼꞇe ᵹeꞇenᵹe.
býþ ꝼoꞃ eoplum æþelinᵹa pýn. hoꝼ hoꞃum planc. ðæꞃ him hæleþe ýmb. peleᵹe on piꞃᵹum pꞃixlaþ ꞃpꞃæce. ꞁ biþ unꞃꞇýllum æꝼꞃe ꝼꞃoꝼuꞃ.
býþ on mýnᵹþe hiꞃ maᵹan leoꝼ. ꞃceal þeah anꞃa ᵹehpýlc oðpum ꞃpican. ꝼoꞃ ðam bꞃýhten pýle bome ꞃine ꝼ eapme ꝼlæꞃc eopþan beꞇæcan.
býþ leobum lanᵹꞃum ᵹehuhꞇ ᵹiꝼ hi ꞃculun neþun on nacan ꞇealꞇum. ꞁ hi ꞃæ ýþa ꞃpýþe bꞃeᵹaþ. anð ꞃe bꞃim henᵹeꞃꞇ bꞃibleꞃ ne ᵹým.
pæꞃ æpeꞃꞇ miþ eaꞃꞇ benum. ᵹe ꞃepen ꞃecᵹun. oþ he ꞃiððan eꞃꞇ. oꝼeꞃ pæᵹ ᵹepiꞇ oꞃꞇ æꝼꞇeꞃ pan. ðuꞃ heaꞃbunᵹaꞃ ðone hæle nembun.
býþ oꝼeꞃ leoꝼ. æᵹhpýlcum men. ᵹiꝼ he moꞇ ðæꞃ. pihꞇeꞃ anð ᵹepýꞃena on bꞃucan on blobe bleabum oꝼꞇaꞃꞇ.
býþ bꞃihꞇneꞃ ꞃonb. beoꞃe mannum. mæꞃe meꞇobeꞃ leohꞇ. mýꞃᵹþ anð to hihꞇ eabᵹum anð eaꞃmum. eallum bꞃice.
býþ on eopþan. elba beaꞃnum. ꝼlæꞃceꞃ ꝼoboꞃ ꞃeꞃeþ ᵹelome oꝼeꞃ ᵹanoꞇeꞃ bæþ ᵹapꞃecᵹ ꝼanbaþ. hpæþeꞃ ac hæbbe æþele ꞇꞃeope.
biþ oꝼeꞃ heah. elbum býꞃe. ꞃꞇiþ on ꞃꞇabule. ꞃꞇebe nihꞇe hýlꞇ. ðeah him ꝼeohꞇan on ꝼiꞃaꞃ moniᵹe.
býþ æþelinᵹa ꞁ eopla ᵹehpæꞃ. pýn anð pýþmæýnb. býþ on piꞃᵹe ꝼæᵹeꞃ. ꝼæꞃꞇlic on ꝼæpelþe. ꝼýpb ᵹeaceꞃa ꞃum.
býþ ea ꝼixa. anð ðeah abꞃuceþ. ꝼoboꞃ onꝼalban. haꝼaþ ꝼæᵹepne eapb. pæꞇpe bepoppen. ðæꞃ he pýnnum leoꝼaþ.
býþ eᵹle eopla ᵹehpýlcun. ðonn ꝼæꞃꞇlice ꝼlæꞃc onᵹinneð. hꞃapcolian hꞃuꞃan ceoꞃan blac to ᵹebebban bleba ᵹeðpeoꞃaþ. pýnna ᵹepiꞇaþ pepa ᵹeꞃpicaþ.

L. l 2   Frat

The first printed version of the Old English *Rune Poem* in Hickes' *Thesaurus*

In editing the text of the Old English *Rune Poem* that appears on page 135 of George Hickes' *Thesaurus*, I have omitted the sound values and the variant rune forms added by Hickes, since it is demonstrable that these were borrowed from Cotton ms Domitian A.ix, fol 11v. The additional runes, without corresponding stanzas, appended at the bottom of Hickes' text have also been omitted, as coming from the same source and hence forming no part of the poem under study. Similarly, the rune names themselves, although retained in this edition, have been placed in parentheses after the runes on account of my strong doubt that these names were inserted in the original written version of the poem. For the rationale behind the above changes in the runic information given see pages 25–6 of the introduction.

Other changes, which require less explanation, include setting out the *Rune Poem* as verse to indicate the metrical division by alliterative lines and half-lines, modernizing punctuation and capitalization, rectifying word division, and expanding standard scribal abbreviations. Where more drastic emendation was required in order to correct errors in Hickes' text, the altered letters have been italicized and an explanation of the change provided in the explanatory notes.

I

ᚠ (feoh) byþ frōfur   fīra gehwylcum;
sceal ðēah manna gehwylc   miclun hyt dǣlan,
gif hē wile for Drihtne   dōmes hlēotan.

II

ᚢ (ūr) byþ anmōd   and oferhyrned,
felafrēcne dēor   – feohteþ mid hornum –
mǣre mōrstapa;   þæt is mōdig wuht!

5

III

ᚦ (ðorn) byþ ðearle scearp,   ðegna gehwylcum
anfengys yfyl,   ungemetun rēþe
manna gehwylcun   ðe him mid resteð.

IV

ᚠ (ōs) byþ ordfruma   ǣlcre sprǣce,
wīsdōmes wraþu   and witena frōfur
and eorla gehwām   ēadnys and tōhiht.

10

V

ᚱ (rād) byþ on recyde   rinca gehwylcum
sēfte, and swīþhwæt   ðām ðe sitteþ onufan
mēare mægenheardum   ofer mīlpaþas.

15

VI

ᚳ (ĉēn) byþ cwicera gehwām   cūþ on fȳre,
blāc and beorhtlīc;   byrneþ oftust
ðǣr hī æþelingas   inne restaþ.

VII

ᚷ (ġyfu) gumena byþ   gleng and herenys
wraþu and wyrþscype;   and wræcna gehwām
ār and ætwist,   ðe byþ ōþra lēas.

20

VIII

ᚹ (wyn)ne brūceþ   ðe can wēana lȳt,
sāres and sorge,   and him sylfa hæfþ
blǣd and blysse   and ēac byrga geniht.

I
Wealth is a benefit to all men;
yet every man must share it freely,
if he wishes to gain glory before the Lord.

II
The aurochs is courageous and has huge horns,
a very fierce beast – it fights with its horns –   5
a notorious moor-stalker; that is a brave creature!

III
The thorn is extremely sharp, painful
for any warrior to grasp, immeasurably fierce
to any man who rests among them.

IV
The mouth is the source of every utterance,   10
the support of wisdom and a comfort to wise men
and the joy and delight of every noble.

V
Riding is easy for warriors sitting in the hall,
and very strenuous for one who bestrides
a powerful horse travelling the long roads.   15

VI
The torch is known to all the living by its flame,
shining and bright; most often it burns
inside where princes sit at ease.

VII
Generosity is a grace in men of position and deserving of praise,
a prop to their honour; and for all the dispossessed   20
it is a help and a means of survival, when they have no other.

VIII
Joy he experiences who knows little of woes,
of pain or sorrow, and has for his own
prosperity and happiness and also the contentment belonging to
                                            fortified communities.

IX

�ᚻ (hægl) byþ hwītust corna;   hwyrft hit of heofones lyfte,   25
wealcaþ hit windes scūra;   weorþeþ hit tō wætere syððan.

X

ᚾ nȳd) byþ nearu on brēostan;   weorþeþ hī ðēah oft niþa bearnum
tō helpe and tō hæle gehwæþre,   gif hī his hlystaþ æror.

XI

ᛁ (īs) byþ oferceald,   ungemetum slidor;
glisnaþ glæshlūttur   gimmum gelīcust;   30
flōr forste geworuht,   fæger ansȳne.

XII

ᚷ (gēr) byþ gumena hiht,   ðon God læteþ,
hālig heofones cyning,   hrūsan syllan
beorhte blēda   beornum and ðearfum.

XIII

ᛇ (ēoh) byþ ūtan   unsmēþe trēow,   35
heard hrūsan fæst,   hyrde fȳres,
wyrtrumun underwreþyd,   wynan on ēþle.

XIV

ᛈ (peorð) byþ symble   plega and hlehter
wlancum ....., ðār wigan sittaþ
on bēorsele   blīþe ætsomne.   40

XV

ᛉ (eolhx) secg eard hæfþ   oftust on fenne,
wexeð on wature;   wundaþ grimme,
blōde brēneð   beorna gehwylcne
ðe him ænigne   onfeng gedēð.

XVI

ᛋ (sigel) sēmannum   symble biþ on hihte,   45
ðonn hī hine feriaþ   ofer fisces beþ,
oþ hī brimhengest   bringeþ tō lande.

IX
Hail is the whitest of grains; it whirls down from heaven's height,   25
and gusts of wind toss it about; then it is transformed to water.

X
Hardship oppresses the heart; yet nonetheless often it is transformed
                                                        for the sons of men
to a source of help and salvation, if only they heed it in time.

XI
Ice is extremely cold and immeasurably slippery;
it glitters clear as glass, very like jewels;   30
it is a floor wrought by the frost, fair to behold.

XII
Harvest is a joy to men, when God,
the holy king of heaven, makes the earth bring forth
bright fruits for rich and poor alike.

XIII
The yew is a tree with rough bark,   35
hard and firm in the earth, a keeper of flame,
well-supported by its roots, a pleasure to have on one's land.

XIV
A table-game is always a source of recreation and amusement
to proud ....., where warriors sit
happily together in the mead-hall.   40

XV
Elk-sedge usually dwells in a marsh,
growing in the water; it gives grievous wounds,
staining with blood every man
who lays a hand on it.

XVI
The sun is always a source of hope to seafarers,   45
when they row the sea-steed over the fish's bath,
until it brings them to land

XVII

↑ (Tīr) biþ tācna sum;   healdeð trȳwa wel
wiþ æþelingas;   ā biþ on færylde
ofer nihta genipu;   nǣfre swīceþ.   50

XVIII

B (beorc) byþ blēda lēas;   bereþ efne swā ðēah
tānas būtan tūdder;   biþ on telgum wlitig,
*h*ēah on helme,   hrysted fægere;
geloden lēafum,   lyfte getenge.

XIX

M (eh) byþ for eorlum   æþelinga wyn,   55
hors hōfum wlanc,   ðǣr him hæle*þas* ymb,
welege on wicgum,   wrixlaþ sprǣce;
and biþ unstyllum   ǣfre frōfur.

XX

M (man) byþ on myrgþe   his māgan lēof;
sceal þēah ānra gehwylc   ō*ð*rum swīcan,   60
for ðām Dryhten wyle   dōme sīne
þæt earme flǣsc   eorþan betǣcan.

XXI

Γ (lagu) byþ lēodum   langsum geþūht,
gif hī sculun nēþun   on nacan tealtum,
and hī sǣȳþa   swȳþe brēgaþ,   65
and se brimhengest   brīdles ne gȳme*ð*.

XXII

ᛝ (Ing) wæs ǣrest   mid Ēast-Denum
gesewen secgun,   oþ hē siððan ēst
ofer wǣg gewāt;   wǣn æfter ran;
ðus heardingas   ðone hæle nemdun.   70

XXIII

ᛟ (ēþel) byþ oferlēof   ǣghwylcum men,
gif he mōt ðǣr rihtes   and gerysena on
brūcan on bo*l*de   blēadum oftast.

XVII

Tir is one of the guiding signs; it keeps faith well
with princes; always it holds its course
above the night-clouds; it never fails.   50

XVIII

The birch has no fruit; nonetheless it bears
shoots without seed; it is beautiful in its branches,
high of crown, fairly adorned;
tall and leafy, it reaches up to touch the sky.

XIX

The steed is the joy of princes in noble company,   55
the charger proud in its hoofs, when warriors,
prosperous ones on horseback, discuss its points;
and to the restless it always proves a remedy.

XX

Man rejoicing in life is cherished by his kinsmen;
yet everyone must betray his fellow,   60
because the Lord purposes by his decree
to commit the wretched human body to the earth.

XXI

Water seems interminable to men,
if they are obliged to venture out in a tossing vessel,
and the sea-billows terrify them exceedingly,   65
and the sea-steed will not respond to the bridle.

XXII

Ing among the East-Danes was first
beheld by men, until that later time when to the east
he made his departure over the wave, followed by his chariot;
that was the name those stern warriors gave the hero.   70

XXIII

The family land is very dear to every man,
provided that there in his own house he may enjoy
everything that is right and proper in constant prosperity.

XXIV

ᛟ (dæg) byþ Drihtnes sond, dēore mannum,
mǣre Metodes lēoht, myrgþ and tōhiht   75
ēadgum and earmum, eallum brīce.

XXV

ᚪ (āc) byþ on eorþan elda bearnum
flǣsces fōdor; fereþ gelōme
ofer ganotes bæþ; – garsecg fandaþ
hwæþer āc hæbbe æþele trēowe.   80

XXVI

ᚫ (æsc) biþ oferhēah, eldum dȳre,
stīþ on staþule; stede rihte hylt,
ðēah him feohtan on fīras monige.

XXVII

ᚣ (ȳr) byþ æþelinga and eorla gehwæs
wyn and wyrþmynd; byþ on wicge fæger,   85
fæstlīc on færelde, fyrdgeatewa sum.

XXVIII

ᛡ (īar) byþ ēafixa; and ðēah ā brūceþ
fōdres on foldan; hafaþ fægerne eard,
wætre beworpen, ðǣr hē wynnum leofaþ.

XXIX

ᛠ (ēar) byþ egle eorla gehwylcun,   90
ðonn fæstlīce flǣsc onginneþ
hrāw cōlian, hrūsan cēosan
blāc tō gebeddan; blēda gedrēosaþ,
wynna gewītaþ, wēra geswīcaþ.

XXIV

Day is sent by the Lord, beloved by mankind,
the glorious light of the Creator, a source of joy and hope   75
to the haves and have-nots, of benefit to everyone.

XXV

The oak nourishes meat on the land
for the children of men; often it travels
over the gannet's bath – the stormy sea tests
whether the oak keeps faith nobly.   80

XXVI

The ash is extremely tall, precious to mankind,
strong on its base; it holds its ground as it should,
although many men attack it.

XXVII

The bow is a pleasure and brings honour
to all princes and nobles; it looks fine on a steed,   85
is reliable on a journey, a kind of army-gear.

XXVIII

The eel belongs to the river-fish; and yet it always takes
its food on land; it has a beautiful dwelling-place,
surrounded by water, where it lives in delight.

XXIX

Earth is loathsome to every man,   90
when irresistibly the flesh,
the dead body begins to grow cold,
the livid one to choose earth as its bedfellow;
fruits fail, joys vanish, man-made covenants are broken.

Explanatory notes

At the head of the columns of runic information which are printed to
the left of the main text of the Old English *Rune Poem* on page 135 of
his *Thesaurus*, George Hickes provides, directly opposite to the first
stanza of the poem, the normal angular form of the rune ᚠ, prefixed
by the usual transliteration into the alphabet equivalent f, and followed by the traditional rune name *feoh* superscript in a hand-
engraved facsimile of insular minuscule (for the physical layout of
the page see the facsimile on page 84 and the discussion on pages
25–7 of the introduction). The majority of the remaining twenty-
eight stanzas are prefaced with equally normal runic information,
including similarly unambiguous rune names. Hence the abbreviated
first sentence of the explanatory notes on the runes which introduce
each stanza usually will do no more than summarize the information
regarding rune form, equivalent alphabet letter, and rune name contained in the *Thesaurus* (with the parenthetical addition of my own
translation of the rune name into Modern English); only where the
runic information provided by Hickes is in some way aberrant will the
first sentence of the stanza note be expanded and its format modified.

Further significant data bearing on runic nomenclature to be included in the stanza note consist of:

1 the etymology of the names of the original twenty-four runes of the
   Common Germanic *futhark* (for the *futhark* symbols see page 4 of
   the introduction);

2 the earliest known forms of the Old English rune names, all of
   which appear in continental manuscripts but point to an Anglian
   original, such as:

a those represented in the brief, but very important treatise on runic cryptography which René Derolez discusses in detail in his *Runica Manuscripta*, pp 89ff, under the title of 'the *isruna* tract' and whose earliest extant versions are found in two ninth century manuscripts, St Gall, Stiftsbibliothek, ms 270 (see Derolez, pp 90ff) and Brussels, Koninklijke Bibliotheek, ms 9565–9566 (see Derolez, pp 95ff and also plate v);

b those listed in the right margin on folio 3v of the ninth century Brussels, Koninklijke Bibliotheek ms 9311–9319 (see Derolez, pp 65ff and also plate iv.b);

c those often attributed to Alcuin's pupil Arn, archbishop of Salzburg, and found on folio 2or of the still much-debated early ninth to tenth century Vienna, Österreichische Nationalbibliothek, ms 795, plus the so-called 'Gothic' letter names found on the verso of the same folio, which clearly are also related in some way to the Old English rune names (see Derolez, pp 52ff and also plate iv.a); and finally

3 the sixteen rune names of the reduced Norse *futhǫrk* (for which see also page 8), as they are found explicated or listed in the other three surviving rune poems, that is, the thirteenth century Norwegian *Rune Poem*, the fifteenth century Icelandic *Rune Poem*, and that curious bit of mnemonic doggerel, the ninth century *Abecedarium Nordmannicum* (for the texts of these three poems see Appendix B; and for a brief discussion of each see pages 34–7.

Summaries of the background information on runic nomenclature derived from these sources will appear in abbreviated form as the second sentence in brackets at the beginning of each stanza note.

STANZA I, LINES 1–3

ᚠ rune, transliteration *f*, name *feoh* (meaning wealth).
[Gmc: *feχu* (cattle, goods); oe: Isruna *feh*, Brussels *fech*, Vienna *fe*, *fech*, and 'Gothic' *fe*; Norse: NRP *fé* (wealth), IRP *fé* (wealth), and AN *feu*.]

From the primary meaning of 'cattle, livestock' (Bosworth-Toller definition 1), the word *feoh* developed the extended sense of moveable property, including 'goods,' 'money,' and the word's own lineal descendant 'fee' (compare the similar background of the Latin word *pecunia*). Tempting though it may be to take up the provocative hint offered by the initial juxtaposition of rune 1, ᚠ *feoh* (tame bovine animal), with rune 11, ᚢ *ūr* (wild bovine animal), and begin to frame yet another hypothesis to account for the characteristic rune order of the original Germanic *futhark* (see, for example, the theories noted in footnote 16 on p 65), such an endeavour could contribute little more than a freakish antiquarian digression to any edition of the Old English *Rune Poem*; for it is obvious from the descriptive stanza that follows the ᚠ rune in lines 1–3 of the poem that the primary meaning of the rune name *feoh* was not the sense understood or intended by the anonymous author, any more than it was the sense understood or intended by Cynewulf in his runic signatures (for which see Appendix A plus the brief discussion of Cynewulf's techniques on p 19). In every instance where the Old English rune name *feoh* has a clearly ascertainable meaning, the appropriate translation appears to be 'wealth,' with the additional connotation of transitory and hence illusory comfort summed up in the term 'worldly goods' or in the Gospel phrase 'treasure upon earth.' These last two attempts at a precise translation of *feoh* point up a distinctly ambivalent attitude toward the word among the Anglo-Saxons, which it should prove instructive to attempt to trace to its source.

There can be little doubt that, when first invented, the initial rune name signified 'cattle,' the most valuable possession of a people still very primitive in comparison with contemporary Mediterranean civilization. For an essentially unlettered society with as yet no practical use for the *futhark*, the property rune ᚠ may well have assumed an auspicious character, perhaps even a formal symbolic function as one of the most important omens of good fortune in the kind of lot-casting ritual that the first century Roman historian Tacitus describes in *Germania*, chapter 10:

Auspicia sortesque ut qui maxime observant. Sortium consuetudo simplex. Virgam frugiferae arbori decisam in surculos amputant, eosque notis quibus-dam discretos super candidam vestem temere ac fortuito spargunt. Mox, si publice consultetur, sacerdos civitatis, sin privatim, ipse pater familiae, precatus deos caelumque suspiciens, ter singulos tollit, sublatus secundum impressam ante notam interpretatur.

(To divination and lot-casting they pay the greatest attention. Their method of casting lots is simple. They lop a branch from a fruit-bearing tree and cut it into slices, which they mark with distinguishing signs and scatter at random without order on a white cloth. Then the priest of the community (if a public consultation is involved) or the father of the family (if the matter is private) invokes the gods and, with eyes lifted to the sky, picks up three slices of wood, one at a time, and interprets them according to the signs previously marked upon them.)

A balanced and well-documented summary of the arguments for and against the magical and oracular uses of the early runes can be found in Musset's *Introduction*, pp 141–155.

Various scholars have attempted to reconstruct, by means of the extant runes and rune names, the ur-Germanic culture of two thousand years ago in which the twenty-four rune *futhark* had its origin. One of the most recent and most ingenious full-scale studies of this type is Karl Schneider's ponderous *Die Germanischen Runenna-men*, where, for example, the ᚠ rune is discussed in the context of primitive cow worship and Nerthus cult, and its form is identified as representing the head of a horned cow in profile (see pp 54–6). As Georges Dumézil points out in his *Les Dieux des Germains*, cattle were sacred to the fertility god, in the later Germanic north called Frey (the Lord), one of the triad of gods, Tyr, Odin, and Frey, who respectively carried on the three Indo-European divine functions of administering the world, giving war-luck, and ensuring the fertility of cattle and crops. Frey, the son of Niord (masculine form or consort of Nerthus), remained consistently the god of fertility. Tyr, who was originally the chief of the gods (like his Greek cognate Zeus), fell to a rank barely distinguishable from that of the crude warrior-god, Thor. Odin, on the other hand, god of the battle-slain, of storm, and hence of all kinds of inspiration including sorcery and poetry, became the special god of the ruling priest-kings and thereby the highest of all the Æsir worshipped in the Germanic north. (For Tyr see the stanza note on rune XVII below; for Odin see the stanza note on rune IV below; for Ing as a possible manifestation of Frey see the stanza note on rune XXII below.) Tyr gave his name to the third of the three *ættir* (families or groups of eight runes) into which the *futhark* was divided (on this tripartite division see pp 51–2, including the references in footnote 12 on p 80). Frey, by association with his sacrificial animal, gave his name to the first of the three *ættir*.

Information and theories bearing on the earliest uses and significances of runes (much of which is conveniently summarized in

Schneider's *Runennamen*, pp 25–42), can make only limited contributions to the interpretation of a work as late and as sophisticated
as the Old English *Rune Poem*; and no judicious editor should be
expected to consider the bulk of the highly speculative reconstruc-
tions of ancient Germanic cult practices proposed by Schneider and
his predecessors as relevant to the immediate topic. Nonetheless,
from time to time in these explanatory notes, I shall insert brief
references to possible lingering pre-Christian overtones, where these
appear almost inescapable. In the present instance, the evidence
compiled by the scholars of ur-Germanic culture would suggest that
the ᚠ rune was, in its earliest context, a completely positive symbol
with no ambivalent aspect, as reflected by its description in the first
line of the Old English *Rune Poem* as *frōfur fīra gehwylcum* (a benefit
to all men).

For the later warrior society that we see mirrored in *Beowulf*, the
word *feoh* appears to retain many positive aspects. Here the term
clearly signifies 'portable wealth' or, to represent the value system of
the poem more accurately, 'portable honour' and includes such ancestral treasures as the banner, helmet, chainmail coat, sword, and
saddle with which the Danish king rewards the young Geatish hero
(lines 1020–45). It is noteworthy that, according to the *Beowulf*
poet's reflection of this stage of the word's development, *feoh* was
valued by the warrior class not so much for its monetary worth as in
terms of its social function: as Vilhelm Grønbech's English translator
phrases it in *The Culture of the Teutons* II, p 34, a gift of *feoh* was 'a
solid lump of honour ... composed of old achievements, old high-
mindedness, old chieftainly prodigality, the glory of the owners and
the words of praise uttered by admirers.' Even the dragon hoard in
Beowulf is not presented as evil in origin, but as having become evil
from disuse, the rust which has eaten through once splendid adornments of honourable men offering unmistakable physical evidence of
its owner's corrosive avarice. The fabulous wealth of the Scyldings,
on the other hand, is shown to be a force for good: in constant use,
circulating freely to ransom the outlaw, encourage youthful heroism,
cement the bonds of loyalty and friendship, and even promote imitative generosity in its recipients, Hrothgar's *ealdgestrēon* (ancient
treasure) maintains its burnish undimmed. As a Roman and thus an
outsider, Tacitus might mistake the prodigal gift-giving of Germanic
chieftains for cynical pandering to the barbaric greed of their follow-

ers (see *Germania*, chapter 21). As a descendant of the Germanic
tribes of whom he writes, the Anglo-Saxon poet applauds the liberal
sharing of treasure in *Beowulf* for an ennobling ritual that bathes
giver, receiver, and beholder in a golden glow of mutual esteem (see
Beowulf, lines 1025–8, 1046–9). Indeed, from his prologue description
of Scyld's young heir (lines 21–5), the *Beowulf* poet makes it the
distinguishing mark not only of regal houses but of all praiseworthy
warriors to win *feoh* readily by means of prowess and then let it flow
freely through their hands for the express purpose of extending the
circle of friendship and inspiring noble deeds. Hrothgar's moving
elegy of Æschere praises that dead thane as much for generosity to
other warriors as for more obvious services to his lord through valour
and good counsel (see lines 1341–4). However destructive it may
prove to the hoarder, *feoh* is a potentially unifying and ennobling
social instrument in *Beowulf*, when used by those over whom it has
no dominion.

The author of the Old English *Rune Poem* need make no great leap
of the imagination in order to reinterpret this socially approved
liberality with *feoh* in the new spiritual context of Christian *contemptus mundi*, where all worldly treasure is viewed as intrinsically
valueless except for its use in ameliorating human suffering and need.
Under his treatment, the profuse gift-giving characteristic of the
Germanic court is transmuted into a religious act: the practical expression of charity through almsgiving in order to win the praise of a
new kind of Lord. The first stanza's closing pun on the similar roles of
the earthly and heavenly *dryhten* in relation to *feoh* is a measure of
how far the intellectual world of one western branch of Germania had
developed from the primitive divination rituals described by Tacitus
in *Germania*, chapter 10 (quoted earlier), where *feoh* perhaps first
came to signify more than just the common name of a valuable
domestic animal. In fact, it is my contention that this pun on the two
realms, mundane and spiritual, sets the tone and approach for the rest
of the poem, which was designed, not merely as a hodge-podge of
disparate mnemonic verses explicating the traditional rune names,
but as one more attempt to extend the policy of pouring new wine
into old bottles established for the mission to the English by Pope
Gregory the Great (see the quotation from his letter to Mellitus on
p 16). Throughout the poem, we see its anonymous author deliber-

ately imitating and refashioning traditional Germanic gnomic utterance so as to declare the glory of God and his works in the at best
religiously neutral context of the Anglo-Saxon *futhorc* (for a detailed
discussion of the poet's approach see pp 55–63).

1 *byþ* third person singular iterative present of *beon* (to be), showing
West Saxon rounding of *i* to *y* in the neighbourhood of a labial (see
Campbell #318) as throughout the poem except in lines 45, 48, 49, 52,
58, and 81. This verb probably would be more accurately conveyed,
not by the neutral verb 'is' of my translation, but by some clumsier
formula such as 'was, is, and ever shall be.' The second word in all but
five of the twenty-nine stanzas (VII, VIII, XV, XVI, and XXII), its
insistent presence constitutes one of the major stylistic links unifying
the poem and identifies the type of utterance to be expected throughout, being the characteristic verb of the so-called *bith*-gnomes, those
traditional wisdom verses on which The Old English *Rune Poem* was
modelled (discussed on pp 38–40).

frōfur for standard West Saxon *frōfor*, as also in lines 11 and 58,
resulting from the falling together of unstressed vowels (see Campbell
#49, 368–87). Bruce Dickins (*Runic Poems*, p 13) gives the customary
translation 'comfort'; Theodor von Grienberger ('Das angelsächsisches Runengedicht,' p 204) prefers *Hilfsmittel* (help); since
the stanza does not suggest that mankind feels either miserable or
weak, this edition uses the more neutral term 'benefit.'

fīra gehwylcum 'to all men,' showing *y* for earlier *e* as also in lines 2,
7, 9, 13, 43, 60, and 90 (for which see Campbell #717). This inclusive
formula accentuates the universality of the concise *bith*-gnome defining *feoh* in line 1a. It is merely the first of many such universalizing
phrases designed to underline the homiletic purpose of the poem as a
collection of moral lessons for Everyman: compare *manna gehwylc*
(line 2), *þegna gehwylcum* (line 7), *manna gehwylcun* (line 9),
eorla gehwām (line 12), *rinca gehwylcum* (line 13), *cwicera
gehwām* (line 16), *oft* (line 27), *niþa bearnum* (line 27), *beornum
and ðearfum* (line 34), *symble* (line 38), *beorna gehwylcne* (line 43),
symble (line 45), *ā* (line 49), *nǣfre* (line 50), *ǣfre* (line 58), *ānra
gehwylc* (line 60), *ǣghwylcum men* (line 71), *oftast* (line 73), *ēad-*

gum and earmum (line 76), *eallum* (line 76), *elda bearnum* (line 77), *gelōme* (line 78), *eorla gehwæs* (line 84), *ā* (line 87), *eorla gehwyl-cun* (line 90).

2 *sceal* third person singular present indicative of *sculan* (shall, must, have to). This is the characteristic verb of the so-called *sceal*-gnomes, which, like the *bith*-gnomes, are found both singly and in collections (for examples see the maxims of the *Exeter Book*, whose opening lines are quoted in footnote 24 on p 77). Where *sceal*-gnomes differ from *bith*-gnomes at all, it is in putting rather more stress on action than on description, that is, on the individual's obligation to fulfil a pre-scribed role in the world pattern by doing what is fit, right, and proper. Grammatically, this shift from passive observation to active participation is reflected in the first stanza when *manna gehwylc*, a variation of the inclusive formula *fīra gehwylcum*, becomes subject instead of indirect object of the verb. Throughout the Old English *Rune Poem*, the verb *sculan* is used only in contexts of apparently unpleasant duty: the paradoxical requirement to give away one kind of good in order to obtain another here in stanza I; the enforced withdrawal of support from loving kinsmen as a result of mortality in stanza xx; and the terrible necessity of placing one's life at the mercy of the sea in stanza xxI. It is significant that at least two (and probably all three) of these occurrences of *sculan* involve the religi-ous mysteries of death and judgement; certainly the first carries almost the force of a Christian commandment. It may not be unwar-ranted speculation, therefore, to assume that the poet chose the verb *byþ* to give gnomic flavour to his verses, but reserved *sceal* to stress instances of divine decree.

ðēah contrastive adverb 'yet,' to underline the shift from observation to exhorted action represented by the successive main verbs *byþ* and *sceal*. Its presence is a signal that this is not ordinary gnomic verse, but that some paradox is involved.

miclun for *miclum*, dative form of the adjective *micel* (big), used as an adverb meaning 'freely, generously.' In this poem, as in most other Old English texts, the normal dative plural ending is well preserved (note the thirty-one forms with -*um* in lines 1, 5, 7, 13, 15, 27, 29, 30,

34 twice, 39, 45, 52, 54, 55, 56, 57, 58, 60, 63, 64, 67, 71, 73, 74, 76 thrice, 77, 81, and 89 in comparison with the eight forms with final -*n* in lines 2, 8, 9, 27, 37 twice, 68, and 90). The -*un* forms, as Frederick Jones suggests on page 86 of his dissertation, may represent a stage in the change from -*um* to -*on*, -*an* described by Alistair Campbell in paragraph 378 of his *Old English Grammar*. Another plausible explanation is that the -*un* forms represent incorrect expansions of the contraction -*ū*, either by some late West Saxon scribe copying an earlier text or at the time of Hickes' edition (see Grienberger, 'Runengedicht,' pp 205–6 for discussion of this point).

hyt for standard *hit* (it) found in lines 25 and 26 (for this alternation see Campbell #703).

3 *for* preposition plus dative, meaning 'before, in the presence of,' intended to summon up the image of a court in support of the pun on earthly and heavenly *dryhten* described in the stanza note above.

Drihtne 'the Lord,' shows unrounding of *y* to *i* before *h* (for which see Campbell #316); compare the normal form *Dryhten* (line 61); see also *Drihtnes* (line 74).

dōmes objective genitive singular of the noun *dōm*, meaning 'glory' or, in the more precise etymological sense, 'favourable judgement.' Like *dryhten*, this is a word capable of operating powerfully at both the secular and the religious levels. In the heroic context mirrored by *Beowulf*, *lof* (praise) and *dōm* (a glorious reputation) are the almost synonymous aims of the warrior class; the goad of the judgement of others, particularly of one's own lord, impels men to seemingly impossible feats in order to establish the secular immortality of a lasting *dom*. In the Christian context, every day's acts should be performed in full consciousness of the kind of judgement they will obtain on *Dōmesdæg* (Doomsday), when the Lord chooses the *heorðdryht* (close, ie, hearth, companions) to share his glorious light for eternity.

hlēotan translated here 'to gain,' literally 'to obtain by lot,' probably retains some overtones of fate or destiny, reinforcing the concept of divine power over men's lives.

STANZA II, LINES 4–6

ᚢ rune, transliteration *u*, name *ūr* (meaning aurochs).
[Gmc: *ūruz* (aurochs); OE: Isruna *uur*, Brussels *ur*, Vienna *ur*, and 'Gothic'
uraz; Norse: NRP *úr* (slag), IRP *úr* (drizzle), and AN *ur*.]

The aurochs (*bos primigenius*) was the original wild ox of Europe
from which domestic cattle are descended. Archaeological evidence,
written accounts over many centuries, and pictorial representations
made not long before its extinction in the early seventeenth century
reconstruct the intimidating image of an enormous black beast,
standing six feet at the shoulder and with great spreading forward-
curving horns (see plate III opposite p 46 in Richard Lydekker's *The
Ox and its Kindred* for two portraits of the aurochs; and consult his
detailed discussion of the animal's appearance and forest habitat on
pp 37–67). Writing at about the period when runes are thought to
have had their origin, Caesar described the size and ferocity of the
aurochs, as well as the important double function of its horns among
the Germani in serving both as trophies of manly courage in the hunt
and, when adorned with silver, as fitting drinking vessels at the most
splendid banquets:

Tertium est genus eorum, qui uri appellantur. Hi sunt magnitudine paulo
infra elephantos, specie et colore et figura tauri. Magna vis eorum est et
magna velocitas, neque homini neque ferae quam conspexerunt parcunt. Hos
studiose foveis captos interficiunt. Hoc se labore durant adulescentes atque
hoc genere venationis exercent, et qui plurimos ex his interfecerunt, relatis
in publicum cornibus, quae sint testimonio, magnam ferunt laudam. Sed
adsuescere ad homines et mansuefieri ne parvuli quidem excepti possunt.
Amplitudo cornuum et figura et species multum a nostrorum boum cornibus
differt. Haec studiose conquisita ab labris argento circumcludunt atque in
amplissimis epulis pro poculis utuntur.

(The third species consists of the ure-oxen so-called. In size these are somewhat smaller than elephants; in appearance, colour and shape they are as
bulls. Great is their strength and great their speed, and they spare neither man
nor beast once sighted. These the Germans slay zealously, by taking them in
pits; by such work the young men harden themselves and by this kind of
hunting train themselves, and those who have slain most of them bring the
horns with them to a public place for a testimony thereof, and win great

renown. But even if they are caught very young, the animals cannot be tamed or accustomed to human beings. In bulk, shape, and appearance their horns are very different from the horns of our oxen. The natives collect them zealously and encase the edges with silver, and then at their grandest banquets use them as drinking cups.) (*Gallic Wars* VI, 28)

It stands as clear testimony to the conservatism of Germanic tradition in Britain that, although the aurochs survived only in the forests of the continent and was therefore unknown to English hunters, the fearsome brute maintained its linkage with the second rune, as well as the major elements of its reputation over the centuries that intervened between the Anglo-Saxon exodus from the continent (traditionally c 450) and the composition of the Old English *Rune Poem* (probably after 950). This resistance to change is particularly striking in view of the obvious temptation to replace the uncommon word *ūr* with some everyday homonym, such as the conveniently available first person plural possessive adjective which many believe that Cynewulf used as a substitute (see the notes on the Cynewulfian signatures in ASPR II, pp 124–5, 150–1, and ASPR III, pp 254–5). Largely in order to explain Cynewulf's use of this rune without requiring any such substitution, Ralph Elliott has proposed an extended meaning for the rune name *ūr*, that is, the manly strength and courage needed to battle the aurochs (see *Runes*, pp 150–1 and also his articles in *English Studies* 34, pp 49ff, 193ff). In rebuttal to his argument, the reader should note the ready substitution of more familiar homonyms meaning 'slag' and 'drizzle' in the Norwegian and Icelandic rune poems. Perhaps the reason for the tenacity of the original Old English rune name should be sought in the Anglo-Saxon veneration of *ealdgestrēon* (ancient treasure), family heirlooms which may frequently have included decorated drinking vessels fashioned out of aurochs horns, such as the pairs of silver-gilt drinking horns found in the Sutton Hoo and Taplow burials in the company of other treasures brought from the continental homeland (see R.L.S. Bruce-Mitford, *The Sutton Hoo Ship-Burial*, plate 19, and also fig 6.a and the main discussion of the horns on pp 33–5; in addition, see D.M. Wilson, *The Archaeology of Anglo-Saxon England*, p 260; for an outline of the sacred and binding Germanic rituals in which such drinking horns played a part, see Grønbech, part II, subsections 6 and 9–12).

Although there is no specific reference to man in the second stanza of the Old English *Rune Poem*, the aurochs is not presented in the neutral tone of wonder at one of the marvels of God that we find, for example, in stanza IX. Instead, the description here is couched in heroic terms; the beast appears as a warrior: *anmōd* (courageous), *felafrēcne* (very fierce), one who *feohteþ* (fights), using his horns as weapons, and lives like a notorious outlaw on the moors beyond human habitation, a *mǣre mōrstapa* (famous moor-stalker) (compare Grendel, the *mǣre mearcstapa* (famous boundary-stalker), whose presence darkens the civilized splendour of Heorot and interrupts its gift-giving ceremonies in the first episode of *Beowulf*). This terminology transforms the aurochs into man's adversary, an adversary viewed with awe verging on admiration, as shown by the emphatic ring of the concluding half-line of the stanza, '*þæt is mōdig wuht*' (that is a brave creature), which clearly belongs to the epic context of such heroic summaries as '*þæt wæs gōd cyning*' (that was a good king) in *Beowulf* (cf lines 11, 863, 1812, and 2390). From this description of the aurochs, the probable place of the second rune in primitive divination emerges fairly clearly; in contrast to *feoh* (cattle), *ūr* (aurochs) must have constituted a challenge and a danger, rather than a tame benefit. It is interesting to note in this connection the similarly uncomfortable overtones preserved in the homonyms substituted for aurochs in the Norwegian and Icelandic rune poems.

4 *and* for Hickes' and no doubt the manuscript's 7, the Tironian symbol used as a contraction for *and* seven times in the poem (lines 4, 20 twice, 24, 58, 65, and 84), as opposed to eighteen instances where the word is spelled out in full.

oferhyrned for Hickes' *ofer hyrned*. Bosworth-Toller and most editors translate 'having horns above.' With Dickins (*Runic Poems*, p 13), I interpret *ofer* as an intensifier (compare *oferceald*, line 29; *oferlēof*, line 71; and *oferhēah*, line 81) and therefore translate 'has huge horns,' viewing the adjective as designed to stress the distinctive aspect of the aurochs for the Anglo-Saxons, who had seen only the great trophies of its horns and not the animal itself (in this context note that line 5b reaffirms the central importance of the aurochs' horns for the poet: *feohteþ mid hornum* (it fights with its horns)).

5 *felafrēcne* 'very fierce' for Hickes' *fela frecne*.

6 *mōrstapa* 'moor-stalker' for Hickes' *mor stapa*. In the literal sense this is an ignorantly inaccurate epithet for a forest creature; but in the symbolic sense it is a telling indicator of the way the aurochs lived like an outlaw, untameable and beyond the hedges of human control.

þæt expanded from Hickes' *þ*, both here and in line 62.

wuht for normal *wiht* (creature); see Campbell #338, note 1 for the appearance of *u* in low sentence stress.

STANZA III, LINES 7–9

Þ rune, transliteration ð (alternatively, insular minuscule *þ*, both equivalent to Modern English *th*), name ðorn (meaning thorn).
[Gmc: *þurnuz (thorn); OE: Isruna ðorn, Brussels *thorn*, Vienna ðorn; versus Gmc:* *þurisaz (giant); Norse: NRP *þurs* (giant), IRP *þurs* (giant), AN *thuris*; versus apparently meaningless Vienna 'Gothic' *thyth* (perhaps from Greek *theta*).]

English and Scandinavian tradition diverge over the name of the third rune, although both names, 'thorn' and 'giant,' are obviously inimical to human comfort, preserving what may have been the original aura of bad fortune in the lot casting. It is usually assumed that the Norse rune name represents the early Germanic significance of the rune and that the Anglo-Saxon rune name was created after the conversion to Christianity, either as part of a monastic attempt to purge the *futhorc* of references to heathen mythology or because the new alliterating name aptly described the spiky shape of a convenient sound symbol which, by the early ninth century, was passing out of the specialized context of the *futhorc* into everyday bookhand (for the earliest firmly dated example of the use of this symbol in insular bookhand see Charter 33 of the Clofesho Council, 803, in Henry Sweet's *The Oldest English Texts*). Although the latter suggested motive may have had some contributory force, it is noteworthy that the Anglo-Saxon monks who preserved the rune names did not find it necessary to replace the religiously innocuous name *wyn* with some more physically descriptive word when the eighth rune likewise became an ordinary sound symbol in insular script. Those interested in the survival of aspects of insular calligraphy will recognize the tenacity of the definite article *þe* (written with the initial runic letter for *th* open at the top) in the still extant *ye* of gratuitously quaint signs, such as 'Ye Olde Tea Shoppe.'

The ðorn is described in stanza III in terms of the human pain it causes, both singly (in grasping one thorn) and collectively (upon lying down in a briar-patch); but in total effect the note of warning is not unmodulated by admiration of the plant's valour, and even perhaps by a touch of grim humour at the plight of those so foolish as to meddle with thorns. It is typical of Schneider's methods of finding evidence in the extant rune poems for his reconstruction of primitive Germanic beliefs that he interprets both the Norse *þurs* and the English ðorn as references to the early thundergod 'Donar' (who appears in later Scandinavian mythology as the huge hammer-bearing Thor) and then proceeds to emend the Old English *Rune Poem* so that ðegna (thanes, men) (line 7) reads *þyrsa* (giants) and *manna* (men) (line 9) reads *mægþa* (maidens); the new stanza thus produced is then translated as a description of the thundergod in his roles as giant-fighter and bringer of fertility, functions further stressed by Schneider's analysis of the rune form as the god's hammer and/or *membrum virile* (see *Runennamen*, pp 388–99 for the full exposition of this extraordinary argument).

8 *anfengys* 'to grasp,' (literally, of grasp) for Hickes' *anfen-gys*. Most English editors, following the suggestion of Grein (in 'Zur Textkritik der angelsächsischen Dichter, p 428), read as two words *anfeng is* (the touch, or the grasping, is); thus Dickins, Dobbie, and Jones. Like Grienberger ('Runengedicht,' p 206), I interpret Hickes' internal hyphen as the thoughtless repetition of one originally placed at the end of a line in the manuscript in order to indicate the continuation of the genitive singular form *anfengys* at the beginning of the next line; this interpretation makes the three descriptive adjectives: *scearp*, *yfel*, and *rēþe* grammatically parallel in the descriptive sequence (for the date when the hyphen was first used in Old English manuscripts see page 31). The late West Saxon variant of *y* for unstressed *e* seen in this word appears also in *ēadnys* (line 12), *recyde* (line 13), *herenys* (line 19), *underwreþyd* (line 37), and *fæylde* (line 49); for this spelling see Campbell #369, fn 1.

ungemetun for the normal adverbial dative *ungemetum* found in line 29, meaning 'immeasurably' (for the -*un* ending see the explanatory note on *miclun* in line 2).

9 *gehwylcun* for the normal dative form *gehwylcum* found in lines 1, 7, and 13 (for the -*un* ending see the note on *miclun* in line 2).

him mid 'among them,' with the preposition placed after the object it governs.

STANZA IV, LINES 10–12

ᚩ rune, transliteration *o*, name *ōs* (meaning mouth, perhaps with some overtones of the divine source of eloquence).
[Gmc: **ansuz* (god); OE: Isruna *oos*, Brussels *os*, Vienna *os*, and 'Gothic' *aza*; Norse: NRP *óss* (rivermouth), IRP *óss* (god, specifically Odin), AN *os*; versus the unrelated Latin homonym *os* (mouth).]

Originally the rune ᚠ stood in fourth position in the twenty-four rune Common Germanic *futhark*, as it continued to do in the later sixteen rune Norse *futhǫrk* (for these two rune sequences see pages 4 and 8); with the sound value *a* and the name **ansuz*, it represented Germanic *a* whatever the phonetic context. In the normal development of the rune name, however, its initial vowel became unrepresentative of the majority of the Old English vowels resulting from Germanic *a*, when Germanic **ansuz* became Old English *ōs* (through loss of the inflectional ending, rejection of the nasal consonant before *s*, and compensatory lengthening and nasalization, followed by rounding of the preceding vowel; for which see Campbell #130). A new rune form was created in order to represent the sound developed in this way, perhaps formally a ligature of ᚠ *a* and ᚾ *n* (as first argued in the 1890's by Hempl, 'The Old English Runes for *a* and *o*,' pp 350–1, and by Grienberger, 'Die angelsächsischen Runenreihen,' pp 19–20, and since accepted by most runologists). Then the original rune ᚠ was suitably renamed and used to represent the fronted *a*, in insular spelling *æ*, which, except where retraction or restoration occurred, is the characteristic product of Germanic *a*. Some indication of the way in which rune lore was transmitted in an oral society emerges from the fact that, when this process of sound differentiation was complete, it was the rune with the original mnemonic name that retained fourth place in the new Anglo-Saxon *futhorc*, whereas the rune with the original form was tacked on at the end of the sequence along with various completely new runes invented to represent distinctively Old English sounds (see the explanatory note on stanza xxvi and also the *futhorc* sequence on p 12). When the initial sound of the name of the original Germanic o-rune (ᚪ *oþil*) changed its value through i-mutation (see the explanatory note on stanza xxiii), the fourth rune came to be used for every Old English o, whatever its source.

The process by which the rune name ōs developed the meaning which it appears to have in the Old English *Rune Poem* requires some explanation. Certainly the meaning '(pagan)god' which the name has in the Icelandic *Rune Poem* seems etymologically to represent the direct Germanic tradition, as contended by Grienberger, 'Runengedicht,' p 207; Arntz, *Handbuch*[2], pp 191ff; Dickins, *Runic Poems*, p 13; Philippson, *Germanisches Heidentum bei den Angelsachsen*, pp 135, 153; Marstrander, 'Om runene og runenavnenes oprindelse,' p 148; Krause, *Runeninschriften im älteren Futhark*, pp 58, 190; and Schneider, *Runennamen*, p 373. Furthermore, it would be foolishly hypercritical to dispute much of the large body of evidence assembled by these and other scholars to demonstrate the influence which the northern imagination supposed the Germanic gods to exert over human life, in particular the close connection that the storm and death-god Odin (Old English Woden), chief of the Æsir, was thought to have with eloquence and wisdom and, notably, with the mysteries of rune lore itself (see the quotations from *Hávamál* on pages 6 and 9; the references in stanza note 1; Schneider, *Runennamen*, pp 371–8; and, for the specifically English evidence, see J.S. Ryan, 'Othin in England,' especially p 462 where Woden's presence in the genealogies of all the Anglo-Saxon royal houses is discussed; A.L. Meaney, 'Woden in England: a Reconsideration of the Evidence;' and, for a very interesting article on the Sutton Hoo artefacts as evidence for a Wodan-descended kingship, K.G. Hauck, 'Herrschaftszeichen eines Wodanistischen Königtums'). Such evidence lends some faint tincture of plausibility to a reading of stanza iv as praise of Woden in his role as god of eloquence (*spræce*), of wisdom (*wīsdōmes, witena*), and of the noble dead (*eorla*) who achieve the warrior's hope (*tō-*

hiht) of feasting with him in Asgard's great hall of the battle-slain, Valhalla (*ēadnys*).

It is historically unlikely, however, that the monasteries responsible for the written preservation of the Anglo-Saxon rune names or the demonstrably Christian author of this poem would knowingly assist in reinforcing the reputation of the Germanic pantheon. Perhaps it was fortunate, then, that by the time of written vernacular records the mnemonic rune name *ōs* had become a rare word in Old English, appearing only in personal names, such as those of the divinely descended Northumbrian kings, Oswald *et al* (for names beginning with *Ōs*- see Searle's *Onomasticon Anglo-Saxonicum*, pp 370–81), and in the oblique nonce form *ēsa* (genitive plural of *ōs*) found in the charm *wið fǣrstice* (against a sudden stitch) (see Dobbie, p 122, line 23), where the mighty Æsir of northern mythology have degenerated to the status of minor physical annoyances. There can be little doubt that it must have been only the unfamiliarity of the Old English simplex *ōs* ([pagan] god), coupled with its fortuitous resemblance to the innocuous Latin word *os* (mouth), that enabled this remnant of pre-Christian religion to survive unchanged in the name lists of monkish scribes and so find its way, with however distorted a reinterpretation, into the Old English *Rune Poem*. I feel quite confident, as a result, in following Kemble's early suggestion ('On Anglo-Saxon Runes,' p 340) and borrowing the false definition 'mouth' for my translation of *ōs*, as do most other editors.

11 *frōfur* for standard *frōfor* (see the note on line 1), the second in a series of four variations on the concept of 'benefit' (*wraþu, frōfur, ēadnys,* and *tōhiht*), furnishing an interesting commentary on the importance of *rǣd* (counsel, wise advice), a concept that also looms large in the heroic poetry, where it often seems to merge directly into action (compare *Beowulf*, lines 172, 278, 1376, 2027, 3080).

12 *tōhiht* 'a delight' or 'a thing hoped for' for Hickes' *to hiht*.

STANZA V, LINES 13–15

R rune (rounded form like capital R instead of normal angular Ʀ), transliteration *r*, name *rād* (meaning riding).

[Gmc: **raiðō* (riding); OE: Isruna *rat*, Brussels *rad*, Vienna *ra(e)d(a)*, and

'Gothic' *reda*; Norse: NRP *ræið* (riding), IRP *reið* (riding), and AN *rat.*]. Note that what appears in the photograph on p 84 to be a cross-stroke transforming the *d* of *rād* to *ð* is actually a mark in the paper and not attributable to Hickes' printer.

All the rune poems mention the horse in describing this rune and stress the strenuous aspect of horsebackriding, thereby leaving little doubt about their authors' common understanding of the fifth rune name (compare the Norwegian and Icelandic rune poems in Appendix B). Nonetheless, a number of commentators have posited other Old English meanings for *rād* in order to account for the contrast on which the stanza turns, a contrast emphasized by the juxtaposition of the alliterating adjectives *sēfte* (easy) and *swīþhwæt* (very strenuous) in line 14. For example, the Bosworth-Toller dictionary suggests a pun on two otherwise unrecorded Old English definitions of *rād* as the 'furniture' of a house and the furniture or 'harness' of a horse; whereas the Grein-Köhler *Sprachschatz* proposes a different pun on *rād* as 'the rise and fall of music' (a possibility supported only by the compound *swegelrād*) and *rād* in its normal significance of 'horsebackriding.' Of course there is a definite riddling quality to all the runic stanzas and certainly some of the rune names are looked at from a number of different aspects (compare stanza xxv, where the oak-tree is described first in terms of its acorns and then as ship-timber); but the search for multiple meanings seems unnecessary here. Surely the humour produced by noting the disparity between thoughts (perhaps even easy boasts) in the mead-hall and hard physical exercise out in the world of action furnishes sufficient explanation for the stressed contrast.

Those who interpret the Germanic *futhark* in terms of its hypothetical cult origins find traces of symbolic significance even here. For example, Helmut Arntz, in the second edition of his *Handbuch*, p 196, connects the *rād*-rune with the journey to the underworld and Ralph Elliott, in *Runes*, p 57, suggests that it may have come to function as 'a journey-charm, whether for the living or for the dead' (for interesting physical evidence of the concept of death as a journey see R.L.S. Bruce-Mitford, *The Sutton Hoo Ship Burial* and Philip Grierson's explanation of the coins and ingots as passage money in 'The Purpose of the Sutton Hoo Coins;' compare also the account of Scyld's funeral in *Beowulf*, lines 26–52). Karl Schneider (in common with Bugge,

Indledning, pp 38–84; Agrell, 'Der Ursprung der Runenschrift und die Magie;' von der Leyen, 'Die germanische Runenreihe und ihre Namen;' and Jungandreas, 'Die germanische Runenreihe und ihre Bedeutung') sees the image of a wheeled vehicle lying behind the shape of the ᚱ rune and painstakingly reconstructs an association with the chariot of the sun-god (see *Runennamen*, pp 116–18).

13 *recyde* with *y* for normal *e*, shows the falling together of unstressed vowels (see Campbell #49, 368ff).

14 *sēfte, and swīþhwæt*: a comma is inserted before *and* to enforce the sense of contrast; another possibility is to translate *and* in an adversative sense as 'but.'

15 *mægenheardum* 'powerful' or 'strong to endure,' for Hickes' *mægen heardum*.

mīlpaþas for Hickes' *mil paþas*, literally 'mile-paths,' meaning the open road which is measured in miles, as opposed to a by-way extending only a short distance: the term is designed to indicate a tedious and exhausting journey, hence translated 'the long roads.'

STANZA VI, LINES 16–18

ᚳ rune, transliteration *c*, name *cēn* (meaning torch).
[Gmc: *kēnaz (pine-torch); OE: Isruna *cen*, Brussels *ken*, Vienna *cen*; versus Gmc: *kaunaz (ulcer); Norse: NRP *kaun* (ulcer), IRP *kaun* (ulcer), AN *chaon*; versus the apparently meaningless Vienna 'Gothic' *chozma*.]

The author of the Old English *Rune Poem* shows no knowledge of the Northumbrian epigraphical runes ᚩ (*calc*) and ᛡ (name unknown), which were invented to distinguish the velar stops represented in insular script by *c* from the affricate [tʃ] that developed before a front vowel and was also represented by the same letter, as in the rune name *cēn* (for the epigraphical runes referred to above see Bruce Dickins, 'A System of Transliteration for Old English Runic Inscriptions').

It is noteworthy that the rare word *cēn* (torch) should survive as the name of the sixth rune in Anglo-Saxon rune lists and in this poem,

despite the pressure from the near homonym *cœn* (keen, brave),
which actually does appear as a variant form in one of the rune lists
on folio 3v of St John's College, Oxford, ms 17 (reproduced in Derolez,
plate III). Even Cynewulf seems to have used the traditional Old
English meaning of 'torch' in his signatures to *Christ, Elene,* and *The
Fates of the Apostles* (see Appendix A and also the references in
stanza note 1, especially Elliott's articles on the Cynewulfian signatures). The Norse tradition (as in the case of rune II) involves a
different Germanic root; but in this case there is no real evidence to
show whether the English rune name or the equally tenacious Norse
one is truer to the original Common Germanic *futhark* nomenclature;
Jungandreas even suggests that both names are corrupt descendants
of Germanic *kanō* (skiff), which he associates with the island-cult of
the fertility goddess Nerthus (see 'Die germanische Runenreihe und
ihre Bedeutung').

It is typical of Karl Schneider's adventurous attempt to recreate
early pan-Germanic cult practices that he links the Old English burning 'torch,' the Old Norse burning 'ulcer,' and even the hitherto
undefined 'Gothic' *chozma* with the cremation burial of Germanic
chieftains described as early as Tacitus' *Germania,* chapter 40, and
exemplified in the closing lines of *Beowulf*; in keeping with this
interpretation, he reads 'ðǣr hī æþelingas inne restaþ' as a reference,
not to the torch-lit hall in which nobles sit at ease, but to the balefire
in which they lie to be consumed after death. Although the word
cwicera (the living) might seem to lend some support to Schneider's
interpretation, readers less committed to the theory of a Germanic
ur-poem tend to see this stanza as belonging to the image of the happy
mead-hall of life, to which the pagan priest alluded in Bede's account
of the Christianization of Northumbria (*Ecclesiastical History,* iii,
13) and which also appears in stanzas I, VII, XIV, and XXIII of this
poem.

17 *byrneþ* for earlier *bierneþ* represents late West Saxon monophthongization (for which see Campbell #299–301).

oftust here and in line 41, as compared to *oftast* in line 73, shows the
falling together of vowels in unstressed syllables (for which see
Campbell #49, 368ff).

STANZA VII, LINES 19–21

Χ rune, transliteration *g*, name *ġyfu* (meaning generosity, abstracted from
the root meaning gift).
[Gmc: *geƀō* (gift); OE: Isruna *gebo*, Brussels *geuo*, Vienna *geofu* and 'Gothic'
geuua; absent from the reduced sixteen rune Norse *futhǫrk* represented by
NRP, IRP, and AN.]

The author of the Old English *Rune Poem* shows no knowledge of the
Northumbrian epigraphical rune Χ or ᚸ (gar), which was invented to
distinguish the velar spirant (and rarer stop), retained in Old English
in the context of back vowels and represented in insular script by *g*,
from the palatal spirant that developed before a front vowel and was
also represented by the same letter, as in the rune name *ġyfu* (see
Dickins, 'A System of Transliteration' cited in stanza note VI above).
The *y* for earlier *ie* in *ġyfu* represents West Saxon monophthongization (see Campbell #300–1).

Gift-giving was central to Germanic life, as illustrated by Tacitus'
remarks on barbarian hospitality in chapter 21 of his *Germania* (see
also my comments in stanza note I on the rune name *feoh*). Generosity was considered a noble attribute that cemented the bonds of
Germanic society, honouring in the process both giver and receiver;
and this apparent readiness to part with worldly goods could easily be
reinterpreted as the Christian virtue of charity. In stanza VII, both the
Germanic and the Christian heritages are evident. The heroic values
of the Germanic warrior class are represented by such terms as *gleng*
(ornament), *herenys* (praise), and *wyrþscype* (honour, literally,
worship, with which term compare Malory's 'worshipful' knights of
King Arthur for a late reflection of the social status and the kind of
aristocratic idealization involved). On the other hand, the Christian
duty of almsgiving to the poor obviously shades the meaning in the
final phrases of the stanza: 'wræcna gehwām/ār and ætwist, ðe byþ
ōþra lēas.' Thus, in this stanza (as in stanza I) we see a further clear
instance of putting new wine into old bottles, that is, giving fresh
religious significance to traditional secular or pagan practices.

19 *gumena* the position of this genitive plural form makes the first break
in the opening syntactic pattern characteristic of the majority of the

stanzas in the poem: 'A (rune name) *byþ* B (definition);' other instances occur in stanzas VIII, XV, XVI, and XXII. Metrical requirements cannot supply a reason, since the reversal of word order to *gyfu byþ gumena* would produce a perfectly acceptable half-line. Perhaps the unusual order is designed to lay stress on *gumena* (men of position), as opposed to *wræcna* (the dispossessed).

herenys for standard *herenes* shows the falling together of unstressed vowels (see Campbell #49, 368ff).

20 *and* expanded from Hickes' 7 twice in this line.

wyrþscype: for *wyrþ* from earlier *weorþ* see Campbell #324; for the meaningless interchange of *i* with *y* in *scype* see Campbell #317.

21 *ār and ætwist* translated 'help and means of survival' (rather than 'shelter and residence,' as argued not very persuasively by Kock, 'Interpretations and Emendations of Early Old English Texts,' pp 307ff).

ōþra genitive plural referring to *ār and ætwist*, or perhaps, as Jones suggests on page 92 of his dissertation, to possessions in general.

STANZA VIII, LINES 22–4

ᛈ rune (rounded form like a capital P; Hickes also adds the more normal angular form ᛈ), transliteration w (Hickes has prefixed *uu* and added superscript an insular minuscule *ρ*), name *wyn* (Hickes *wen*, meaning joy, possibly with the connotation clan-joy).
[Gmc: *ụunịō (joy); OE: Isruna *huun*, Brussels *uung*, Vienna *uyn*, and 'Gothic' *uuinne*; absent from the reduced sixteen rune Norse *futhqrk* represented by NRP, IRP, and AN.]

The w-rune ᛈ (like the *th*-rune ᚦ) was adopted into insular bookhand as a useful sound symbol; it began to replace the doubled *u* borrowed from Latin texts as early as 742–3 (see Charter 1 in Sweet's *The Oldest English Texts*). The substitution of *wen* for the normal rune name *wyn* probably represents a dialectal variant resulting from the Kentish unrounding and lowering of *y* to *e* (see Campbell

#288–92). As the other Old English name lists make clear, this word should not be read as the near-homonym *wēn* (hope); therefore, to avoid possible confusion, I have normalized its form in the printed text to standard West Saxon. It is easily demonstrable that the spelling of the rune name with an *e* cannot be attributed to the writer of the main text of the poem, who consistently spells the same word with a *y* throughout (see lines 37, 55, 85, 89, and 94). Possibly Hickes (or the manuscript's copyist, Humphrey Wanley) borrowed the rune name *wen* from Cotton ms Domitian A.ix (the only extant manuscript in which such an anomalous form of *wyn* appears and the source of many of Hickes' other additions); or else this name, along with the rest of the rune names, may have been inserted into the manuscript by some later hand than that of the original scribe in answer to the twenty-nine riddles posed by the poem (see George Hempl's discussion of the question of extraneous borrowings in 'Hickes's Additions to the Runic Poem,' and also the discussion on pp 25–6 of this edition. In support of the argument that *wen* and the other rune names were later additions, note that neither the unique manuscript of the Norwegian *Rune Poem* nor the earliest manuscript of the Icelandic *Rune Poem* contained any vernacular name glosses of the rune symbols (see notes 10 and 12 on pp 75 and 76).

'Joy' is the generally accepted meaning of the rune name, although Helmut Arntz has argued for possible connections with Germanic **winjō* (pasture) and **wulþuz* (glory) (see *Handbuch*[2], pp 203ff), and Karl Schneider would postulate *die Sippe* (the clan) as the underlying concept (*Runennamen*, pp 60–7). Schneider's interpretation may have some validity in view of the fact that all joy appears to have been seen by the Germanic people as having its source within the peaceful bonds of human community, whether family unit or *dryht* (band of men, ie, Tacitus' *comitatus* or band of companions); there was no joy lying about loose in the wilds (on this point see Grønbech, *The Culture of the Teutons*, part 1, section 1, under *friþ*). However, *wyn* certainly can be found in various Old English contexts not involving the family or *dryht*, as Bosworth-Toller records: compare, for example, Psalm 94:2 ('We sealmas him singan mid wynne,' translating *in psalmis jubilemus ei* (we rejoice to him in songs)) and also the use of the rune symbol as a grammalogue for *wyn* in Psalm 99 of the Junius Psalter, where ᚹ *sumiaþ* translates *jubilate*; in Exeter Riddle 91, where the compound *mōd · ᚹ ·* appears (for *mōdwyn* (that which rejoices the heart)); and two instances in *Elene*, *weroda* ᚹ in line 788 (for *weroda wynn* (joy of hosts)) and *wuldres* ᚹ in line 1089 (for *wuldres wynn* (joy of heaven)). Of course the Cynewulfian signatures to *Christ II*, *Elene*, and *The Fates of the Apostles* furnish additional examples (see Appendix A). In the Old English *Rune Poem*, wyn appears as the antithesis of *wēana* (woes), *sāres and sorge* (pain and sorrow) and is equated with *blǣd and blysse* (prosperity and happiness); it also is associated with *byrga*, which involves the protection afforded by an established community.

22 *ne* the complete identification and interchangeability of rune symbol and rune name are underlined here by the direct addition of the genitive singular inflectional ending -*ne* to the rune itself (see Derolez, pp 410–12 for a discussion of similar practices in the *Durham Ritual* gloss).

brūceþ 'experiences or enjoys,' taking the genitive *wynne* as direct object. This construction makes the second break in the opening formulaic pattern (see the note on line 19) and the first time that the gnomic verb *byþ* is altogether missing from a stanza. One reason is not far to seek: unlike most of the rune names, 'joy' cannot be linked with an object or action – it is a subjective experience; therefore the poet is reduced to describing *wyn* by means of opposites (*wēana*, *sāres*, and *sorge*), by means of equally abstract synonyms (*blǣd* and *blysse*), and finally through the image of a man enjoying the satisfaction of a secure and comfortable life, unlike the *wrǣcna* of the preceding stanza.

23 *sorge* for Hickes' *forge* (as demanded by both alliteration and sense), correcting a copyist's error easily accounted for by the physical simi-larity of the two letters in insular script.

sylfa for earlier West Saxon *selfa* (see Campbell #325), a nominative singular masculine weak declension adjective referring back to and emphasizing the pronoun ðe (who).

hæfþ here (as in line 41) shows loss of the unaccented vowel of the verb ending (for such contractions see Campbell #732). Compare the uncontracted form *hafaþ* in line 88.

24 *and* expanded from Hickes' 7.

blysse for *blisse* (for which see Campbell #318).

byrga geniht 'the contentment belonging to fortified communities' (literally, of strongholds the enoughness), usually translated (following Grienberger, 'Runengedicht,' p 209) 'the abundance characteristic of cities'; but note also the translation 'a good enough house' (Dickins, *Runic Poems*, p 15). My translation underlines the need for the protection of living in a strong and well-established settlement and avoids the misleading elegance of terms like 'cities' (see Dobbie, p 155) and 'castles' (see Jones, p 81).

STANZA IX, LINES 25–6

ᚻ rune (Hickes adds the more usual variant ᚺ and the very rare form ᛡ), transliteration *h*, name *hægl* (meaning hail).
[Gmc: * χagalas (hail, sleet); OE: Isruna *hagal*, Brussels *hagal*, Vienna *hægil*, and 'Gothic' *haal*; Norse: NRP *hagall* (hail), IRP *hagall* (hail), and AN *hagal*.]

This may have constituted the first of a triad of potentially menacing runes in the original Germanic context of divination. It is noteworthy, however, that the author has transmuted hail, normally one of the formulaic attributes of winter's terror in the elegiac poetry and a symbol of fallen man's plight (for the symbolism involved see E.G. Stanley, 'Old English Poetic Diction') into a natural portent to be pondered over because of its rapid changes: the movement from heaven to earth, the metamorphosis from solid to liquid. Here is a point where gnomic nature wisdom and marvel at God's wonders merge easily. The *hægl* stanza serves as a natural instance of the process of transmutation into a benefit to be dealt with on a spiritual level in the *nȳd* stanza immediately following.

Stanza IX presents the first deviation from the three-line norm established in the first eight stanzas. However, since each of the four hypermetric half-lines here is equivalent to three, rather than the usual two, alliterative feet or measures, the net weight of this stanza remains the same as for the previous ones, that is, twelve measures. The reason for the shift from normal to hypermetric lines is not easy to determine. Perhaps the crowded couplet is intended merely to accentuate the rapid movement and change involved as hail goes through its various manifestations. It is also possible that the unmistakable shift has a major structural function, being designed to mark the beginning of the second of the three *ættir* (families or groups of eight runes) into which the original twenty-four rune *futhark* was divided from early times (for these groups see the discussion on pages 49–52). Karl Schneider contends (in *Runennamen*, pp 152ff) that Hagal was a divine being, associated with the creation of the world, whose name was given by the Germani to rune IX and by extension to the second group of eight runes, just as Frey's name, symbolized by his sacred animal *feoh*, was given to rune I and by extension to the first *ætt* (see the explanatory note on stanza I), and Tyr's name was given to rune XVII and by extension to the third *ætt* (see the explanatory note on stanza XVII). It is noteworthy, however, that the Old English *Rune Poem* betrays no awareness of the existence of the god Hagal.

25 *hwītust corna* 'whitest of grains.' The fact that all the rune poems refer to hail as a kind of grain (compare the Norwegian *Rune Poem*: *kaldastr korna* (coldest of grains) and the Icelandic *Rune Poem*: *kaldakorn* (cold grain)) could be thought to suggest that the device of memorizing runes by means of alliterative formulas in a kind of rudimentary mnemonic verse may be much older than any of the extant poems. More likely, however, it is merely further evidence of the wide currency of Germanic poetic formulas (see the discussion on pages 37–8 of the introduction, especially the reference in note 14 on page 76 to the appearance of the same *corn* formula in *Seafarer*, line 32).

hwyrft from *hwyrfeþ* by syncopation and assimilation (for which see Campbell #732–5). The root vowel *y* for earlier *ie* represents late West Saxon monophthongization (see Campbell #209–301).

scūra Hickes' form of this word has not been emended in this edition to the more regular masculine nominative plural *scūras* (as, for example, by Dobbie, p 155, following Grimm and Ettmüller); instead, it is assumed to be a feminine form, as in the cognate Gothic *skūra* and Old Norse *skúr*.

STANZA X, LINES 27–8

ᛀ rune (Hickes adds a unique variant form ᛀ, probably miscopied from Cotton Domitian A.ix where there is a mark, not by the scribe, looking like a second bar), transliteration *n*, name *nȳd* (need, hardship, constraint). [Gmc: **nauþiz* (need); OE: Isruna *nod*, Brussels *not*, Vienna *naed*, and 'Gothic' *noicz*; Norse: NRP *nauðr* (need), IRP *nauð* (need), and AN *naut*.]

The spelling of the rune name as *nȳd* for earlier *nīed* represents West Saxon monophthongization (see Campbell #300–1). As described in the Norwegian and Icelandic rune poems, the rune name involves suffering and inability to act. This concept of *nȳd* is reinforced by its description in *Solomon and Saturn*, line 13, as the worst lot one can obtain in life ('nēd bið wyrda heardost') and possibly in *Elene*, line 1261, as the *enge rūne* (constraining rune) associated with the experience of *nearusorge* (oppressive grief) (for this last reference and for the use of *nȳd* in the other Cynewulfian signatures see Appendix A). It is interesting that the *nȳd* rune should be placed between the two winter symbols of *hægl* (hail) and *īs* (ice), since both hail and ice normally occur in Old English poetry in contexts of human constraint (compare the way that winter imprisons Hengest at the court of Finn and inhibits retributive action in *Beowulf*, lines 1127–33, and the way that it physically reinforces both the Wanderer's and the Seafarer's recognition of what amounts to their emotional solitary confinement in an alien world). In such contexts, usually God is presented as the only agent with power to loose the fetters of winter and free man from tribulation and impotence: compare lines 74–5 of the *Exeter Maxims*: 'ān sceal inbindan/forstes fetre, felameahtig God' (one shall unbind fetters of frost, very mighty God) or the description of the melting sword-blade in *Beowulf*, lines 1607–10:

> þæt wæs wundra sum
> þæt hit eal gemealt   īse gelīcost,
> ðonne forstes bend   Fæder onlæteð,
> onwindeð wælrāpas.

(It was a miracle that it melted completely, just like ice, when the Father releases the bond of frost, unties the deadly ropes.)

Significantly, in stanza x emphasis is laid on *nȳd*, not merely as something to be endured (its role in both the Norwegian and Icelandic rune poems), but as a moral test or trial that can turn out well, given the right attitude on the part of the sufferer. Thus, this potentially menacing rune is put to Christian didactic purpose.

27 *brēostan* for *brēostum* (in the heart). For the -*an* ending see the explanatory note on *miclun*, line 2.

ðēah contrastive (as also in line 2) to underline the paradoxical disparity between worldly appearance and spiritual reality.

28 *hǣle* meaning 'salvation' (literally, healing, making whole) as in the term *se Hǣlend* (the Saviour), a further indication of the poem's perspective on the divine purpose of earthly tribulation.

gehwæþre for Hickes' *ge hwæþre*, meaning 'nonetheless' (reinforcing the paradox signalled in *ðēah*).

his hlystaþ ǣror 'heed it in time' (literally, listen to it before). As outlined in the introduction to the *Exeter Maxims* (quoted in note 24 on page 77 of this edition), the purpose of piling up gnomic statements was not to collect random fragments of knowledge about the world, but to acquire wisdom that would throw light upon our experience and thus ameliorate human life and perhaps save one's soul. Here the poet is stressing the hard-won truth that even the worst temporal lot can be transmuted by wise men into an eternal benefit. So runes as disparate as *feoh* and *nȳd* can be made to direct men's thoughts to the same spiritual end and ultimately teach the same moral lesson about the things of this world.

STANZA XI, LINES 29–31

| rune, transliteration *i*, name *īs* (meaning ice).
[Gmc: **īsa* (ice); OE: Isruna *iis*, Brussels *is*, Vienna *is*, and 'Gothic' *iiz*; Norse: NRP *ís* (ice), IRP *iss* (ice), and AN *is*.]

According to later Norse mythology, ice was the primal material from which life emerged. In the *Prose Edda* it gives birth to the frost-giant Ymir:

Ginnungagap, þat er vissi til norðrættar, fyltisk með þunga ok hǫfugleik íss ok hríms ok inn í frá úr ok gustr; en enn syðri hlutr Ginnungagaps léttisk móti gneistum ok síum þeim, er flugu ór Múspellzheimi ... ok þá er mœtti hríminu blær hitans, svá at bráðnaði ok draup – ok af þeim kviku-dropum kviknaði með krapti þess, er til sendi hitann, ok varð mannz líkandi, ok er sá nefndr Ymir, en hrímþursar kalla hann Aurgelmi, ok eru þaðan komnar ættir hrím-þursa. (*Gylfaginning*, chapter 5)

(Ginnungagap, which faced toward the northern quarter, became filled with heaviness, and masses of ice and rime, and from within, drizzling rain and gusts; but the southern part of the Yawning Void was lighted by those sparks and glowing masses which flew out of Muspellheim ... and when the breath of heat met the rime, so that it melted and dripped, life was quickened from the yeast-drops by the power of that which sent the heat, and became a man's form. And that man was called Ymir, but the Rime-Giants call him Aurgel-mir, and thence come the races of the Rime-Giants.)

Following Ymir's birth, in chapter 6 of *Gylfaginning*, the cow Auðumla (who also sprang from the melting ice to feed him with her milk) produced Búri, the grandfather of Odin, by licking the salty ice-blocks for three successive days until a whole human shape emerged. See also the other evidence for Germanic belief in ice as the cosmic ur-matter in Schneider's *Runennamen*, pp 149ff.

The birth process fancifully presented in *Gylfaginning* is re-enacted each year in the spring, when the ice breaks up on lakes and streams once frozen solid in cold immobility and life seems to begin again. After the growth cycle of the year is complete, the return of the ice brings apparent death to the agricultural world once more. This latter transformation of water from moving, life-giving liquid to solid floor or bridge seems to have fascinated the authors of the Old English, Norwegian, and Icelandic rune poems, who obviously all viewed it as a mystery. Compare also the attitude to this process evinced in the passage in the *Exeter Maxims* immediately preceding the three half-lines on God's power to unbind the fetters of frost quoted in stanza note x above: 'Forst sceal frēosan ... īs brycgian/wæter helm wegan, wundrum lūcan/eorþan cīþas' (Frost shall freeze ... ice form a bridge, water wear a cover, mysteriously lock up the growing things of earth) (lines 71–4). The author of the Old English *Rune Poem*, however, stresses the beauty, rather than the potential terror, of this natural wonder, thereby rendering it relatively harmless; his horror is reserved for different concepts, such as that of rune xxix: ᛠ *ēar* (the earth [as man's grave]).

29 *oferceald, ungemetum slidor* for Hickes' *ofer cealdunge metum slidor*, a nonsensical word division.

30 *glæshlūttur* for Hickes' *glæs hluttur*, with final -*ur* for standard West Saxon -*or* showing the falling together of vowels in unstressed syllables (see Campbell #49, 368ff).

gelīcust for *gelīcost*, showing the falling together of vowels in unstressed syllables (Campbell #49, 368ff).

31 *geworuht* 'wrought' for Hickes' meaningless *ge worulit*, no doubt a minim stroke error in copying. Note also the intrusion of the parasitic vowel *u* (for which see Campbell #360).

fæger ansȳne 'fair to behold' (literally, fair in aspect), stressing the beauty of the created world, even in winter. The *ȳ* for earlier *īe* represents late West Saxon monophthongization (for which see Campbell #301).

STANZA XII, LINES 32–4

ᚷrune (rounded form instead of normal angular ᛄ), transliteration *g* (Hickes *ge*, corresponding to Modern English initial *y*), name *gēr* (meaning year and, more specifically, a fruitful year or harvest).
[Gmc: **jēra* (year); oe: Isruna *ger*, Brussels *iar* and *ger*, Vienna *gaer*, and 'Gothic' *gaar*; Norse: NRP *ár* (harvest), IRP *ár* (summer), and AN *ar*.]

The rune that stood twelfth in the twenty-four rune Common Germanic *futhark* was only half-sized and represented the semi-vowel [*j*] as in Modern English 'year' (see page 4; also see Elliott, *Runes*, p 16, and, for examples, Table II and the photographic end-plates II, figs 3, 4, 5, and III, fig 6). In the process of extension to full size, this rune appears to have taken variant forms, including ᚷ, which is found in the Old English *Rune Poem* and in all manuscript *futhorcs*, and ᛄ, which is found in all Old English runic inscriptions, except for the *futhorc* on the blade of the Thames scramasax where the variant ✝ appears (see Elliott, *Runes*, plate III, fig 7). In Norse tradition, this rune appears as ✝, ↑, or ⌐ with a new value *a*, resulting from the loss of the rune name's initial semi-vowel (see page 8 and also the Norse rune poems in Appendix B). Because the rune form ♦ does not appear in the primary epigraphical tradition on Anglo-Saxon objects of stone, metal, wood, or bone, Page calls it a 'pseudo-rune' (see *English Runes*, pp 42–3); it is, however, the normal form for the twelfth rune in the Old English manuscript tradition, where the epigraphical form ☩ makes only an infrequent appearance near the end of the expanded *futhorc* with the name *īor* or *īar* (see the explanatory note on stanza XXVIII below). In any case, both ♦ and ☩ became somewhat redundant symbols when the initial sound of rune name VII (*ġyfu*) grew indistinguishable from the initial sound of rune name XII (*ġēr, īar*) (for instances of epigraphical confusion over how to represent this sound see Page, *English Runes*, p 48). The *ē* in *ġēr* (for earlier *ġēar*) represents late West Saxon smoothing (see Campbell #312).

It is clear from the context in the Old English *Rune Poem*, as well as from the word's appearance elsewhere in Old English and from its Norwegian and Icelandic cognates, that *ġēr* did not imply the entire calendar year of twelve months, but referred only to the warm growing season. In *Beowulf*, lines 1132–4, the word seems to signify the onset of that season in the spring: 'winter ȳþe belēac/īsgebinde, oþ þæt ōþer com/gēar in geardas' (winter locked the waves in fetters of ice, until another spring came into those habitations). In the Icelandic *Rune Poem*, the rune is defined as the height of the growing season: *sumar* (summer). Finally, in both the Norwegian *Rune Poem* and the Old English *Rune Poem*, the rune is associated with the produce of the growing season and hence perhaps is best translated as 'fruitful year' or 'harvest.' The twelfth rune stands in distinct contrast with the preceding three runes of winter and constraint; and the corresponding stanzas in the Old English, Norwegian, and Icelandic rune poems reflect an uninhibited human delight in fruitfulness. The author of the Old English *Rune Poem* takes great care, however, to attribute the earth's bounty to *god* (God), who is further defined by the appositive epithet *hālig heofones cyning* (the holy king of heaven) in order to ensure that the reference is unambiguously Christian.

32 *hiht* 'hope, joy,' the happy consummation to which men look forward
and whose arrival they celebrate with thanksgiving; the *i*-spelling is
an example of the unrounding of *y* before *h* (for which see Campbell
#316).

ðon may represent an abbreviation (ðoñ for ðonne) as suggested by
Grienberger, 'Runengedicht,' p 210. The metre does not absolutely
require the expanded form, however; and for the use of ðon without
expansion see Dobbie's note to this line (*Minor Poems*, p 155) plus the
supporting citations in the note on *Exeter Riddle 54*, line 9 (ASPR III,
p 349).

33 *syllan* the *y* for earlier *e* represents a late West Saxon change common
to the *sel* group (for which see Campbell #325).

34 *beornum and ðearfum* 'for rich and poor' (literally, men of position
and the needy). This universalizing phrase is parallel to the references to *gumena* and *wræcna* in stanza VII; it belongs to the Christian
rather than to the heroic context and is intended to emphasize the
limitless bounty of God (compare also *ēadgum and earmum* in
line 76).

STANZA XIII, LINES 35-7

⅄ rune (rather like a capital Z; Hickes adds the more usual reversed variant
ᛇ), transliteration *eo*, name *ēoh* (meaning yew-tree).
[Gmc: *eiχuaz* (yew); OE: Isruna *ih*, Brussels *ih* and *inc*, Vienna *ih*, and
'Gothic' *uuaer*; absent from the reduced sixteen rune Norse *futhǫrk* represented by NRP, IPR, and AN, but compare rune XV.]

The spelling of the rune name with final *h* is a variant of the more
common Old English *īw* (as, by Verner's law, beside *īw*, *ēow* we also
find *īh*, *īoh*, *ēoh*; for which alternation see Campbell #412). Page
argues that the word represents the renaming of an original high front
vowel rune in order to designate medial and final [χ] (see 'The Old
English Rune *ēoh*, *īh*, "yew tree",' pp 125-36), an argument given
some support by the Vienna manuscript transliteration of ᛇ as both *i*
and *h* (*i&h*) (see Derolez, plate IV.a). Insular inscriptions appear to
bear out the suggestion of shifting values: compare, for example, the

use of this rune for the vowel *i* on the Dover stone (see Elliott, *Runes*, pp 82–3 and fig 31), its use for the voiceless palatal spirant in *almehttig* on the east side of the Ruthwell cross (see Elliott, *Runes*, pp 90, 95, and fig 40), and its possible use as equivalent to palatalized *g* on the Thornhill в fragment (see Elliott, *Runes*, pp 87–8 and fig 36; also Page, *English Runes*, p 48). Dickins established a reasonable compromise transliteration by adopting the symbol ʒ (yogh), which represents both the voiced and voiceless spirants in Middle English (see his 'A System of Transliteration for Old English Runic Inscriptions,' p 16). Appropriately enough, the term 'yogh' is the lineal descendant of rune name XIII, which was applied by the Anglo-Saxons to the Irish letter *g* on account of its formal resemblance to the Old English rune (see Anna Paues, 'The Name of the Letter ʒ,' for details).

Considerable evidence has been assembled to document the prized status of the yew-tree and especially the protective qualities attributed to it both in the Germanic and in the Celtic worlds (see Elliott, 'Runes, Yews and Magic,' pp 250–61). Schneider contends that the world-tree Yggdrasil itself was originally not an ash but the venerable and evergreen yew (*Runennamen*, pp 277–80); and, in keeping with this interpretation, he emends *hyrde fȳres* (guardian of flame) in line 36 to *hyrde fēres* (normally *fēores* (guardian of life); *Runennamen*, p 282), as an epithet more accurately descriptive of this magical eternity symbol. Certainly the reference to the yew-tree's value as firewood fits somewhat awkwardly into a series of descriptions of the living tree; but the later stanzas on the oak and the ash (stanzas XXV and XXVI) are characterized by equally rapid shifts in perspective, and it is noteworthy that in line 32 the Norwegian *Rune Poem* also sees fit to comment on the yew's burning qualities: 'vant er, er brennr, at svíða' (it sputters when it burns) (see Appendix B). The poet's laudatory attitude towards the firm, tenacious, and useful yew-tree is summed up in the antepenultimate word *wynan* (a delight).

37 *wyrtrumun* for *wyrtrumum* (by its roots); for the dative ending in *-un* see the note on *miclun*, line 2.

underwreþyd for standard *underwreþod* (supported from beneath), shows the falling together of vowels in unstressed syllables (for which see Campbell #49, 368ff).

wynan on ēþle usually assumed to be a dittographic error for *wyn on ēþle* and emended accordingly. The form *wynan* could also be an adverbial dative (for standard *wynnum*) as suggested by Grienberger in 'Runengedicht,' p 211 (compare *brēostan*, line 27 and *māgan*, line 59); certainly the unemended form is metrically better than *wyn* and therefore is retained in this edition.

STANZA XIV, LINES 38–40

ᚹ rune (Hickes gives this uncommon broken form instead of the normal ᚸ), transliteration *p*, name *peorð* (meaning unknown: some kind of game?). [Gmc: *perþ? 'meaning unknown'; oe: Isruna *perd*, Brussels *pert*, Vienna *peord*, and 'Gothic' *pertra*; absent from the reduced sixteen rune Norse *futhąrk* represented by NRP, IRP, and AN.]

The word *peorð* appears outside this poem only in lists of rune names, which by their nature provide no context for definition. Various meanings have been proposed, ranging from the more or less plausible 'pawn, in chess' (Grimm, *Ueber deutsche Runen*, pp 239ff), 'chessman' (Dickins, *Runic Poems*, p 17), and 'dice-box' (Schneider, *Runennamen*, pp 411–35) to the less likely 'throat, gullet' (Grienberger, 'Die germanische Runennamen 1,' p 212), 'apple-tree' (Marstrander, 'Om runene og runenavnenes oprindelse,' pp 138ff), and a handful of others, including 'penis,' recorded by Philippson in 'Runenforschung und germanische Religionsgeschichte,' p 331. It is always possible that, since *p* was not a common sound in native Germanic words (as reflected by the omission of the ᚸ rune from the Vadstena bracteate, where the ᛒ rune takes its place [see Elliott, *Runes*, plate 11, fig 4]), the name *peorð* may represent an early borrowing from some foreign language: Marstrander's rather far-fetched suggestion that *peorð* is a doublet of the equally indefinable rune name *cweorð* rests upon the assumption that it was borrowed from a Gaulish *p* variant of the Irish ogham name for apple-tree (*ceirt*). The fact that the only defective line in the poem occurs in the *peorð* stanza subtracts that much more evidence for arriving at an accurate definition of the author's understanding of this rune name. Nonetheless, whatever the exact denotation of *peorð* may be, as one of the elements contributing to hall-joy, it clearly has both aristocratic and unqualifiedly pleasant connotations in this poem.

38 *symble* 'always' as in line 45, rather than the other possibility [*æt*]
symble (at a banquet).

hlehtor for *hleahtor* represents late West Saxon smoothing (see
Campbell #312).

39 *wlancum* ... (for proud ...) represents a metrically defective half-line.
Some editors would supply an alliterating noun here (see Ettmüller's
willgesīðum (willing companions) and Grienberger's *werum*
(men)); others insert an adverbial phrase (see Rieger's *on winge-
drince* (at their wine-drinking) and Grein's *on middum* (in the
midst), the latter accepted by Kluge and Dickins); Dobbie opts for
'*and* and another adjective; for example *wlancum and wīsum* ["for
the proud and the wise"]' (see ASPR VI, p 156). Since the evidence is
inconclusive, no emendation whatsoever is made in this edition,
where the lacuna is indicated by dots.

40 *bēorsele* for Hickes' *beor sele* (beer-hall), translated here as 'mead-
hall' to avoid pejorative modern connotations of the literal translation.

ætsomne for Hickes' *æt somne*.

STANZA XV, LINES 41–4

ᛉ rune (with semi-rounded arms instead of normal angular ᛉ), trans1itera-
tion *x*, name *eolhx* (meaning uncertain, perhaps elk).
[Gmc: **alhiz/algiz?* (elk?); OE: Isruna *elux*, Brussels *ilix*, Vienna *ilcs*; versus
Gmc: **eiχu̯az* (yew); Norse: NRP *ýr* (yew), IRP *ýr* (yew-bow), and AN *yr*;
versus apparently meaningless 'Gothic' *ezec* (perhaps from Greek *zeta*).]

The confusions apparent above probably result from the instability of
the Germanic sound *z*, exemplified by the original fifteenth rune
name, coupled with its final position in that name (a position neces-
sitated by the fact that, unlike the sounds exemplified by most other
rune names, *z* could not occur initially). Germanic final *z* developed regularly into Norse final *R*; but the Primitive Old Norse rune
name **algiR* appears to have been replaced by the name of the
thirteenth rune, *ýr* (from Primitive Old Norse **īhwaR*, which also

contained a final *R* and which otherwise would have disappeared altogether, when the rune it had named was deleted in forming the reduced sixteen rune *futhqrk*). Hence Norse *ýr*, cognate with Old English *ēoh/īw* (yew), was transferred to a new association with the Norse rune ᛉ, an inverted form of ᛦ (for further clarification, see the convenient tables of correspondence in Musset, *Introduction*, p 130 and Elliott, *Runes*, pp 48–9). Since Germanic final *z* did not come down into Old English at all (see Campbell #404), the Anglo-Saxons were left with a spare rune, which they chose to use to represent *x* in runic inscriptions of Latin texts, such as the Christ symbol ᛁ ᚻ ᛦ ᛦ ᚳ ᛦ (IHS XPS) on the seventh century coffin of St Cuthbert (for which see Page, *English Runes*, pp 172–4 and fig 35).

If the root of the rune name that survives in The Old English *Rune Poem* did indeed go back to an original Germanic name *alhiz* (elk), it must have lost any relationship with the sound once exemplified by that name long before runes were used in Old English Christian inscriptions or their mnemonic names listed in writing by monks. There can have been only a fossil association between ᛦ and *eolh*, preserved by the fact that runes were taught orally in a fixed traditional sequence. How, then, could this useless fossil name be manipulated or distorted so as to manifest some relationship to the new sound *x* arbitrarily assigned to the rune? Two more or less plausible hypotheses have been offered. The Bosworth-Toller dictionary initially reflected the opinion of earlier editors that *eolhx* might be an alternative spelling for the genitive singular of *eolh*, ie, *eolces*, whose closing sounds approximate the contemporary pronunciation of Latin *x* [*ks*]; but, since this would involve a highly abnormal variant of the expected genitive singular *ēoles* (see Campbell #574.2 for the normal declension of *eolh* with loss of *h* and compensatory lengthening of the root vowel in inflected forms), the 1921 Bosworth-Toller supplement retracted the suggestion, substituting the compound *eolhsecg* without any explanation of the deleted letter *x*. Page also has proposed that the rune name may have been originally *eolh* (elk), 'to which was added the new value of the rune, *x*' (see *English Runes*, p 80), a process which could account for the appearance of *x* (rarely the alternative spelling *cs*) throughout the rune name lists. In addition, this latter suggestion might explain the poet's inability to define the rune name *eolhx*, now rendered meaningless as an Old English word, and his consequent need to substitute a compound word that reproduced the same combination of sounds.

Other not very convincing etymologies and definitions have been suggested for *eolhx*, including Cockayne's 'seaholly' (*Leechdoms, Wortcunning and Starcraft of Early England* III, p 324), Redbond's *helix* (willow) ('Notes on the Word "eolhx,"' p 55), Arntz' *Alces* (twin divinities) named in Tacitus' *Germania*, chapter 43 (*Handbuch*[2], pp 213ff), Elliott's **algiz* (protection, defence) (*Runes*, pp 52–3), and Schneider's **elkiz* (swan) as symbol of Odin's hand-maidens, the Valkyrie (*Runennamen*, pp 402–9).

Whatever the origin and meaning of the rune name itself, the Old English *Rune Poem* does not pretend to define that name as a simplex, but instead defines a compound containing it which also appears in various Old English glosses for the Latin noun *papiluus* (papyrus or water-reed), spelled both with and without the x characteristic of the rune name lists (see, for example, *papiluus: ilugsegg* (Epinal), *papilus: ilugseg* (Erfurt) in Sweet's *Oldest English Texts*, and *papiluus: eolugsecg, papilluum: eolxsegc* in Wright-Wülker's *Anglo-Saxon and Old English Vocabularies*). On balance, despite the possibility that the uncompounded rune name may have had no meaning at all by the time the Old English *Rune Poem* was composed, the translator's best course seems to be to render *eolhxsecg* as 'elk-sedge,' perhaps signifying (as Rieger suggested in his *Alt-und angel-sächsisches Lesebuch*, p 138) a kind of marsh-grass on which the elk was accustomed to sleep or browse.

Stanza xv is the first of the four-line stanzas found in the poem. It is difficult to explain why such a heavy stanza was interjected here; perhaps only for variety, perhaps (as suggested on p 52 above) to throw into relief the following two stanzas describing the final rune of the second *ætt* (group of eight): ᚼ (*sigel*) and the first rune of the third *ætt*: ↑ (*Tīr*), both of which retained a good deal more of their original significance and importance than rune xv. Another distinctive aspect of the stanza is the absence of the gnomic verb *byþ*: the poet's difficulty is defining the rune name *eolhx* is emphasized by his inability to employ the customary opening formula '*A* (rune name) *byþ B* (definition).'

41 *eolhxsecg eard hæfþ* 'elk-sedge has its dwelling' for Hickes' *eolhx seccard hæfþ*, following most editors since Grimm (*Ueber deutsche Runen*, p 221) in interpreting *seccard* as the erroneous telescoping by a copyist of the two distinct words *secc* (for more common *secg* (sedge)) and *eard* (dwelling).

Although it is not impossible to wrest a kind of sense out of the word division given by Hickes (the elk has its reed-habitat), stanza xv as a whole seems to be describing a plant rather than an animal (note that the subject *wexeð on wature* (grows in the water)); moreover, the aggressive vocabulary used in the description of this plant does not necessarily connote movement or volition, but is markedly similar to the vocabulary used in stanza iii to describe the thorn and shows a certain admiration for the warrior-like qualities of the marsh-grass in defence of its watery home.

hæfþ for this contracted verb form see the explanatory note on line 23 above.

42 *wexeð* for earlier *weaxeð* represents late West Saxon smoothing (see Campbell #312).

wature for *wætere* (compare line 26) may represent the late tenth century falling together in pronunciation of front and back *a* (see Campbell #363ff and 329.3, fn 2), accompanied by harmony of the medial vowel (*u*).

43 *brēneð* is shown in the Bosworth-Toller supplement as a form of *bærnan* (to burn), an interpretation adopted by Jones (p 101), but rejected as unsuitable to the context both by Dickens, who proposes instead *beerneð/beyrneð* (covers) (p 17), and by Dobbie (p 157), who (following Grein-Kohler and Grienberger) sees it as 'a (Kentish?) form of a verb *brȳnan*, otherwise unrecorded but to be taken as a causative verb from *brūn*, i.e. "makes brown with blood"' (see Campbell #288 for this unrounding and lowering of *y* to *e*). Any one of these translations would make reasonable sense, since blood is represented in Old English poetry as hot (compare 'Flōd blōde weol ... / hātan heolfre' (blood and hot gore bubbled up in the water) in *Beowulf*, lines 1422–3), flowing over surfaces (compare 'drihtnes rōd bið blōde beurnen' (the Lord's cross is covered with blood) in Napier's edition of Wulfstan, pp 182–3), and producing a dark stain (compare the possible use of *dænnede* for *dunnode* to mean 'darkened' in the description of the field of slaughter in *The Battle of Brunanburh*, line 12). Since a heavy first syllable would produce a better metrical line here and in order to avoid the need for *r*-metathesis, this edition has adopted Dobbie's interpretation and therefore gives *brēneð* (em-

browns or stains). The etymology of the word *secg* lends some support to this reading on account of its relationship to *secg* (sword) (compare also the Latin words *gladius* (sword) and *gladiolus* (little sword, referring to the sharp blades of the plant)).

44 *him ǣnigne onfeng gedēð* 'lays a hand on it' (literally, puts any grasp on it).

STANZA XVI, LINES 45–7

ᚻ rune, transliteration *s*, name *sigel* (meaning sun).
[Gmc: *sōṷulō/seꬶilan?* (sun?); OE: Isruna *sigi*, Brussels *sigil*, Vienna *sygil*, and 'Gothic' *sugil*; Norse: NRP *sól* (sun), IRP *sól* (sun), and AN *sol*.]

This rune has several variant forms not noted by Hickes, including the fairly common ᛋ , an earlier form ᛉ , and the rare form ᚦ found on the Thames scramasax (see Elliott, *Runes*, plate III, fig 7), on the coffin of St Cuthbert (see Page, *English Runes*, fig 35), and in the *futhorc* listed on folio IIv of Cotton ms Domitian A.ix (see Derolez, plate I), which was the source of the other variant rune forms found on page 135 of the *Thesaurus*. Normally it is assumed (as by Elliott, *Runes*, p 56) that the etymologies of the Norse rune name *sól* and the Old English rune name *sigel* are different, although the meaning of the two names is identical. Schneider, however, makes an adventurous attempt to derive both, as well as Old English *swegl* (sky), from the same Indo-European compound *ṷesṷkuol* (-os/om) (good wheel) (a reference to ᛋ, the swastika as ancient sun-cult image): *sól* he traces to this compound's Primitive Germanic descendant *sōṷulō*; *swegl* and *sigel* to two cognate forms *sṷeꬶalan* and *seꬶilan*. The fact that not only the meaning, but also the main consonants *s* and *l* are identical, coupled with the known instability of intervocalic *g*, provides at least some basis for this kind of etymological speculation about the original rune name; therefore I have tentatively reproduced it here. Of course, it is also possible that the Old English rune name was contaminated by the Latin-based word *sigel* (jewel) and used in the figurative sense of 'circular shining object in the sky' (for this possibility see J.R.R. Tolkien, 'Sigelwara Land').

Whatever the etymology of the rune name, there is no question but that *sigel* does have the meaning 'sun' in Old English, both as a separate word (note its equation with *woruldcandel* (world-candle) in *Beowulf*, line 1965) and in compounds (compare *sigelbeorht* for *solio fulget* (it shines like the sun) and *sigelhwerfe* for *solsequium vel heliotropium* (sun-follower or plant that turns toward the sun) cited in the Bosworth-Toller dictionary). Despite the seafaring context of this stanza, it is extremely unlikely that *sigel* could mean 'sail' in any poem defining rune names (for the suggestion that it may do so, see Grein, *Bibliothek der angelsächsischen Poesie* II, p 352; Arntz, *Handbuch*², p 215, note 3; and Jungandreas, 'Zur Runenreihe,' p 229). As supporting evidence for the identification of the rune name *sigel* with 'sun', note that rune XVI stands at the end of the *Exeter Book* sun riddle in answer to its cryptic lines (see ASPR III, p 184 [Riddle 6] and the editorial note on p 325).

45 *sēmannum* for Hickes' *se mannum*: the *ē* for normal West Saxon *ǣ* is probably a Kenticism (see Campbell #288). Note that the insertion of this word in line 45a necessitates the postponement of the gnomic verb *biþ* to the b-verse, thus breaking up the opening formula '*A* (rune name) *byþ B* (definition).' It may seem difficult to understand why the seafaring image need enter this definition at all. One possible explanation could lie in its common metaphorical identification with the state of fallen man seeking to return to the Paradise from which he was exiled (see the explanatory notes on stanza XXI below); in this context *sigel* (the sun) becomes a divine symbol (as in stanza XXIV, for which see the explanatory notes below).

on hihte 'a source of hope.' The medieval lack of navigational aids must have made clear weather and good visibility essential for seafarers. Note also the relevance of 'hope' to the possible Christian interpretation of voyaging referred to above under *sēmannum*. Schneider emends this phrase to *on hiehðe* (on high), in support of his image of the swastika or 'good wheel' set high on the masts of ships, both of living seafarers and of those making their funeral journey (*Runennamen*, p 97; on the concept of death as a journey, see the references in the explanatory note on stanza V above). The form *hihte* shows unrounding of *y* to *i* before *h* (for which see Campbell #316).

46 *ðonn* possibly should be expanded to *ðonne*, as by Dickins, p 17 and Grienberger, p 212 (compare *ðon* in line 32, however).

hine the masculine accusative singular pronoun referring to
brimhengest (as in Dobbie, p 157, following Grienberger, p 212).
Dickins (p 17) reads *hine* as a variant form of *heonan* (hence, away)
in order to avoid the awkwardness of a delayed referent; this interpretation would make *feriaþ* an intransitive verb as in *The Battle of
Maldon*, line 179.

fisces beþ 'fishes' bath' with *e* for normal West Saxon *æ* in *beþ*
probably is another Kenticism (for which see Campbell #288). Like
ganotes baeþ in line 79, this phrase is a traditional poetic kenning for
sea (see Hertha Marquardt, *Die altenglischen Kenningar*, pp
164–74).

47 *hī brimhengest* for Hickes' *hibrim hengest*. The compound
brimhengest (sea-horse) is a traditional kenning for ship (see
Marquardt, pp 226–9); in a Christian interpretation, this ship would
be the Church, which often was equated with Noah's ark, carrying
its freight of those saved from God's wrath.

STANZA XVII, LINES 48–50

↑ rune, transliteration *t*, name *Tīr* (meaning, the name of a guiding planet,
star, or constellation).
[Gmc: *teiẉaz* (the god Tiw); oe: Isruna *ti*, Brussels *ti*, Vienna *ti*, and 'Gothic'
tyz; Norse: NRP *Týr* (the god Tyr), IRP *Týr* (the god Tyr), and AN *tiu*.]

Initially, Tiw was the supreme Germanic god (parallel to the Greek
sky-god with the cognate name Zeus); when his place was usurped by
the Frankish storm and death-god *Uoðanaz* (Old English *Woden*, Old
Norse *Odin*), he degenerated into a mere war-god (for Tiw's early role
and changing functions see Dumézil [cited in explanatory note 1] and
also the discussion and references in Schneider, *Runennamen*, pp
359–65). It is noteworthy that his cosmic role is to some extent
reflected in later Norse mythology, in that he remained the only god
prepared to sacrifice a hand to the maw of Fenriswolf in order to save
the world from destruction (note the use of the distinguishing epithet
'one-handed' in both the Norwegian and the Icelandic rune poems in
Appendix B). Tiw's early identification with the Roman war-god Mars
is reflected in the regular Old English gloss *tiig* for *mars, martis* (see
the Epinal, Erfurt, and Corpus glossaries in Sweet's *Oldest English*

Texts, pp 77–8) as well as in the renaming of the weekday sacred to the Roman god (*dies Martis*) as *Tiwesdæg* (Tuesday) (for further examples see R. Jente, *Die mythologischen Ausdrücke im altenglischen Wortschatz*, pp 86–9). This interchangeability of names may have been facilitated by the marked similarity of the rune ↑ to the symbol for the planet Mars ♂. It is worth remarking that the Norse name for the war-god was *Týr* (with Germanic final z retained as *R*; compare OE *ēoh/īw* versus ON *ýr* in the explanatory note on rune xv), a name not dissimilar in pronunciation to the etymologically unrelated Old English noun *tīr* (glory). In a society that by the tenth century was very much in contact with Norsemen and where glory traditionally had been associated with martial prowess, it is not impossible that some fusion of terminology took place. The rune name ending in *r*, invariably found in the eleventh century insular manuscripts which contain our only extant native *futhorc* name lists, is totally uncharacteristic of the ninth century continental copies of much earlier Old English *futhorc* name lists; hence it may represent a late assimilation of *Tīw*, *Týr*, and *tīr* (for the runic content and dates of the insular *futhorc* manuscripts Cotton Domitian A.ix and St John's College, Oxford, 17 see Derolez, pp 3ff, 26ff; for the relevant continental manuscripts, Vienna 795, Brussels 9311–19, and the various versions of the *isruna* tract, see Derolez, pp 52ff, 63ff, 89ff). This widespread insular spelling of rune name xvii can hardly be attributed (as Dickins appears to suggest in *Runic Poems*, p 18) to a single misreading of *tīw* with minuscule 'wynn' as *tīr* with the not dissimilar insular minuscule long *r*.

Further evidence for the meaning of this rune name must be sought in the descriptive stanza itself. Line 48a gives the definition *tācna sum* (one of the signs). As Bosworth-Toller amply documents, the kind of 'sign' involved can vary enormously: it may refer to a man-made symbol, significant in physical shape; it may denote an astronomical constellation or 'sign of the zodiac'; it may imply an omen of the future; or it may even mean an act of supernatural intervention in human affairs. The ingenious reader would have little difficulty in detecting any or all of these kinds of 'sign' behind the description of *Tīr* in stanza xvii as one of the signs, as keeping faith well with princes, as always journeying across the night sky, and as never failing. First, the form of the inscribed rune itself might be referred to in its function as victory-charm (see Elliott, *Runes*, p 55 for this interpretation of the repeated use of ↑ on the Lindholm amulet).

Second, the war-god might be described in relation to the battle-aid he renders to glory-seeking followers (a sense not completely distinguishable from the first). Next, the renamed planet Mars (or, as Dickins and Dobbie suggest, following Botkine, *La Chanson des Runes*, p 19, some circumpolar constellation to which the same name was transferred) might be presented in a somewhat more naturalistic description of its visible movement across the night sky. Finally, the concept of reliability, already stressed in the phrase *healdeð trȳwa wel* (it keeps faith well), is repeated in *nǣfre swīceþ* (it never fails), where this concept might be taken as applying not only to the god, but to both his inscribed and astronomical symbols as well. It seems unlikely, however, that the Christian poet, seen so obviously at work in stanzas I, VII, X, and XII, would compose a paean in praise of a heathen god, endorsing in the process the heretical notions of magic and astrological influence. Therefore, with Page (following Dickins, Dobbie, and most other editors), I restrict the meaning of rune name XVII to 'a guiding planet, star, or constellation, useful in navigation,' translated 'one of the guiding signs.' It should be noted that Jones avoids all connection with the god Tiw and with the planet Mars by interpreting the rune name as equivalent to the common noun *tīr* meaning 'honour' (see p 103 of his dissertation).

48 *healdeð* 'holds, keeps'; for this uncontracted verb form see Campbell #734.

trȳwa 'faith,' with *ȳ* for earlier *īe* represents late West Saxon monophthongization (see Campbell #299–301).

49 *biþ on færylde* for Hickes' *biþ onfærylde* (holds its course; literally, is on its journey); note the falling together of medial vowels, when compared with *færelde*, line 86 (for which see Campbell #49, 368ff).

50 *nǣfre swīceþ* 'it never fails'; like all celestial objects above the moon, this planet, star, or constellation was viewed as constant and incorruptible.

STANZA XVIII, LINES 51–5

ᛒ rune (rounded form, like a capital B instead of normal angular ᛒ), transliteration *b*, name *beorc* (meaning birch-tree).

[Gmc: * *ƀerkana* (birch); OE: Isruna *berg*, Brussels *berc*, Vienna *berc*, and 'Gothic' *bercna*; Norse: NRP *bjarkan* (birch), IRP *bjarkan* (birch), and AN *brica*.]

The second of the stanzas on trees (compare stanza XIII), this appears to combine botanical description and aesthetic admiration with some sense of wonder at a natural miracle. Considerable evidence has been gathered to demonstrate that, as the pre-eminent deciduous tree in northern forests and the first to turn green in the spring, the birch played an important part in Germanic fertility rites (on the continuity of this tradition see Elliott, *Runes*, pp 47–50, and on the birch-tree goddess as manifestation of Mother Earth see Schneider, *Runennamen*, pp 262–71; both draw heavily on *Der Baumkultus der Germanen und ihrer Nachbarstämme*, volume I of W. Mannhardt's comprehensive *Wald- und Feldkulte*). Accordingly, both Grienberger and Schneider read stanza XVIII as a description of the birch, interpreting the opening phrases as a reference to the catkins which the tree bears and its lack of edible fruit. Most editors follow Dickins in pointing out that the mysterious reproductive system alluded to in *blēda lēas* (without fruit) and 'bereþ ... tānas būtan tūdder' (bears shoots without seed) better describes the poplar. The obvious Anglo-Saxon confusion between these trees, as reflected in the equation of Latin *populus* (poplar) with vernacular *birciae, birce, byrc*, and *byric* (birch), is noted by Dickins, who goes on to suggest that the tree described in this stanza actually may be the 'grey poplar (*populus canescens*), indigenous to England and Western Europe, [which] is a large tree attaining 100 ft or more in height (*lyfte getenge*) and 15 ft in girth' (*Runic Poems*, p 19). Whichever of the two trees (birch or poplar) was envisaged by the poet as he wrote, he clearly called that tree *beorc* (birch) (as my translation also does) and he found something worthy of comment about the way that it flourished, apparently without fruit or seed.

With this stanza begins a sequence of five four-line stanzas. These expanded stanzas may be designed merely to break a potentially monotonous uniformity in stanza length; but the fact that they form the bulk of the third eight rune division of the original *futhark* leads one to speculate whether the expansion in stanza length might be deliberate, serving to stress by contrast the opening and closing runes of Tyr's *ætt* (see page 52 for a discussion of this structural possibility).

52 *tūdder* for standard *tūddor* shows the falling together of unstressed vowels (see Campbell #49, 368ff).

53 *hēah* 'high' emended from Hickes' *þeah* (though), both for reasons of sense (compare *lyfte getenge* (reaching up to touch the sky)) and to reinforce the *h* alliteration of line 53.

hrysted metathesized variant of *hyrsted* (adorned) (for which see Campbell #459).

54 *geloden lēafum* 'grown tall and leafy' (literally, grown with leaves). This phrase is something of a *hapax legomenon*, being variously translated 'for it is generated from its leaves' (Dickins) and '*beladen mit Blättern,*' (ie, laden with leaves) (Schneider). The latter translation involves the emendation of *geloden* (from *lēodan* (to grow or spring)) to *gehloden* (more normally (*ge*)*hladen*, from *hladan* (to load)); in view of the alliterative requirement for *l* rather than *hl* here, Schneider's otherwise sensible suggestion must be rejected. Dickins' imaginative notion that this phrase reinforces the folklore about the poplar-tree's mysterious method of reproduction by means of underground suckers also seems unnecessary, especially when we compare the similar phrase in *Elene*, 1225–7: 'Mǣrost bēama/ þāra þe of eorðan up awēoxe/ geloden under lēafum' (the most glorious of earthly trees arose, grown tall under its leafy cover), for the Cross was not reputed to be made of poplar-wood.

STANZA XIX, LINES 55–8

M rune, transliteration *e*, name *eh* (meaning horse).
[Gmc: **eχu̯az* (horse); OE: Isruna *eh*, Brussels *hec*, Vienna *eh*, and 'Gothic' *eyz*; absent from the reduced sixteen rune Norse *futhǫrk* represented by NRP, IRP, and AN.]

The normal West Saxon form of the noun for 'horse' is *eoh*, which, according to Hickes, appeared as the rune name corresponding to M in Cotton ms Galba A.ii (see his *Thesaurus*, 'Grammatica Islandicae Rudimenta,' Tab. VI and the analysis in Derolez, pp 34ff); the regular form of the rune name in both continental and insular manuscripts shows *e*, rather than *eo*, no doubt a product of Anglian smoothing (see Campbell #222 and 227), and perhaps preserved in southern

manuscripts in order to underline the traditional sound value involved and avoid confusion with the thirteenth rune name (*ēoh*).
The likelihood of uncertainty about this name was enhanced when
the initial sound of rune name XXIII (*œþel*) became *ē*; thus we see
eþel being mistakenly substituted for *eh / eoh* by the second scribe of
Cotton ms Domitian A.ix, folio IIV (reproduced in Derolez, plate
1). It should be noted, however, that the rune M appears correctly for
e twice in the Cynewulfian signatures, once in the *Vercelli Book*,
Elene, line 1261, and once in the *Exeter Book*, *Juliana*, line 706
(for which two occurrences see the full texts of the signatures in
Appendix A).

A good deal of evidence has been assembled to demonstrate the
significance of the horse as a Germanic cult-animal (see Elliott,
Runes, p 56; Krause, *Beiträge zur Runenforschung* II, pp 65ff, and
Schneider, *Runennamen*, pp 378ff). Stanza XIX shows no awareness
of this or any other kind of religious significance, but describes the
horse in the context of aristocratic life: as a source of pleasure to
princes in the company of nobles, as a topic of conversation for
wealthy mounted warriors, and as an outlet for pent-up human
energy. The variations in name (*eh, hors, wicg*) belong to the language of epic poetry, a fact which reinforces the purely secular impact
of the stanza.

56 *hors hōfum wlanc* 'the charger proud in its hoofs' gives an excellent
picture of the noble bearing of this much-prized animal. Schneider
emends *hors* to the plural *horsu* and reads *hofum* (with a short vowel),
translating the phrase as 'Die beiden Rosse auf den Häusern (sind)
glänzend' (the two horses [are] shining on the buildings), in order to
reflect his identification of rune XIX as the equine cult-symbol of the
two divine brothers mentioned in Tacitus' *Germania* (see the reference to these *Alces* in the explanatory note on *eolhx*, rune name XV),
who are seen here figuring as horse-head gable ornaments (see
Runennamen, p 381, also on p 384, figs 1 and 2).

hæleþas ymb for Hickes' *hæleþe ymb*. Both words are emended by
most editors to *hæleþ ymbe* for grammatical and metrical reasons: in
order to regularize the abnormal nominative plural form of the noun
(usually either *hæleþ* or the analogical formation *hæleþas*, for which
see Campbell #637), and to improve the metre by substituting the
form of *ymb* commonly found in postposition (for these arguments

see Sievers, 'Zur Rhythmik,' p 519, followed by Kluge, Dickins, Grienberger, and Dobbie). It is not impossible, however, to scan the phrase
with a third weak syllable in the noun and only one syllable in the
preposition; for example, using Robert Creed's simplification of
Pope's isochronous method, line 52 might be scanned as follows:

hors / hōfum wlanc // ðǣr him / hæleþe ymb.

Therefore I have made the smallest emendation consonant with
grammatical sense by regularizing the noun ending to -as and leaving
the preposition unemended. It does not seem scribally impossible that
an original hæleþas was replaced by a false dative singular form
intruded on account of the deceptive proximity of following ymb
(which actually governs him) and reinforced by the -e ending of the
substantive adjective welege (wealthy ones), which stands in appos-
ition to Hickes' hæleþe (warriors).

58 and is expanded from Hickes' 7.

unstyllum for unstillum: for this meaningless interchange of y and i
see Campbell #317.

frōfur for standard frōfor, for which see the explanatory note on
line 1.

STANZA XX, LINES 59–62

ᛗ rune, transliteration m, name man (Hickes gives an, with the rune itself
replacing the letter m) (meaning man).
[Gmc: *mannaz (man); OE: Isruna man, Brussels man, Vienna mon, and
'Gothic' manna; Norse: NRP maðr (man), IRP maðr (man), and AN man.]

Hickes adds erroneously above m the transliteration d and beside it
the name deg (day). No doubt this false information was borrowed
from the transcription of Cotton ms Domitian A.ix, fol 11v, which is
reproduced immediately following the Old English Rune Poem on
page 136 of his Thesaurus (for the original see plate 1 in Derolez,
where the second Domitian scribe's confusion about the similarly
shaped runes for m and d is clearly evident; also read Hempl's comments on the source of the alternative rune names in 'Hickes' Additions to the Runic Poem.' There can be no real question about the

traditional rune name; like ᛈ *wynn* and ᚦ *ðorn*, this rune and its
meaning were widely known, as shown by the fact that the rune was
used as a grammalogue in various manuscripts to replace the word
man (note, for example, *gefean* ᛗ *meahte* (man might rejoice) in
Vercelli Homily XIII; · ᛗ · *dreama full* (full of human joys) in the
Exeter Book poem entitled *The Ruin*, line 23; and also the ten occurrences in the *Durham Ritual*, all cited in Derolez, pp 396–7 and 402).

Elliott suggests that the rune name may 'refer either literally to the
race of men or perhaps symbolize the legendary progenitor of the
human race; cf. Tacitus, *Germania*, ch. 2' (*Runes*, p 58). Schneider
carries this idea still further by identifying Tacitus' *Mannus* with
Vater Himmel (Father Heaven), the consort of Mother Earth
(*Runennamen*, pp 258ff); he even emends *on myrgþe* (in mirth) to *on
moldan* (on earth) in order to assist this reading (p 259). It seems
clear from the context, however, that the rune name in the Old
English *Rune Poem* refers, not to a divine or semi-divine being, but to
a man, and specifically to one who shares the joys of living within the
bonds of the closest human community, the family (note also the
similar concept of the source of man's pleasure in the Icelandic *Rune
Poem*: 'maðr er manns gaman' (man is his fellow man's joy)). Germanic kinship bonds were inviolable, making the whole extended
family into a kind of psychological unity; betrayal of kinsmen was an
unspeakable crime, for which the Germanic law codes provided no
recompense (for fuller details see Grønbech, *The Culture of the
Teutons* part 1.i on *friþ*, *sib*, and *mandream*; as an Old English poetic
example, note the helpless despair of Hrethel when one of his sons
slays another in *Beowulf*, lines 2435–72). The poet uses the horror of
the unthinkable idea of failing the family in order to underline the
impotence of man in the face of his own mortality. Ultimately, he
insists, we all must withdraw our support from one another (*ōðrum
swīcan*), when the dead desert the living and their strong bodies,
which once protected the family like staves in a fence, are buried and
rot in the grave. In a thoroughly orthodox way, the poet attributes
human mortality to the judgement of the Judaeo-Christian God
(compare *Genesis* 3:19 where Yahweh pronounces on fallen man the
following sentence: 'In the sweat of thy face shalt thou eat bread, till
thou return unto the ground; for out of it wast thou taken: for dust
thou art, and unto dust shalt thou return'). It is interesting to see that
both the Norwegian and Icelandic rune poems also connect man with

the earth, although in their case the formula *moldar auki* (augmentation of dust) appears to refer more to our creation from that material than to our necessary dissolution into the same element from which we were created (see Appendix B for the two *maðr* stanzas).

59 *māgan* for *māgum* (kinsmen); for this form of the dative compare *wynan*, line 37, and *brēostan*, line 27, and the explanatory note on *miclun*, line 2.

60 *sceal* 'must' is used in effective contrast to the gnomic verb *byþ* (as in stanza I, line 2) to indicate a divine requirement.

þēah 'nevertheless' contrastive (as in stanzas I and X) in order to emphasize the paradoxical difference between natural human inclination and spiritual necessity.

61 *Dryhten wyle dōme sīne* 'the Lord intends by his decree.' For the meaningless interchange of *y* and *i* in *wyle* here (as compared to *wile* in line 3) see Campbell #317. Note how the linking of *Dryhten* (Lord) and *dōm* (judgement), seen first in stanza I, is echoed here in one of the most explicitly homiletic of all the stanzas in the poem.

62 *þæt earme flǣsc eorþan betǣcan* 'the wretched human body commit to the earth'; *þæt* is expanded from Hickes' *þ*. This is the first open reference to the overall theme of the transitory nature of life on earth, expounded at length in stanza XXIX and culminating in the last half-line of the poem with the breaking of all merely human covenants.

STANZA XXI, LINES 63–6

⌐ rune, transliteration *l*, name *lagu* (meaning water, sea).
[Gmc: **laguz* (water); OE: Isruna *lago*, Brussels *lago*, Vienna *lagu*, and 'Gothic' *laaz*; Norse: NRP *lǫgr* (water), IRP *lögr* (water), and AN *lagu*.]

With the exception of Krause's unlikely proposal that the original rune name was **laukaz* (leek), there is universal agreement on **laguz* (water) for the original Common Germanic root. As Elliott reminds us, water was associated with 'the nether realms of early

Germanic cosmology' (*Runes*, p 56). We have only to compare the
description of Grendel's mere and its monstrous denizens to confirm
the continuity of this linkage (see *Beowulf*, lines 1361–75). Schneider
fits the ᚱ rune into the context of ship burial, citing relevant archaeological finds and also literary accounts, including the burial of
Scyld Sceafing in *Beowulf*, lines 26–52; he interprets the obvious fear
of seafaring voiced in stanza XXI as the terror involved in man's
helpless journey to the underworld of the dead (see *Runennamen*,
pp 83ff). Seafaring was, of course, a normal practice for the island-
dwelling Anglo-Saxons: their trade with the continent, their contact
with the Mother Church in Rome and other important shrines of
pilgrimage, and even their quickest domestic routes were all by
water. In the poetry, seafaring takes on another dimension as one of
the motifs of heroic adventure (compare Beowulf's sea journey to
Denmark in lines 210–28 and Elene's voyage to the Holy Land in lines
237–50). It also functions as a powerful image for the uncertainty and
tribulations of man's mortal life as sinful exile seeking to return to
Paradise (compare the citations listed in note 24 on page 80, especially *Genesis B*, lines 828–35, where Adam, the first human exile
from his Lord's favour, vows to Eve (ASPR I, p 28):

Gif ic Waldendes   willan cūðe,
hwæt ic his to hearmsceare   habban sceolde,
ne gesāwe þu nō snīomor,   þēah mē on sǣ wadan
hete heofones God,   heonone nū þā
on flōd faran,   nǣre hē firnum þæs dēop,
merestrēam þæs micel,   þæt his ō mīn mōd getwēode,
ac Ic to þām grunde genge,   gif Ic Godes meahte
willan gewyrcean.

(If I knew the Lord's will, what penalty I must receive
from Him, never would you behold a swifter response;
although the God of heaven should command me
to traverse the sea, to journey now from here upon
the flood, never would it be so fearfully deep, the
ocean-current so great, that my mind ever would hesitate
at it, but I would plunge to the very bottom, if I might
do God's will.)

What is pictured in stanza XXI is the essential untrustworthiness of
the sea: the turbulence which makes a stormy passage seem endless;

the lack of any stable point of reference on the small pitching vessels of the period; and, surpassing the rest, the voyager's sense that his direction and even his survival are completely beyond his own control. Those who are forced to venture upon the waves in this stanza are not presented very heroically; instead we appear to be given a fairly naturalistic description of the perils and challenges of the sea, perhaps coloured by the author's recognition of seafaring as an image for the pilgrimage of postlapsarian man to his eternal home. It should also be noted that, where the ᚠ rune occurs in the Cynewulfian signatures, it is related to the changeable aspect of human life on earth (compare *Christ*, line 806; *Elene*, line 1268; and *The Fates of the Apostles*, line 102 in Appendix A).

63 *byþ* ... *langsum geþūht* 'seems interminable,' as in 'his loccas and his beard wǣron gylden geþūht' (his hair and his beard seemed golden) cited by Bosworth-Toller, p 458.

64 *sculun nēþun* for normal West Saxon *sculon nēþan* (are obliged to venture) shows the falling together of unaccented *a, o,* and *u* in late Old English manuscripts (for which see Campbell #49, 368ff).

65 *and* expanded from Hickes' 7.

sǣȳþa for Hickes' *sǣ yþa*.

swȳþe for *swīþe*: for the rounding of *ī* to *ȳ* in the neighbourhood of a labial see Campbell #318.

66 *brimhengest* for Hickes' *brim hengest*, meaning literally 'sea-horse,' ie, 'ship;' for this common kenning see the explanatory note on line 47.

brīdles 'bridle' shows loss of the medial vowel before *l* (see Campbell #388ff).

gȳmeð 'heeds' for Hickes' *gym*, as required by both grammar and metre. Perhaps, as Grienberger suggests ('Runengedicht,' pp 215–6), the word was first scribally shortened to *gymð* and then the final voiceless consonant was omitted.

STANZA XXII, LINES 67–70

ᛜ rune (square-armed form; Hickes adds the more normal variant ᛝ), transcription *ng* (Hickes *ing*), name *Ing* (Hickes *iug*; meaning the culture hero Ing).
[Gmc: **inguz* (Ing); OE: Isruna *inc*, Brussels *hinc*, Vienna *iug*, and 'Gothic' *enguz*; absent from the reduced sixteen rune *futhǫrk* represented by NRP, IRP, and AN.]

This stanza makes the poem's first and only unambiguous reference to a figure out of Germanic mythology (compare stanzas IV and XVII, where the references to Woden and Tiw are debatable). Ing is clearly a man-like being, and his attributes belong to mythology rather than to history. The four-line stanza in which Ing is described is strongly reminiscent of the brief stanzas on Welund, Beaduhild, Maethild, Theodoric, and Eormanric which compose the bulk of the lament of the fictional Germanic scop, Deor (see ASPR III, pp 178ff), or the expanded sections of the *thulas* (or mnemonic catalogues of kings, tribes, and heroes) recited by the equally fictional Germanic scop, Widsith, where the usual identifying half-line or full-line reference swells into a little vignette when describing the most important figures, such as Offa or Hrothulf and Hrothgar (see ASPR III, pp 149ff). The information about Ing presented in lines 67–70 forms a similar little vignette and is equally likely to be based on traditional oral verse. Probably the information contained here owes its survival to the early anthropomorphism of a fertility deity into the legendary ancestor of the Swedes, since the curious details recorded find a parallel in the equally legendary attributes of Scyld Sceafing (the eponymous progenitor of the Scylding dynasty) who brought prosperity to the Danes and whose mysterious arrival and departure are recorded as historical facts and without any apparent religious qualms by the Christian author of *Beowulf* (lines 26–52). Note, in support of this suggestion, that the only other appearance of the name 'Ing' in Old English is as part of the compound *Ingwine* (friends of Ing), an epithet sometimes applied to the Danes in *Beowulf* (lines 1044 and 1319).

Ample evidence has been gathered from outside England to document the widespread Germanic belief in a being called Ing: from Tacitus' reference in the first century to the Germanic tribe living nearest to the Baltic Sea as *Ingaevones* (see *Germania*, chapter 40) to Snorri Sturlusson's comment in the thirteenth century that the fertility god Frey had a further name *Yngvi* and that his descendants were called *Ynglingar* (see the *Ynglinga Saga*, chapter 20). Frey's custom of travelling in a chariot and the fact that he was known as the son of Niord (whose name is etymologically identical with that of the goddess Nerthus, described by Tacitus in chapter 40 of his *Germania* as also making her ritual progress in a sacred car) forms the circumstantial basis for detailed accounts of Ing as early Germanic fertility god found in Chadwick, *Origin of the English Nation*, pp 230ff, 287ff; Klaeber, 'Die Ing-Verse im angelsächsischen Runengedicht;' Krappe, 'Le Char de Ing;' and, most recently, Schneider, *Runennamen*, pp 333ff, 365ff (see also the explanatory note to stanza 1).

Since Ing belonged, not to the observable world of contemporary Anglo-Saxon England, but to the legends of the Germanic past, the opening formula '*A* (rune name) byþ *B* (definition)' could hardly be employed in this stanza. The only way to use it would have been to state that *Ing byþ rūnstæf* (Ing is a runic letter). Instead the poet uses the past tense and recounts something of what he has heard about this legendary culture hero of the pre-Christian continental homeland.

67 *mid Ēast-Denum* for Hickes' *mid east denum* (among the East-Danes), identifying the place where Ing first manifested himself to men; perhaps, with Dickins and Grienberger, to be localized as the island of Zealand, which Chadwick identified with the island in the sea where Tacitus said that a confederation of Baltic tribes were accustomed to worship Nerthus (or Mother Earth) with full sacrificial rites (see *Germania*, chapter 40).

68 *gesewen* 'seen' for Hickes' *ge sewen*.

secgun for *secgum* (by men); for the dative plural ending *-un* see the explanatory note on *miclun*, line 2.

ēst 'east' as in Hickes, although some editors emend to *eft* (again, back). The root vowel *ē* for earlier *ēa* may represent late West Saxon monophthongization (see Campbell 329.2). On the reasonableness of 'east' as the direction for Ing's departure see Schneider, *Runennamen*, pp 366ff.

70 *heardingas* is shown in the text without an initial capital and translated 'warriors' (as in *Elene*, lines 25 and 130). For the proper noun
with an initial capital and the identification of the people involved as
in some way connected with the Old Norse *Haddingjar* and the
Asdingi, a section of the Vandals, see Dickins, *Runic Poems*, p 20.
Schneider interprets the last line of this stanza as stressing the fact
that the fertility god had other names, but that 'Ing' was the name
given to him by the remnant of the Vandals that stayed in Jutland
when the bulk of the tribe began its long migrations (see *Runennamen*, p 369 and note 21).]

hæle 'hero,' a term that could be applied to a divine being, even to the
Christian God (compare *geong hæleð* (the young hero) for Christ in
The Dream of the Rood, ASPR II, p 62, line 39).

STANZA XXIII, LINES 71–3

ᛟ rune (round-headed form with squared arms instead of normal angular
ᛟ), transliteration oe, name *ēþel* (meaning inherited estate, landed property, home).
[Gmc: *ōþila* (landed property); OE: Isruna *odil*, Brussels *odil*, Vienna *oedil*,
and 'Gothic' *utal*; absent from the reduced sixteen rune Norse *futhqrk* represented by NRP, IRP, and AN.]

The name of the Common Germanic rune that was used to represent
all *o* sounds in early inscriptions can be reconstructed as *ōþila*. In
Old English, however, *o* was fronted to *œ* by following *i* and later
unrounded to *e* (see Campbell #198 and 288); hence there are two
forms of the Old English rune name: the earlier *œþel* and the later
West Saxon and Kentish *ēþel*, which are reflected in the contradiction
between Hickes' sound value *oe* (no doubt borrowed from Cotton ms
Domitian A.ix, fol 11v) and the name-equivalent *eþel* (probably
borrowed from some other source, for which see page 25). As a result
of this and other sound changes, ᚩ *ōs* took over the sound value *o* (see
the explanatory note on stanza IV) and ᛟ *ēþel* tended to be confused
with ᛗ *eh* (see the explanatory note on stanza XIX). Despite these
facts, the equation ᛟ : *ēþel* still remained widely known, as witnessed
by the use of the rune as a grammalogue for *ēþel* in *Waldere*, line 31
('sēcan ealdne. ᛟ.' (to seek his old home), Dobbie p 5), in *Beowulf*,

lines 520 ('hē gesōhte swǣsne. ᛟ.' (he sought his own home)), 913 ('. ᛟ. Scyldinga' (the home of the Scyldings)), and 1702 ('eald . ᛟ. weard' (old guardian of the homeland)), and also in the Lauderdale (or Tollemache) manuscript of King Alfred's translation of Orosius ('seo wæs on ǣrdagum heora ieldrena ᛟ' (which was in earlier days the home of their ancestors)); for the full texts of these citations see Derolez, pp 399ff.

ᛟ was normally the twenty-fourth rune, from the earliest Germanic *futharks* (see the fifth century Kylver stone reproduced in Elliott, *Runes*, plate III, fig 3) to the latest Old English manuscript *futhorcs* (see the late eleventh or early twelfth century St John's College, Oxford ms 17, folio 5v reproduced in Derolez, plate III). Thus the original sequence of runic symbols could be interpreted as being bounded by the two agricultural values of ᚠ (cattle) and ᛟ (land) (see Elliott, *Runes*, p 58, and Schneider, *Runennamen*, pp 54–6 for this interpretation). Exceptions to the traditional order are (probably) the sixth century Vadstena bracteate, which omits ᛗ (see Elliott, *Runes*, plate II, fig 4, and Musset, *Introduction* #49) and the *futhorc* in the ninth century Brussels ms 9311–9319 which, like the Old English *Rune Poem*, reverses the order of ᛗ and ᛟ (see Derolez, plate IV.b). It is noteworthy that, as if to mark the original ending of the *futhark*, the stanza length reverts here from four to three lines (for further discussion see page 52).

Like the other stanzas dealing with the peaceful enjoyment of one's property (compare stanzas I and VIII), these lines are characterized by words for pleasure. It is interesting that the poet stresses the importance of proper conduct (and possibly also of rightful inheritance) as necessary to this enjoyment.

71 *oferlēof* for Hickes' *ofer leof* (very dear). The possibility that *ofer* might have connotations of excess appears to be discounted by the moderation of the phrase *rihtes and gerysena* (what is right and proper).

ǣghwylcum men 'to every man,' a universalizing phrase designed to emphasize the gnomic truth of the statement about *ēþel*.

72 *rihtes and gerysena* 'what is right and proper' for Hickes' *rihter and gerysena*, no doubt a copying error resulting from the similarity of

insular *r* and *s*. For the meaningless interchange of *y* for *i* in *gerysena* see Campbell #317. The compound phrase is the genitive direct object of the verb *brūcan* (to enjoy).

on interpreted as part of a verb *onbrūcan* by Bosworth-Toller (see under *gerisene*, p 432), making for an unnecessarily awkward line division. It is better taken, as by Dickins, Grienberger, and Dobbie, for an adverb reinforcing ðǣr and connected with the following adverbial phrase *on bolde* (in his own house).

73 *on bolde* 'in his own house' for Hickes' *on blode* (in the blood). For the suggestion that this phrase should remain unemended and be read with emended *blēadum* as *on blōde blēaðum* (with gentle blood, a metaphor for peacefully) see Grienberger's comments in 'Runengedicht,' p 217.

blēadum 'in prosperity,' usually taken as an adverbial dative meaning 'prosperously' (thus Dickins 'in constant prosperity' and Dobbie 'with prosperity'); but see also Grienberger's suggested emendation recorded in the previous note. Schneider reads as the concrete 'fruits, harvest,' rather than the abstract 'prosperity' (*Runennamen*, p 57), thereby bringing the stanza closer to early agricultural life.

STANZA XXIV, LINES 74–6

ᛗ rune, transliteration *d*, name dæg (meaning day).
[Gmc: *dagaz* (day); OE: Isruna *tag*, Brussels *dag*, Vienna *daeg*, and 'Gothic' *daaz*; absent from the reduced sixteen rune Norse *futhqrk* represented by NRP, IRP, and AN.]

Hickes adds erroneously above *d* the transliteration *m* and beside it the name *mann*; compare stanza XX for the reverse error, no doubt from the same source, Cotton ms Domitian A.ix, fol 11v. The true name was well established, however, as can be seen from the frequency with which the rune is used as a grammalogue for *dæg* in the *Durham Ritual*, even in oblique cases with inflectional endings such as ᛗ *es* and ᛗ *e* (for citations see Derolez, pp 400–1).

Elliott reminds us of the obvious connection of this rune with the sun and sun-worship (*Runes*, p 57). Schneider (*Runennamen*, pp 384ff) associates the rune, instead, with the cult of the divine twins (Tacitus' *Alces* mentioned in the explanatory note on line 56 and in the stanza note on rune xv), this time in their heavenly manifestation as *der Tagstern*, ie, the morning and evening stars recognized as one 'Daystar'. The actual content of stanza xxiv points to a much more important link for the poet with the Judaeo-Christian God, whose first command to the dark and unformed universe was 'Let there be light' (*Genesis* 1:3) and whose son (or human manifestation) was later sent to perform a similar function: see *John* 8:12 where Christ says, 'I am the light of the world; he that followeth me shall not walk in darkness, but shall have the light of life.' The possibly deliberate reversal of the normal *futhorc* order, which gives ᛗ twenty-fourth instead of twenty-third place, has been so arranged as to bring the third *ætt* (and with it the original *futhark* sequence) to a close on a very spiritual note, as opposed to the potentially carnal associations of ᛟ (*ēþel*): *dæg* being specifically equated with *leoht* (light), the first and least tangible, yet most universally desired gift of God.

74 *Drihtnes* 'the Lord's,' a word that obtains part of its resonance from the image of secular kingly power, as in line 3. For the unrounding of *y* to *i* before *h* see Campbell #316.

 sond a nominal formation from the verb *sendan* (to send), variously read as either a person or a thing sent, ie, 'the messenger' or 'the message.' I follow Dickins in avoiding this irrelevant issue through the translation 'is sent by.'

75 *Metodes*, from the verb *metan* (to measure or mete out), is an epithet for God, in his roles both as Creator and as Judge. Although it may seem somewhat difficult to distinguish whether it is the light of creation or the light of promised salvation on Judgement Day that emanates from him here, the context (particularly the word *eallum* (to all)) suggests the former.

 myrgþ and tōhiht 'a source of joy and hope' for Hickes' *myrgþ and to hiht*, showing unrounding of *y* to *i* before *h* in *tōhiht* (for which see Campbell #316). Note the poet's stress on the undiluted joy of *dæg*.

76 *ēadgum and earmum* 'to the haves and the have-nots,' a universalizing phrase, expanding the unspecified *mannum* in line 74b by linking
the polar extremes of human experience; this phrase seems even more
explicitly Christian than the parallel, but somewhat more heroic-
sounding references to *gumena* and *wrǣcna* in stanza VII and *beornum and ðearfum* in stanza XII.

eallum 'to everyone,' a reinforcement of the preceding *ēadgum and
earmum*.

brīce 'of benefit' (literally, useful), ie, a gift to be enjoyed by all.

STANZA XXV, LINES 77–80

ᚪ rune, transliteration *a*, name *āc* (meaning oak-tree).
[This rune was not part of the original Common Germanic *futhark*; OE: Isruna
ac, Brussels *ac*, Vienna *ac*, but absent from the 'Gothic' alphabet; also absent
from the reduced sixteen rune Norse *futhqrk* represented by NRP, IRP, and AN.]

ᚪ is a completely new rune, found only in Old English and Frisian
inscriptions (for the latter see the sixth or seventh century Arum
'sword' and the sixth century Harlingen coin reproduced in Elliott,
Runes, plate IV, fig 9, and plate V, fig 12 respectively). The sound
value of the rune includes *a* from original Germanic *ai* (see Campbell
#134) and *a* from primitive Old English *æ*, either by retraction before
certain consonants and consonant groups (see Campbell #139) or by
restoration before a back vowel (see Campbell #157). It has been
plausibly argued (by Hempl in 'The Old English Runes for *a* and *o*,'
pp 348ff and by Grienberger in 'Die angelsächsischen Runenreihen,'
pp 19ff) that this rune represents a ligature of original Germanic ᚠ
(*a*) with ᛁ (*i*), as reflected in the rune name itself, Old English *ac*
from Germanic **aik* (oak); but Guinn reminds us that the ᚪ rune
may represent no more than 'a simple diacritical marking of the
regular vocalic rune "a",' since no form of the rune intermediate
between ᚠ ᛁ and ᚪ has been found to support the theory of such a
ligature's development (see his *English Runes and Runic Writing*,
p 33).
   With ᚪ commences a final series of five new runes, representing
distinctively Old English vowels and diphthongs. Significantly, the

beginning of this addition to the original twenty-four rune Germanic *futhark* is marked by a four-line stanza (see page 52 for a discussion of this). Interesting parallels have been drawn between these added runes and the structure of the Celtic *ogham* alphabet, where a series of vowels make up the fourth *aicme* (family) (compare the Norse term *ætt* (family or group of eight)) and are followed by a supplementary series of diphthongs (for a thorough review of the connections between runes and *ogham* consult Helmut Arntz, 'Das Ogom,' and R. Thurneysen, 'Zum Ogom'; for a brief, but excellent summary of the relevant material see Musset, *Introduction* #96–103). In the context of the parallels between runes and *ogham*, it is interesting to note that the Old English names for the first two additional runes, like a large proportion of the vegetation nomenclature for *ogham* letters which may have served as their model, consist of words for common trees (*āc* (oak) and *æsc* (ash)); in this connection see G. Calder, *Auraicept na n'éces*, pp 275ff or H. Meroney, 'Early Irish Letter-Names.'

Stanza xxv presents the oak quite naturalistically, if in a more overtly riddling manner than usual in this poem. The tree is described from two aspects: first in terms of the usefulness of its acorns as mast for pigs, that in turn are food for men ('elda bearnum flæsces fōdor'); then in terms of its value as the stoutest kind of ship-timber – thus the oak becomes a kind of amphibian: *on eorþan* (on earth) and *ofer ganotes bæþ* (upon the sea). One particularly telling piece of evidence against Karl Schneider's methods in *Die Germanischen Runennamen* lies in the way he endeavours to fit even this late rune name into his reconstruction of primitive Germanic beliefs (see his discussion on pp 290–2 of oak as the raw material from which man was created). The only non-naturalistic aspect of the description of oak in this stanza is occasioned by the somewhat heroic terminology traditionally associated with seafaring, which tends to impart anthropomorphic qualities (eg, *æþele trēowe* (a noble good-faith)) to any ship that might be made from the tree; but, as J.R. Hall has pointed out in 'Perspective and Wordplay in the Old English *Rune Poem*,' pp 456–7, the latter phrase could be interpreted as a pun on *trēow* (faith) and *trēow* (tree, wood), thus offering a clear hint that the subject described so heroically in the second half of the stanza is indeed a tree. To underline the true meaning, for the only time in the entire poem, the rune name itself is used in the stanza describing it.

79 *ganotes bæþ* 'gannet's bath,' a traditional kenning for 'sea' (consult Hertha Marquardt, *Die altenglischen Kenningar*, p 173 for this kenning; also compare the parallel term *fisces beþ* (fishes bath) in stanza XVI).

STANZA XXVI, LINES 81–3

ᚫ rune, transliteration *ae*, name *æsc* (meaning ash-tree).
[This name was not associated with the ᚫ rune in the original Common Germanic *futhark* (see the explanatory note on rune IV); OE: Isruna *asc*, Brussels *e..* (name partially destroyed), Vienna *aes*, and for the 'Gothic' letter name see rune IV; also for the Norse rune name see rune IV.]

ᚫ was originally the fourth rune in the Germanic *futhark*, with the sound value *a* and the name **ansuz* (god). Except under certain circumstances (see the explanatory notes on runes IV and XXV), Germanic *a* appears in Old English in the spelling *æ*, which indicates the early Anglo-Frisian fronting of this vowel (see Campbell #131–3). Since this fronting did not occur in the case of the original rune name **ansuz* (which became Old English *ōs* and acquired an altered rune form to reflect its new initial vowel), it was necessary to invent another acrophonic name for ᚫ. Once again, for front *a*: ᚫ (*æsc*) as for back *a*: ᚪ (*āc*), a tree name was selected (see the explanatory note on stanza XXV for the possible Irish source of this choice).

Stanza XXVI has a number of points in common with the preceding stanzas on tree names. It describes the ash as tall like the birch (see stanza XVIII) and as both highly prized and firmly rooted like the yew (see stanza XIII). In a manner similar to the stanza on the oak (stanza XXV), its final section takes on distinctively riddling characteristics and also employs heroic terminology in portraying the ash as holding its ground properly although many men fight against it (probably a reference either to the usefulness of ash-wood for weapons, especially spears, as suggested by Grienberger 'Runengedicht,' p 218, or to the difficulty experienced in felling the tree, as implied by Dickins' translation in *Runic and Heroic Poems*, p 23: 'With its sturdy trunk it offers a stubborn resistance'). Although poetically stylized in this way, the description of the ash-tree contained in stanza XXVI remains completely naturalistic. For the contention that, nonetheless, it does have ritual content, see Schneider's association of his unusual reading of the stanza with the world-ash Yggdrasil (*Runennamen*, pp 274–7).

81 *oferhēah* for Hickes' *over heah*, translated 'very tall,' rather than the contextually unlikely 'too tall.'

82 *staþule* for standard *staþole* shows the falling together of unstressed vowels (see Campbell #49, 368ff).

   hylt for *healdeþ* by syncopation and assimilation (see Campbell #732–5).

83 *ðēah him feohtan on fīras monige* 'although many men attack it' furnishes an example of the late postposition of *on*, which governs *him* (it). Grienberger emends *ðēah* to *dēah* (from the verb *dugan* (to be good for)) and translates 'ist tüchtig, taugt, manche Männer zu bekämpfen' (is good for fighting against many men) ('*Runengedicht*,' p 218).

STANZA XXVII, LINES 84–6

ᚣrune (with medial bar, as opposed to earlier ᚣ), transliteration *y*, name *ȳr* (meaning uncertain, perhaps bow).
[This rune was not part of the original Common Germanic *futhark*; OE: Isruna *yur* (but misapplied to a different rune, as shown in Derolez, plate v), Brussels name missing (transliteration *y* only), Vienna *yr*, but absent from the 'Gothic' alphabet; absent also from the reduced sixteen rune Norse *futhqrk*, but compare the Norse name for rune xv as represented in NRP *ýr* (yew), IRP *ýr* (yew-bow), and AN *yr*.]

ᚣ is a completely new rune, created to represent the vowel resulting from the fronting of *u* by following *i* (see Campbell #199). In the simplest early forms it appears to consist of rune II: ᚢ, ᚢ, or ∧ (*u*) with subscript rune XI: ᛁ (*i*) (see Vienna ms 795, folio 20r, reproduced in Derolez, plate IV.a); hence it could be interpreted formally as a ligature of the two, especially since *ui* is often found instead of *y* in early Old English manuscripts (see Campbell #42, 199). Later forms show various styles of subscript *y*, as here, where the top of the *y* is flattened to form a medial bar. This new rune was well established at least by the beginning of the eighth century (note its use in the word *wylif* (she-wolf) on the left side of the Franks Casket and in the

word *kyningc* (king) on the east side of the Ruthwell Cross, as shown
in Elliott, *Runes*, plates XXII and XVII); and it appears regularly in
twenty-seventh position in the extended *futhorc*, as represented by
the ninth century Thames scramasax (see Elliott, *Runes*, plate III, fig
7), as well as by all native manuscript *futhorcs* and most continental
versions (note, however, the unusual reversal: ᛏ *eor*, ᛤ *yr*, in Vienna
ms 795).

Although the name *ȳr* was regularly associated with this rune, its
meaning remains a matter for debate. Probably the easiest assumption is that the new rune name was initially meaningless in itself,
being simply a by-form of rune name II: *ūr*, devised to represent an
i-umlaut of the relevant vowel *u* (for this view see Joan Blomfield,
'Runes and the Gothic Alphabet,' p 220). Noting that the Old English
word thus produced resembles the Norse rune name *ȳr*, which has the
meaning 'yew-bow' in the Icelandic *Rune Poem*, numerous readers
have been tempted to speculate about the possibility of a borrowed
definition: that is, whether the Anglo-Saxon poet, faced with a traditional rune name that was otherwise unknown in his vernacular,
could have taken his interpretation of its meaning from the
homophonic name of the final Norse rune, which by this time had lost
all connection in form and sound with the thirteenth Old English
rune (see the explanatory notes on stanzas XIII and XV above and, as
some indication of the long history of this 'bow' theory, see also W.
Grimm, *Ueber deutsche Runen*, pp 233, 344; Bosworth-Toller under
ȳr; Keller, 'Zum altenglischen *Runengedicht*,' pp 145ff; Arntz, *Handbuch*², pp 207ff, 231; and Dobbie's edition of the Old English *Rune
Poem*, p 159). For the possibility that Cynewulf may have used the
rune with this same meaning see Elliott's articles on 'Cynewulf's
Runes;' and compare the Cynewulfian signatures printed in Appendix A. The identification of *ȳr* with 'bow' works reasonably well in
the context of stanza XXVII's opening and closing comments: a bow
could be termed a kind of war-gear and, both in sport and in battle, it
could bring joy and honour to nobles. The identification works less
well in the context of the middle two comments; for, while a decorated bow conceivably might be described as looking fine on a horse
(see May Keller's references to the splendor of decorated Germanic
yew-bows in *The Anglo-Saxon Weapon Names*, pp 48ff), it hardly
would be termed *fæstlīc on færelde* (firm, secure or reliable on a
journey), unless that journey were interpreted (in the light of a bow's

primary function) as the straight flight of any arrow shot from it. Hence the meaning 'yew-bow' has frequently been rejected and various alternative definitions proposed, including 'horn' (Holthausen, 'Zu den altenglischen Rätseln,' p 176, and the Grein-Köhler Sprachschatz), 'saddle' from 'yew-wood saddle-bow' (Grienberger, 'Runengedicht,' p 219), 'adornment' (von Friesen, Runorna, p 62), 'female aurochs' (Keller, 'Zur Chronologie der altenglischen Runen,' p 29), 'axe-iron' (Dickins, Runic Poems, p 22), and 'gold buckle' (Schneider, Runennamen, pp 240ff). Unsurprisingly, Schneider discovers underlying cultic affiliations for even this patently secular stanza; see his linkage of *ȳr* (gold buckle) with *ūr* (*semen virile*) seen as a symbolic reference to Heimdall/Hagal (*Runennamen*, pp 237–42).

In default of any more satisfactory definition and etymology, this edition maintains the traditional translation of *ȳr* as 'bow.' As befits a stanza dealing with the bow or any other kind of war-gear, the vocabulary used in lines 84–6 is aristocratic and heroic (compare *æþelinga* (princes), *eorla* (nobles), *wyrþmynd* (honour), and *wicge* (steed)).

84 *and* expanded from Hickes' 7.

86 *fyrdgeatewa* for Hickes' *fyrd geacewa*, whose *c* probably arose from scribal miscopying of *t*, which it resembles in insular script.

STANZA XXVIII, LINES 87–9

⟊ rune, transliteration *io*, name *īar/īor* (Hickes shows a superscript correction of the initial letters of *iar* to *io*) (meaning uncertain, probably some kind of fish or fish-like creature (an eel or a newt?).
[This rune was not part of the original Common Germanic *futhark*; OE: Isruna absent, Brussels absent, Vienna both rune and 'Gothic' letter absent; also absent from the reduced sixteen rune Norse *futhqrk* represented by NRP, IRP, and AN.]

⟊ is another completely new rune, but one that is not well represented in Old English manuscript *futhorcs*. Moreover, its position as rune XXVIII is unique to the Old English *Rune Poem*: normally it does not appear amongst the four runes (ᚪ *āc*, ᚫ *æsc*, ᚣ *ȳr*, and ᛠ *ēar*) which are thought to constitute the first extension of the original twenty-four rune Common Germanic *futhark* (for this chronology see Elliott, *Runes*, pp 33–5). Where ✚ appears at all in Old English manuscript *futhorcs*, it is appended after ᛠ *ēar*, in company with some or all of the other relatively unnecessary runes (ᚹ (or more commonly ᚣ) *cweorð*, ᚳ *calc*, ᛥ *stan*, and ᚷ or ᚸ *gar*) which are thought to constitute a later and less widely known extension of the Anglo-Saxon *futhorc* to its ultimate total of thirty-three runes (see the complete thirty-three rune *futhorc* in Cotton ms Domitian A.ix, fol 11v, reproduced in Derolez, plate 1, and also the discussion of the last five runes in Elliott, *Runes*, pp 36–8 and Page, *English Runes*, pp 42–3). Even the place of ✚ in this second extension was by no means fixed, as demonstrated by the English *futhorc* with names from Cotton ms Galba A.ii, reproduced in Hickes' *Thesaurus*, 'Grammaticae Islandicae Rudimenta,' Tab.VI, which shows ✚ *ior* in thirty-first position (see Derolez, p 46 for this *futhorc*).

As outlined in the explanatory note on rune XII, ✚ appears to be the epigraphical variant of ᛄ *gēr*. Hence it is not absolutely impossible that the aberrant rune name *īar* which Hickes records in his facsimile may have originated as a doublet for rune name XII *gēr*, the smoothed form of normal West Saxon *gēar* (see Dickins' suggestion to this effect in *Runic and Heroic Poems*, p 23). Keller maintained that the duplication of rune names came about as a result of deliberate borrowing from Norse nomenclature (see 'Zum altenglischen Runengedicht,' pp 148ff). Militating against any connection with the name of rune XII, whether in its Old English form *gēar* or its Norse form *ár*, are the twin facts that someone (either Hickes or some scribal predecessor) has corrected the name *īar* to correspond with the sound value *io* and that the resultant name *īor* (not *īar*) was indeed the normal one in Old English manuscript *futhorcs* (compare the insular *futhorcs* where ✚ appears, ie, Cotton mss Domitian A.ix, fol 11v and Galba A.ii (folio unknown) cited in notes 94 and 96 on pp 72–3). As suggested on page 28, it is always possible that *īar* may be a Kenticism; but, if *īor* is the true West Saxon name, then the linguistic contortions required to connect it with the name of rune XII are beyond the powers of this and most other editors. Joan Blomfield cuts the etymological knot by suggesting that the name of ✚ is 'purely phonetic,' in other words, that *īar/īor* (along with *ēar*) was 'formed on the same model' as the immediately preceding rune *ȳr*, the relevant vowel being made into the semblance of a word by the addition of the same consonant, r (see 'Runes and the Gothic Alphabet,' pp 219–20).

The content of stanza XXVIII leaves the rune name's meaning for the Anglo-Saxon poet as debatable as its proper spelling and etymology. Neither *īar* nor *īor* appears outside *futhorc* name lists in Old English records. Generations of editors and dictionary-makers from the time of Grimm (*Ueber deutsche Runen*, p 244) have tentatively translated the apparently amphibious creature described in this stanza as 'eel' or 'newt' (see Grein, *Bibliothek der angelsächsischen Poesie* II, p 353; Bosworth-Toller under *īor*; Holthausen, *Altenglisches etymologisches Wörterbuch* under *īor*; Dickins, *Runic Poems*, p 23; Grienberger, 'Runengedicht,' p 220; and Dobbie, p 159). Schneider has produced an extensive, but unconvincing etymology to justify his translation of *īor* as 'serpent' and his interpretation of stanza XXVIII as a description of *Midgarðsormr* (the World-Serpent) of Norse cosmic mythology (*Runennamen*, pp 293ff). Elliott makes the aesthetically appealing suggestion that, since the rune name *īar/īor* was meaningless to the poet, he created a new definition 'by simply attaching to it the first of the two meanings of *ēar*, namely, "ocean, sea"' (see *Runes*, p 54). This imaginative solution has the attraction of enabling the editor to leave *ēa fixa* unemended as a poetic kenning for 'sea' (literally, river of fishes); it also reminds us of parallels in some of the more interesting Old English riddles, where enormous entities like 'storm,' 'sea,' or even 'creation' itself are presented as animate beings with habits and emotions comprehensible to men (compare the Exeter *Riddles* 1–3, 5, and 11 in ASPR III, pp 180ff).

87 *ēafixa* for Hickes' *ea fixa*, as suggested by Grienberger, 'Runengedicht,' p 220, meaning 'of or belonging to the riverfish.' Note the late West Saxon metathesis of [sk] to [ks], when compared with *fisces*, line 46 (for which see Campbell #440). Dobbie (p 160) rejects this genitive plural in predicate position and emends to the nominative singular *ēafix* (for *ēafisc* (a riverfish)), following Grimm, Ettmüller, Kluge, Rieger, Dickins, and most other editors. Grein emends to the rather clumsy *ēafixa sum* (one of the riverfish), followed by Wülker. Elliott leaves Hickes' phrase unemended as *ēa fixa* (a river of fishes) (see 'The Runes in the Husband's Message,' pp 1ff, and the main stanza note on *īar/īor* above). Jones emends to *ēafix ā* (ever a riverfish), thereby lending unusual importance to the vowel

which most editors delete altogether, making it parallel to the adverb *ā* in verse 87b, which bears full stress and sets the alliterative pattern for the entire line; he sees this emendation as reinforcing the amphibious nature of the creature described (see p 111 of his dissertation).

ðēah 'yet, nonetheless' contrastive to indicate a paradoxical truth, as in lines 2 and 60.

ā brūceþ for Hickes' *abruceþ*, an emendation required by the alliterative stress pattern and made by all editors since Grimm.

88 *fōdres* shows loss of the medial vowel after a long syllable (see Campbell #392).

on foldan 'on land' for Hickes' *onfaldan*: the vowel *a* is regularized to normal West Saxon *o* to avoid any possible confusion with *on falde* (in a sheep-fold), which would be a completely nonsensical reading.

hafaþ 'has,' compare *hæfþ*, lines 23 and 41: for this uncontracted verb (see Campbell #762).

89 *wætre* compare the forms *wætere* in line 26 and *wature* in line 42; shows loss of the medial vowel after a short syllable (for which see Campbell #388).

STANZA XXIX, LINES 90–4

ᛠ rune, transliteration *ea* (Hickes *ear*), name *ēar* (Hickes *car*; meaning earth).
[This rune was not part of the original Common Germanic *futhark*; OE: Isruna *aer*, Brussels name missing (transliteration *eo* only), Vienna *eor*, but absent from the 'Gothic' alphabet; absent also from the reduced sixteen rune Norse *futhqrk* represented by NRP, IRP, and AN.]

This is the final member of the first and best known extension of the Common Germanic *futhark* (note its appearance in twenty-eighth position in the Anglo-Saxon *futhorc* on the blade of the Thames scramasax reproduced in Elliott, *Runes*, plate III, fig 7). It represents the Old English diphthong *œa* (written *ea*) resulting from primitive Germanic *au* (see Campbell #131, 135, 275–6), which sometimes is confused in Northumbrian dialects with *eo*, as in the evidence from Brussels ms 9311–19 and Vienna ms 795 cited above (for other examples of this confusion see Campbell #278). Formally, this rune resembles rune xxv: ᚪ (*āc* from **aik-*) and rune iv: ᚩ (*ōs* from **ans-*), both of which are thought to have originated as ligatures of ᚨ (Germanic *a*) with a following sound (for more details on these ligatures see the explanatory notes on stanzas iv and xxv above). It is not impossible, therefore, that ᛠ (*ēar* from **aur-*) may have been constructed on the same model. For the argument that the original sound represented by this new construct could have been an early Anglo-Frisian monophthong see Page, 'The Old English Rune *ear*.'

Hickes' evidence for the rune name is complicated by an error in transcription: *car* for the very similar *ear*, compounded by his borrowing of the rune name *tir*, erroneously attributed to ᛠ by the second scribe of Cotton ms Domitian A.ix, fol 11v, which Hickes adds to the left of the rune (compare the stanza notes on runes xx and xxiv above for similar errors borrowed from this source). Other insular manuscripts, however, leave little room for doubt that the Old English rune name was *ēar* (compare St John's College, Oxford ms 17, fol 5v, Cotton ms Galba A.ii, and the information provided by the first scribe of Cotton ms Domitian A.ix, folio 11v as shown in Derolez, pp 38ff, 45ff, 9ff, and plates III and I). Like the new rune names described in stanzas xxvii and xxviii, *ēar* is etymologically obscure. It has been argued that the name was a meaningless phonetic formation on the same model as *ȳr* and *īar/īor* (see Arntz, *Handbuch²*, pp 229ff, and Blomfield, 'Runes and the Gothic Alphabet,' pp 219–20). Blomfield takes this argument further in attributing a learned definition 'the end' to the otherwise meaningless *ēar*: noting how the regular appearance of ᛠ *ēar* at the end of the *futhorc* led to its frequent equation by alphabetizers with the final Latin letter *z*, she hypothesizes the rune's acquisition of this meaning 'simply by position' (see page 225 of her article cited above and compare the similar use of the Greek letter names *alpha* and *omega* for 'the beginning' and 'the end' in Revelations 22:13). Schneider painstakingly reconstructs an Indo-European root **aur-* (*os/om*) (house, dwelling), which he relates to Old English *ærn* (habitation) and whose secondary meaning 'house for the dead, grave' he sees as lying behind the rune name *ēar* (*Runnennamen*, pp 72–4). Most editors, however, follow Grein (*Bibliothek* II, p 353) in explaining Old English *ēar* as cognate with Old Norse *aurr* (clay, loam). Page translates Old Norse *aurr* as 'wet clay' and the related *eyrr* as 'gravelly bank,' thereby establishing at least a tenuous link with the more common meaning of Old English *ēar*, ie, 'sea or ocean' (which Elliott suggested may have been transferred to *iar/ior*, as described in the explanatory notes on stanza XXVIII above). Dickins translates *ēar* in his edition of the Old English *Rune Poem* as 'the grave,' an interpretation that gains some etymological reinforcement from the parallel Gothic term *aurahjons* (tomb).

Clearly *ēar* (earth) and its synonym *hrūsan* in line 92 have no connection with the fruitful Mother Earth of early Germanic fertility cults. What stanza XXIX presents is the earth or 'dust' of the Christian burial service (quoted from God's curse on fallen man in Genesis 3:19, 'dust thou art and unto dust thou shalt return'). The physical revulsion at the thought of returning to this element, which is so obvious in the poet's choice of terminology in the last stanza, is strongly reminiscent of contemporary sermon literature (compare the examples cited in note 26 on pp 80–1) and also akin to medieval pictorial representations of death and Doomsday, all of which were designed to encourage the rejection of worldly ties (*contemptus mundi*). In the final three phrases of the poem, everything that earth can offer to man, including all the wonders and pleasures celebrated in the preceding twenty-eight stanzas, is shown to be an ephemeral and untrustworthy illusion. Thus the poet affords his audience the best possible reason for his insistent exhortation from the very first stanza of the Old English *Rune Poem* to give away all those earthly things on which humans are tempted to rely.

In order both to underline his message and to bring the poem to a strong close, the poet has made use of several striking metrical effects in stanza XXIX. First, he has expanded this final stanza to five lines, making it the longest one in the poem. Next, he has used heavy alliteration, particularly in the transverse alliteration of the antepenultimate line. Finally, he has used the device of parallelism in the infinitives *cōlian/cēosan* and especially in the third person plural verbs *gedrēosaþ/gewītaþ/geswīcaþ*, so as to create a series of rhymes which reinforce the alliteration and impart a sense of finality.

90 *eorla gehwylcun* 'to every man.' For the *-un* dative ending see the explanatory note on *miclun*, line 2. This universalizing phrase carries

more than gnomic weight, reminding one forcibly of the Middle
English play *Everyman*, where a representative human being also
faces the ultimate deprivation of death.

91 ðonn perhaps a contraction for ðonne, as in lines 32 and 46 above.

fæstlīce 'firmly, irresistibly,' an adverb designed to underline man's
impotence when confronted with his body's mortality (compare the
same concept in stanza xx).

93 blāc 'pallid, livid,' nominative singular to agree with flǣsc and/or its
appositive hrāw, rather than with the nearest noun hrūsan, which is
accusative singular (thus also Dobbie, p 160, correcting Dickins,
Runic Poems, p 23, where he translates hrūsan ... blāc as 'dark earth').

tō gebeddan 'as its bedfellow, ie, consort, wife or bride' (compare
Beowulf, line 63: healsgebedda). Normally a symbol of fleshly comfort, this image reinforces the horrible contrast between the flushed
warmth of life and the cold pallor of death.

blēda literally, 'fruits' and forming part of an image of late autumn,
blēda gedrēosaþ (fruits fail), which Dickins reads abstractly as 'prosperity declines' (compare the concrete use of blēda in lines 34, 51 with
the abstract use of blǣd in lines 24, 73). The employment of fall and
winter imagery to indicate the passing away of human life and
earthly values was common in Old English elegiac poetry (compare
Wanderer and *Seafarer*, ASPR III, pp 134ff, 143ff).

94 wēra for standard West Saxon wǣra (covenants), an interpretation
adopted in the Grein-Köhler *Sprachschatz*, p 755, and followed by
most editors. This raising of ǣ to ē may be a sign of Kentish influence
(see Campbell #288); but for the other possibilities see also Campbell
#291 and 292. Compare the concept of involuntary breaking of the
social bond in stanza xx, where the topic of man's death was first
unambiguously broached.

Glossary

GLOSSARIAL NOTE

Every occurrence of a word in the Old English *Rune Poem* is noted in this glossary by a numerical line reference; *a* or *b* following the line reference refers to the first half-line or second half-line respectively. Where the same word appears in distinctively different forms, there is cross-referencing to the main form (for example, *anfengys* is cross-referenced to *onfeng*) and the relevant grammatical information is given only under that main form. Words beginning with the *æ* digraph are alphabetized to appear after the complete list of words beginning with *a*. Similarly words beginning with *þ* or *ð* are alphabetized to appear after the complete list of words beginning with *t*. The grammatical information given is abbreviated as follows:

a accusative
adj adjective
adv adverb
anom anomalous
art article
athem athematic
conj conjunction
d dative
def definite
dem demonstrative
dir direct
f feminine
g genitive
ind indicative
indecl indeclinable
indef indefinite
inf infinitive
lit literally
m masculine
n neuter
nom nominative

obj object
pl plural
poss possessive
pp past participle
prep preposition
pres present
pret preterite
pret-pres preterite-present
pron pronoun
refl reflexive
rel relative
s singular
st strong
sub subjunctive
subst substantive
superl superlative
vb verb
wk weak
(Roman numerals refer to verb types)

ā *adv* always 49, 87

āc *m a-stem noun* oak: *as rune name* 77; *nom sg* 80

ān *numeral used as subst* one (person or thing): *g pl* ānra gehwylc: everyone (*lit* each of ones) 60

and *conj* and 4, 11, 12a, 12b, 14, 17, 19, 20a, 20b, 21, 23a, 23b, 24a, 24b, 28, 34, 38, 58, 65, 66, 72, 75, 76, 84, 85, 87 (*italicized references indicate expansion from the Tironian symbol 7*)

anfengys *see* onfeng

anmōd *adj* resolute, courageous: *nom m sg* 4

ansȳn *f i-stem noun* sight, aspect: *g sg* ansȳne 31

ār *f ō-stem noun* help, benefit, kindness: *nom sg* 21

æfre *adv* ever, always 58

æfter *adv* after 69

æghwilc *adj* every: *d sg m* æghwylcum 71

ælc *adj* each, every: *g sg f* ælcre 10

ænig *adj* any: *a sg m* ænigne 44

ærest *adv* first, at first 67

æror *adv* formerly, before, in time 28

æsc *m i-stem noun* ash-tree: *as rune name* 81

ætsomne *adv* together 40

ætwist *f i-stem noun* sustenance, means of survival: *nom sg* 21

æþele *adj* noble: *a sg f* 80

æþeling *m a-stem noun* prince, nobleman: *nom pl* æþelingas 18; *g pl* æþelinga 55, 84; *a pl* æþelingas 49

bæþ *n a-stem noun* bath: *a sg* ganotes bæþ: sea 79; fisces beþ: sea 46

bearn *n a-stem noun* child, son: *d pl* bearnum 27, 77

bēon *anom vb* to be: *3rd sg pres ind* is 6; byþ 1, 4, 7, 10, 13, 16, 19, 21, 25, 27, 29, 32, 35, 38, 51, 55, 59, 63, 71, 74, 77, 84, 85, 87, 90; biþ 45, 48, 49, 52, 58, 81; *3rd sg pret ind* wæs 67

beorc *f ō-stem noun* birch-tree (or perhaps poplar): *as rune name* 51

beorht *adj* bright: *a pl f* beorhte 34

beorhtlīc *adj* bright: *nom sg m* 17

beorn *m a-stem noun* nobleman, prosperous man, warrior, man: *g pl* beorna 43; *d pl* beornum 34

bēorsele *m i-stem noun* mead-hall (*lit* beer-hall): *d sg* bēorsele 40

beran *st vb* IV to bear, produce: *3rd sg pres ind* bereþ 51

betǣcan *wk vb* I to commit, assign: *inf* 62

beþ *see* bæþ

beweorpan *st vb* III to surround: *pp* beworpen 89

biþ *see* bēon

blāc *adj* shining, pale, livid: *nom sg m* 17; *nom sg n* 93

blǣd *m i-stem noun* prosperity: *a sg* blǣd 24; *d pl* blēadum 73

blēadum *see* blǣd

blēd *f ō-stem noun* fruit: *nom pl* blēda 93; *g pl* blēda 51; *a pl* blēda 34

blīþe *adv* happily; *or nom pl m of adj* happy 40

blōd *n a-stem noun* blood: *d sg* blōde 43

blyss *f jō-stem noun* bliss, happiness: *a sg* blysse 24

bold *n a-stem noun* house, building: *d sg* bolde 73

brēgan *wk vb* I to terrify: *3rd pl pres ind* brēgaþ 65

brēnan *wk vb* I (*for* brȳnan *from* brūnian) to make brown, stain: *3rd sg pres ind* brēneð 43

brēost *n a-stem noun* breast, heart: *d pl* brēostan 27

brīce *adj* useful, of benefit: *nom sg m* 76

brīdels *m a-stem noun* bridle: *g sg* brīdles 66

brimhengest *m a-stem noun* ship (*lit* sea-steed): *nom sg* 47, 66

bringan *st vb* III to bring: *3rd sg pres ind* bringeþ 47

brūcan *st vb* II to enjoy, experience, eat, *with gen of dir obj: inf* 73; *3rd sg pres ind* brūceþ 22, 87

burh *f a them noun* fortified dwelling: *g pl* byrga 24

būtan *prep with a* without 52

byrga *see* burh

byrnan *st vb* III to burn: *3rd sg pres ind* byrneþ 17

byþ *see* bēon

can *see* cunnan

ċēn *m a-stem noun?* torch: *as rune name* 16

cēosan *st vb* II to choose: *inf* 92

cōlian *wk vb* II to cool, grow cold: *inf* 92

corn *n a-stem noun* grain: *g pl* corna 25

cunnan *pret-pres vb* to know: *3rd sg pres ind* can 22

cūþ *adj* known: *nom sg m* 16

cwic *adj used as subst* the living, the quick: *g pl m* cwicera 16

cyning *m a-stem noun* king: *nom sg* 33

dæg *m a-stem noun* day: *as rune name* 74

dǣlan *wk vb* I to share, deal, or dole out: *inf* 2

dēor *n a-stem noun* wild animal, beast: *nom sg* 5

dēore *adj* dear, beloved, precious: *nom sg m* 74; *also mutated nom sg m* dȳre 81

dōm *m a-stem noun* judgement, favourable judgement, honour, glory: *g sg* dōmes 3; *d sg* dōme 61

Dryhten *m a-stem noun* lord (whether secular or heavenly): *nom sg* 61; *g sg* Drihtnes 74; *d sg* Drihtne 3

dȳre *see* dēore

ēac *conj* also 24

ēadig *adj* happy, blessed, prosperous, *used as subst* the rich, the 'haves': *d pl m* ēadgum 76

ēadnys *f jō-stem noun* joy: *nom sg* 12

ēafix *m a-stem noun* river-fish: *g pl* ēafixa 87

eall *adj used as pron* all: *d pl* eallum 76

ēar *m a-stem noun?* earth (as grave): *as rune name* 90

eard *m u-stem noun* dwelling, home: *a sg* 41, 88

earm *adj* poor, wretched: *a sg n* earme 62; *used as subst* the poor, the have-nots: *d pl m* earmum 76

Ēast-Dene *m i-stem noun* East-Dane: *d pl* Ēast-Denum 67

efne *adv* even: efne swā ðēah nonetheless (*lit* even so though) 51

egle *adj* loathsome: *nom sg m* 90

eh *n a-stem noun* horse, steed: *as rune name* 55

elde *m i-stem pl noun* men: *g pl* elda 77; *d pl* eldum 81 ēoh *m a-stem noun* yew: *as rune name* 35

eolhx-secg *m a-stem noun* elk-sedge (ie, some kind of sharp-bladed marsh-grass), *a compound made up of* secg (sedge) *and the rune name* eolhx (elk?) 41

eorl *m a-stem noun* nobleman, man: *g pl* eorla 12, 84, 90; *d pl* eorlum 55

eorþe *f n-stem noun* earth, land: *d sg* eorþan 62, 77

ēst *adv* eastward, to the east 68

ēþel *m n-stem noun* one's own property, inherited land or estate, home: *as rune name* 71; *d sg* ēþle 37

fæger *adj* fair, fine, beautiful: *nom sg m* 31, 85; *a sg m* fægerne 88

fægere *adv* fairly 53

færeld *m and n a-stem noun* journey, course: *d sg* færylde 49; *d sg* færelde 86

fæst *adj* firm, fast: *nom sg n* 36

fæstlīc *adj* firm, fast, reliable: *nom sg m* 86

fæstlīce *adv* firmly, irresistibly 91

fandian *wk vb* II to test, find out: *3rd sg pres ind* fandaþ 79

felafrēcne *adj* very fierce, savage: *nom sg n* 5

fenn *n ja-stem noun* fen, marsh: *d sg* fenne 41

feoh *n a-stem noun* wealth, portable property (*from the root-meaning* cattle): *as rune name* 1

feohtan *st vb* III to fight, attack: *inf* 83; *3rd sg pres ind* feohteþ 5

feran *wk vb* I to fare, travel: *3rd sg pres ind* fereþ 78

ferian *wk vb* II to convey, row: *3rd sg pres ind* feriaþ 46

fīras *m ja-stem pl noun* men: *nom pl* 83; *g pl* fīra 1

fisc *m a-stem noun* fish: *g sg* fisces 46

flǣsc *n i-stem noun* flesh, meat, body: *nom sg* 91; *g sg* flǣsces 78; *a sg* flǣsc 62

flōr *m a-stem noun* floor: *a sg* flōr 31

fōdor *n a-stem noun* food, nourishment: *nom sg* 78; *g sg* fōdres 88

folde *f n-stem noun* earth: *d sg* foldan 88

for *prep with a* before, in the presence or company of 3, 55

forst *m a-stem noun* frost: *d sg* forste 31

forðām *conj* because 61

frōfur *f ō-stem noun* benefit, comfort, remedy: *nom sg* 1, 11, 58

fȳr *n a-stem noun* fire: *g sg* fȳres 36; *d sg* fȳre 16

fyrdgeatwe *f wō-stem noun* army gear: *g pl* fyrdgeatewa 86

ganot *m a-stem noun* gannet: *g sg* ganotes 79

gārsecg *m a-stem noun* sea (*lit* spear-man, hence the sea in its destructive aspect, ie, stormy sea): *nom sg* 79

gebedda *f n-stem noun* bed-fellow, consort, bride: *d sg* gebeddan 93

gedēð *see* gedōn

gedōn *anom vb* to do, put, lay: *3rd sg pres ind* gedēð 44

gedrēosaþ *st vb* II to fall, fail: *3rd pl pres ind* gedrēosaþ 93

gehwā *pron* each one, every, all: *g sg m* gehwæs 84; *d sg m* gehwām 12, 16, 20

gehwæþere *adv* yet, nonetheless: gehwæþre 28

gehwylc *pron* each one, every one, any one, all: *nom sg m* 2, 60; *a sg m* gehwylcne 43; *d sg m* gehwylcum 1, 7, 13, gehwylcun 9, 90

geléodan *st vb* II to grow, spring: *pp* geloden 54

gelīc *adj* alike, like to: *nom sg n* superl gelīcust 30

gelōme *adv* often 78

geniht *n i-stem noun* fulness, sufficiency, contentment: *a sg* geniht 24

genip *n i-stem noun* cloud, darkness, night-cloud: *a pl* genipu 50

gēr *n a-stem noun* fruitful year, harvest: *as rune name* 32

gerysne *n ja-stem noun* what is fitting, proper: *g pl* gerysena 72

gesēon *st vb* v to see, behold; *pp* gesewen 68

gesewen *see* gesēon

geswīcan *st vb* I to fail, be broken: *3rd pl pres ind* geswīcaþ 94

getenge *adj* near to, pressing upon, reaching up to touch: *nom sg fem* getenge 54

geþūht *see* geþyncan

geþyncan *wk vb* I to seem: *pp* geþūht 63

gewītan *st vb* I to depart, vanish, die: *3rd pl pres ind* gewītaþ 94; *3rd sg pret ind* gewāt 69

geworuht *see* gewyrcan

gewyrcan *wk vb* I to make, work, build: *pp* geworuht 31

gif *conj* if, provided that 3, 28, 64, 72

gimm *m a-stem noun* gem, jewel: *d pl* gimmum 30

glæshlūttur *adj* clear as glass: *nom sg n* 30

gleng *f ō-stem noun* ornament, grace: *nom sg* 19

glisnian *wk vb* II to glisten, glitter: *3rd sg pres ind* glisnaþ 30

God *m a-stem noun* God: *nom sg* 32

grimme *adv* grimly, grievously 42

guma *m n-stem noun* warrior, man: *g pl* gumena 19, 32

gyfu *f ō-stem noun* gift, giving, generosity: *as rune name* 19

gȳman *wk vb* I to heed, respond to, with *g of dir obj*: *3rd sg pres ind* gȳmeð 66

habban *wk vb* III to have, keep: *3rd sg pres sub* hæbbe 80; *3rd sg pres ind* hæfþ 23, 41; *3rd sg pres ind* hafaþ 88

hæbbe *see* habban

hæfþ *see* habban

hægl *m a-stem noun* hail, sleet: *as rune name* 25

hǣl *n athem noun* healing, salvation: *d sg* hǣle 28

hæle(þ) *m athem noun* warrior: *a sg* hæle 70; *nom pl* hæleþas 56

hafaþ *see* habban

hālig *adj* holy: *nom sg m* 33

hē, hēo, hit *3rd person pron* he, she, it: *nom sg m* hē 3, 68, 72, 89; *g sg m* his 28, 59; *d sg m* him 23 (refl), 44, 56, 83; *a sg m* hine 46; *nom pl m* hī 18, 28, 46, 65; *d pl m* him 9; *a pl m* hī 47, 65; *nom sg f* hī (Kentish for hīo?) 27; *nom sg n* hit 25, 26b; *a sg n* hit 26a, hyt 2. *See also the poss* sīn

hēah *adj* high, lofty: *nom sg f* 53

healdan *st vb* VII to hold, keep, maintain: *3rd sg pres ind* healdeð 48; *3rd sg pres ind* hylt 82

heard *adj* hard, firm: *nom sg n* 36

hearding *m a-stem noun* warrior:
nom pl heardingas 70

helm *m a-stem noun* crown, over-
shadowing foliage: *d sg* helme 53

help *f ō-stem noun* help: *d sg* helpe
28

heofon *m a-stem noun* heaven: *g sg*
heofones 25, 33

herenys *f jō-stem noun* praise: *nom*
sg 19

hī *see* hē

hiht *m i-stem noun* joy, hope: *nom*
sg 32; *d sg* hihte 45

him *see* hē

hine *see* hē

his *see* hē

hit *see* hē

hlehter *m a-stem noun* laughter,
amusement: *nom sg* 38

hlēotan *st vb* II to obtain (by lot):
inf 3

hlystan *wk vb* I to listen, pay heed,
with g of dir obj: *3rd pl pres ind*
hlystaþ 28

hōf *m a-stem noun* hoof: *d pl* hōfum
56

horn *m a-stem noun* horn: *d pl* hornum 5

hors *n a-stem noun* horse, charger:
nom sg 56

hrāw *m or n a-stem noun* dead body:
nom sg 92

hrūse *f n-stem noun* earth: *d sg* hrūsan 36; *a sg* hrūsan 33, 92

hrystan *wk vb* I to decorate, adorn:
pp hrysted 53

hwæþer *conj* whether 80

hweorfan *st vb* III to turn, go, whirl:
3rd sg pres ind hwyrft 25

hwīt *adj* white: *nom sg m superl*
hwītust 25

hwyrft *see* hweorfan

hylt *see* healdan

hyrde *m ja-stem noun* guardian,
keeper: *nom sg* 36

hyt *see* hē

Īar *m a-stem noun?* some kind of
river-fish, eel?: *as rune name* 87

Ing *m a-stem noun?* the culture-hero
Ing: *as rune name* 67

inne *adv* inside 18

is *see* bēon

īs *n a-stem noun* ice: *as rune name*
29

lǣtan *st vb* VII to make, cause to: *3rd*
sg pres ind lǣteþ 32

lagu *m u-stem noun* water, sea: *as*
rune name 63

land *n a-stem noun* land, earth: *d sg*
lande 47

langsum *adj* long-lasting, interminable: *nom sg m* 63

lēaf *n a-stem noun* leaf: *d pl* lēafum
54

lēas *adj* without, void of, *with g* 21,
51

lēod *m a-stem noun* man: *d pl*
lēodum 63

lēof *adj* beloved, cherished: *nom sg*
m 59

leofaþ *see* libban

lēoht *n a-stem noun* light: *nom sg*
75

libban *wk vb* III to live: *3rd sg pres*
ind leofaþ 89

lyft *m or fem i-stem noun* sky, the air
above, *hence* height: *d sg* lyfte 25,
54

lȳt *n indecl adj used as subst with g*
little 22

mægenheard *adj* powerful: *d sg m*
mægenheardum 15

mǣre *adj* famous, glorious, notorious: *nom sg m* 6; *nom sg n* 75

māga *m n-stem noun* relative, kinsman: *d pl* māgan 59

man(n) *m athem noun* man: *as rune name* 59; *d sg* men 71; *g pl* manna 2, 9; *d pl* mannum 74

mearh *m a-stem noun* horse: *d sg* mēare 15

Metod *m a-stem noun* God, as Creator: *g sg* Metodes 75

micel *adj* much, great: *adverbial d pl* miclun, freely 2

mid *prep* with, among 5, 9, 67

mīlpæþ *m a-stem noun* road measured in miles, hence long road: *a pl* mīlpaþas 15

mōdig *adj* brave, bold, high-spirited: *nom sg m* 6

monig *adj* many: *nom pl m* monige 83

mōrstapa *m n-stem noun* moorstalker: *nom sg* 6

mōtan *pret-pres* VI to be allowed to, may: *3rd sg pres ind* mōt 72

myrgþ *f ō-stem noun* mirth, joy, rejoicing: *nom sg* 75; *d sg* myrgþe 59

naca *m n-stem noun* ship, vessel: *d sg* nacan 64

nǣfre *adv* never 50

ne *adv* not 66

-ne *gen sg inflectional ending see* wyn

nearu *adj* oppressive (*lit* narrow): *nom sg fem* 27

nemnan *wk vb* I to name, call: *3rd pl pret ind* nemdun 70

nēþun *wk vb* I to venture out: *inf* 64

niht *f athem noun* night: *g pl* nihta 50

niþ(þ)as *m a-stem pl noun* men: *g pl* niþa 27

nȳd *f i-stem noun* need, hardship, constraint: *as rune name* 27

of *prep with d* out of, from 25

ofer *prep with a* over (*denoting motion in a direction across*) 15, 46, 50, 69, 79

oferceald *adj* extremely cold: *nom sg n* 29

oferhēah *adj* extremely tall: *nom sg m* 81

oferhyrned *adj* exceedingly horned, having huge horns: *nom sg m* 4

oferlēof *adj* exceedingly loved, very dear: *nom sg m* 71

oft *adv* often 27; *superl* oftust 17, 41, oftast 73

on *prep with d* on, in, by, with, against 13, 16, 27, 37, 40, 41, 42, 45, 49, 52, 53, 57, 59, 64, 73, 77, 82, 83, 85, 86, 88; *also in postposition with* ðǣr, therein, thereon 72

onfeng *m a-stem noun* grasping, laying hold of: *nom sg* 44; *g sg* anfengys 8

onginnan *st vb* III to begin: *3rd sg pres ind* onginneþ 91

onufan *prep with dat* upon, on top of 14

ordfruma *m n-stem noun* source, origin: *nom sg* 10

ōs *noun* (*gender and declension unknown*) mouth: *as rune name* 10

oþ *conj* until 47, 68

ōþer *indef pron used as subst* other: *g pl* ōþra 21; *d pl* ōðrum 60 peorð *noun (gender and declension unknown)* a table-game, perhaps chess?: *as rune name* 38

plega *m a-stem noun* play, recreation: *nom sg* 38

rād *f ō-stem noun* riding: *as rune name* 13

ran *see* rinnan

recyd *n a-stem noun* hall, building: *d sg* recyde 13

restan *wk vb* I to rest, sit at ease: *3rd sg pres ind* resteð 9; *3rd pl pres ind* restaþ 18

rēþe *adj* fierce: *nom sg m* 8

riht *n a-stem noun* what is right, lawful: *g sg* rihtes 72

rihte *adv* rightly, as it should 82

rinc *m a-stem noun* man, warrior: *g pl* rinca 13

rinnan *st vb* III to run: *3rd sg pret ind* ran 69

sǣ̅ȳþ *f jō-stem noun* sea-wave, sea-billow: *nom pl* sǣ̅ȳþa 65

sār *n a-stem noun* soreness, pain: *g sg* sāres 23

sceal *see* sculan

scearp *adj* sharp: *nom sg m* 7

sculan *pret-pres vb* IV to be obliged to, must: *3rd sg pres ind* sceal 2, 60; *3rd pl pres ind* sculun 64

scūr *f ō-stem noun* shower, gust: *nom pl* scūra 26

se, sēo, þæt *def art, dem and rel pron* the, that, that one, who: *nom sg m* se 66; *a sg m* ðone 70; *d sg m* ðām 14; *nom sg n* þæt 6; *acc sg n* þæt 62; *nom m sg of the rel indecl particle* ðe 9, 14, 21, 22, 44. Note that þæt always appears in the contracted form þ̵

secg *m or n a-stem noun* sedge: *appears compounded with the rune name* eolhx 41

secg *m a-stem noun* warrior man: *d pl* secgun 68

sēfte *adj* soft, easy: *nom sg f* 14

sēmann *m athem noun* seaman, seafarer: *d pl* sēmannum 45

sigel *n a-stem noun?* sun: *as rune name* 45

sīn *3rd person refl poss adj* his, hers, its *d sg m* sīne 61

sittan *st vb* V to sit, bestride: *3rd sg pres ind* sitteþ 14; *3rd pl pres ind* sittaþ 39

siððan *adv* afterwards, later, then, 68; syððan 26

slidor *adj* slippery: *nom sg n* 29

sond *f i-stem noun* sending, person or thing sent: *nom sg* 74

sorg *f ō-stem noun* sorrow: *g sg* sorge 23

sprǣc *f jō-stem noun* speech, utterance, discussion: *g sg* sprǣce 10; *a sg* sprǣce 57

staþul *m a-stem noun* base, fixed position: *d sg* staþule 82

stede *m i-stem noun* place, ground: *nom sg* 82

stīþ *adj* stiff, strong: *nom sg m* 82

sum *pron* a certain, one of, a kind of 48, 86

swā *adv* so, thus: *used in* efne swā ðēah, nonetheless (*lit* even so though) 51

swīcan *st vb* I *with d of dir obj*, to fail, break faith with, betray: *inf* 60; *3rd sg pres ind* swīceþ 50

swīþhwæt *adj* very strenuous: *nom sg f* 14

swȳþe *adv* very, exceedingly 65

sylf *pron* self: *nom sg masc refl with d* sylfa 23

syllan *wk vb* I to give, bring forth for: *inf* 33

symble *adv* always 38, 45

syððan *see* siððan

tācn *n a-stem noun* token, guiding sign: *g pl* tācna 48

tān *m a-stem noun* shoot, sprout: *a pl* tānas 52

tealt *adj* tilting, tossing: *d sg m* tealtum 64

telga *m n-stem noun* branch, bough: *d pl* telgum 52

Tir *m a-stem noun?* the name of a guiding planet, star, or constellation named after the god Tiw: *as rune name* 48

tō *prep with d* to, towards, into, for, as 26, 28 (*twice*), 47, 93

tōhiht *masc i-stem noun* hope, glad expectation, delight: *nom sg* 12, 75

trēow *n a-stem noun* tree: *nom sg* 35

trēow *f wō-stem noun* truth, faith: *a sg* trēowe 80; *a pl* trȳwa 48

trȳwa *see* trēow

tūddor *n a-stem noun* fruit, progeny, hence seed: *a sg* tūdder 52

ðǣr *adv* there, where 18, 56, 72, 89; ðār 39; *in combination with* on, therein, thereon 72

þæt *see* se

ðām *see* se

ðe *see* se

ðēah *adv* yet, though, nonetheless 2, 27, 51, 87; þēah 60; ðēah *conj* although 83

ðearfa *adj used as subst* poor or needy person: *d pl* ðearfum 34

ðearle *adv* extremely 7

ðegn *m a-stem noun* thane, person of rank (*hence a complimentary poetic term for* man): *g pl* ðegna 7

ðon *see* ðonn

þone *see* se

ðonn *conj* when: ðon 32; ðonn 46, 91

ðorn *m a-stem noun* thorn: *as rune name* 7

ðus *adv* thus 70

underwreþþan *wk vb* I to support: *pp* underwreþyd 37

ungemet *adj used adverbially* immeasurably: *d pl* ungemetun 8; ungemetum 29

unsmēþe *adj* unsmooth, rough: *nom sg n* 35

unstylle *adj* restless: *d pl m* unstyllum 58

ūr *m a-stem noun* aurochs, extinct wild ox: *as rune name* 4

ūtan *adv* on the outside 35

wǣg *m a-stem noun* wave: *a sg* wǣg 69

wǣn *m a-stem noun* waggon, chariot: *nom sg* 69

wæs *see* bēon

wæter *n a-stem noun* water: *d sg* wætere 26, wature 42, wætre 89

wature *see* wæter

wēa *m n-stem noun* woe: *g pl* wēana 22

wealcan *st vb* VII to toss, roll: *3rd pl pres ind* wealcaþ 26

wel *adv* well 48

weleg *adj* wealthy, prosperous: *nom pl m* welege 57

weorþan *st vb* III to become, be
transformed into: *3rd sg pres ind*
weorþeþ 26, 27

wēr *f ō-stem noun* treaty, covenant:
nom pl wēra 94

wexan *st vb* VII to wax, grow: *3rd sg*
pres ind wexeð 42

wicg *n ja-stem noun* horse: *d sg*
wicge 85; *d pl* wicgum 57

wiga *m n-stem noun* warrior, man:
nom pl wigan 39

willan *anom vb* to wish, desire, in-
tend, purpose: *3rd sg pres ind* wile
3; *3rd sg pres ind* wyle 61

wind *m a-stem noun* wind: *g sg*
windes 26

wīsdōm *m a-stem noun* wisdom: *g*
sg wīsdōmes 11

wita *m n-stem noun* wise man,
counsellor: *g pl* witena 11

wiþ *prep with acc* towards, with 49

wlanc *adj* proud, high-spirited: *nom*
sg 56; *dat pl?* wlancum 39

wlitig *adj* beautiful: *nom sg f* 52

wrǣcna *see* wrecca

wraþu *f ō-stem noun* prop, support:
nom sg 11, 20

wrecca *m n-stem noun* wretch,
homeless or dispossessed person: *g*
pl wrǣcna 20

wrixlan *wk vb* I to exchange: *3rd pl*
pres ind wrixlaþ 57

wuht *n i-stem noun* creature, being:
nom sg 6

wundian *wk vb* II to wound: *3rd sg*
pres ind wundaþ 42

wyle *see* willan

wyn(n) *f jō-stem noun* joy, pleasure, delight: *nom sg* wyn 55, 85; *g*
sg as inflected rune name wynne
22; *nom pl* wynna 94; *d pl* wynan
37; *d pl* wynnum 89

wyrtrum *m a-stem noun* root: *d pl*
wyrtrumun 37

wyrþmynd *f ō-stem noun* honour:
nom sg 85

wyrþscype *m i-stem noun* worship,
honour: *nom sg* 20

yfyl *adj* painful *nom sg m* 8

ymb *prep with d* about, concerning:
in postposition governing him 56

ȳr *m or n noun of unknown declension* yew-wood bow?: *as rune name*
84

Appendixes
Bibliography

Appendix A
The Cynewulfian Signatures

THE FATES OF THE APOSTLES, LINES 96–106
THE VERCELLI BOOK, FOLIO 54r

Hēr mæg findan   fōreþances glēaw,
se ðe hine lysteð   lēoð giddunga,
hwā þas fitte fēgde. · ᚠ· þær on ende standeþ,
eorlas pæs on eorðan brūcaþ;   ne mōton hīe āwā ætsomne,
woruldwunigende. · ᚹ· sceal gedrēosan;
· ᚢ· on ēðle   æfter tōhrēosan;
læne līces frætewa,   efne swā · ᛚ· tōglīdeð.
þonne · ᚳ· ond · ᛁ·   cræftes nēotað
nihtes nearowe,   on him · ᚾ · līgeð,
cyninges þēodom.   Nū ðu cunnon miht
hwā on þām wordum wæs   werum oncȳðig.

(Here anyone who takes pleasure in songs, if he is sharp of mind, may discover
who composed these verses. There at the end stands *feoh* (wealth), which
nobles enjoy on earth; but they cannot have it forever, dwelling in this world.
Wyn (joy) must pass away; then those things accounted *ūr* (ours) on our own
land, the transitory adornments of the body, must perish, even as *lagu*
(water) glides away. When *cēn* (torch?) and *ȳr* (bow?) perform their duty in
the confines of the night, *nȳd* (necessity), the service of the king, lies upon
them. Now you may know who was made known to men in these words.)

ELENE, LINES 1256–71
THE VERCELLI BOOK, FOLIO 133r

      Ā wæs secg oð ðæt
cnyssed cearwelmum, ᚺ · drūsende,
þēah he on medohealle māðmas þege,
æplede gold. · ᚻ· gnornode
· ᛏ · gefēra, nearusorge drēah,
enge rūne, þær him ·ᛗ· fore
mīlpaðas mæt, mōdig þrægde
wīrum gewlenced. · ᛇ· is geswiðrad,
gomen æfter gēarum; gēogoð is gecyrred,
ald onmēdla. · ᚾ· wæs gēara
gēogoð hādes glǣm. Nū synt gēardagas
æfter fyrstmearce forð gewitene,
līfwynne geliden, swā · ᚱ· tōglīdeð,
flōdas gefȳsde. · ᚠ· ǣghwām bið
lǣne under lyfte; landes frætwe
gewītaþ under wolcnum winde gelīccost.

(Until then [when he learned the story of St Helena's discovery of the Cross] the man was always buffeted by sorrow-surges, like a failing *ċēn* (torch), although he received treasures of apple-shaped gold in the meadhall. *Ȳr* (bow?) lamented, the companion of *nyd* (need), endured oppressive misery, constraining secrets [or, if *rūne* can mean *rūnstæf*, the constraining rune, referring to *nȳd*], even where before him *eh* (the horse) measured the mile-long roads, the proud one raced in its filigreed trappings. *Wyn* (joy) is diminished, pleasure with the passage of years; youth is changed, the pride of former days. Once the splendour of youth was *ūr* (ours). Now the old days are gone in the fullness of time, our life's joys departed as *lagu* (water) glides away, the hastening streams. For all men under heaven *feoh* (wealth) is fleeting; the adornments of earth vanish like wind under the clouds.)

CHRIST II, LINES 793–814
THE EXETER BOOK, FOLIO 19v

            Ic þæs brōgan sceal
gesēon synwræce,   þæs þe ic sōð talge,
þær monig beoð   on gemōt læded
fōre onsȳne ēces dēman.
þonne · ᚳ · cwacað, gehȳreð cyning mæðlan,
rodera ryhtend,   sprecan rēþe word
þām þe him ǣr in worulde wāce hȳdron,
þendan · ᚢ · ond · ᚾ · ȳþast meahtan
frōfre findan. þær sceal forht monig
on þam wongstede wērig bīdan
hwæt him æfter dǣdum dēman wille
wrāþra wīta. Biþ se · ᚹ · scæcen
eorþan frætwa. · ᚢ · wæs longe
· ᚱ · flōdum bilocen, līfwynna dǣl,
· ᚠ · on foldan. þonne frætwe sculon
byrnan on bǣle; blāc rāsetteð
recen rēada lēg,   rēþe scrīþeð
geond woruld wīde. Wongas hrēosað,
burgstede berstað. Brond bið on tyhte,
ǣleð ealdgestrēon unmurnlice,
gǣsta gīfrast, þæt gēo guman hēoldan,
þenden him on eorþan onmēdla wæs.

(I shall behold the terror of the retribution for sin, for I believe it true, when many shall be brought in a host into the presence of the eternal Judge. Then *ćēn* (torch?) will tremble, will hear the King, the Ruler of heaven, speak, pronounce stern words to those who obeyed him negligently before in this world, when *ȳr* (bow?) and *nȳd* (need) could very easily find comfort. There in that place must many a weary one await in terror what harsh punishment he intends to adjudge them according to their deeds. *Wyn* (joy) in earthly treasures will have gone. For a long time *ūr* (our possessions), our share of life's joys, were surrounded by *lagu-flōdum* (flowing streams of water), our *feoh* (wealth) upon this earth. Then such adornments must burn in the funereal holocaust; bright and swift, the red flame will rage, angrily spread far and wide through the world. The meadows will perish, the fortified dwellings will burst apart. Fire will be on the move; that greediest of enemies will burn without compunction all the ancestral heritage that men once possessed, while earth's glory was theirs.)

JULIANA, LINES 699–711
THE EXETER BOOK, FOLIO 76r

          Mīn sceal of līce
sāwul on sīðfæt,   nāt ic sylfa hwider,
eardes uncȳðgu;   of sceal ic þissum,
sēcan ōþerne   ǣrgewyrhtum,
gongan ïudǣdum.   Gēomor hweorfeð
·ᚻ·ᚻ· ond ·ᛏ·   Cyning biþ rēþe,
sigora syllend,   þonne synnum fāh
·ᛗ·ᚹ· ond ·ᚢ·   acle bīdað
hwæt him æfter dǣdum   dēman wille
līfes to lēane.   ·ᛚ·ᚠ· beofað,
seomað sorgcearig.   Sār eal gemon,
synna wunde,   þe ic sīþ oþþe ǣr
geworhte in worulde.

(My soul must travel out of my body, I know not where, to the undiscovered country; from here I must go to seek another dwellingplace according to my former works, journey where my earlier deeds take me. Sadly, *ćēn* (torch?), *ȳr* (bow?), and *nȳd* (need?) will depart. The King will be stern, the giver of victories, when, stained with sins, *eh* (horse?), *wyn* (joy?), and *ūr* (our?) await in terror what he intends to adjudge to them according to their deeds, as a reward for the lives they have lived. *Lagu-feoh* (water-wealth? ie, the earth encompassed by the sea?) will tremble, lie troubled. I shall remember all the injury to my soul, the wounds of sin, that I persisted in inflicting while in this world.)

Appendix B
The Norse Rune Poems

THE *ABECEDARIUM NORDMANNICUM*
(based on the facsimile in René Derolez, *Runica Manuscripta*, p 78)

Text

ᚠ(feu) forman;
ᚢ(ur) after;
ᚦ(thuris) thritten stabu;
ᚩ(os) is themo oboro;
ᚱ(rat) endos uuritan;
ᚲ(chaon) thanne cliuot.

ᚼ(hagal) ᚾ(naut) habet,
ᛁ(is), ᛅ(ar), ᛌendi (sol).

ᛏ(tiu), ᛒ(brica) ᛘendi (man) midi,

ᛚ(lago) the leohto;
ᛣ(yr) al bihabet.

Translation

ᚠ(wealth) first;
ᚢ(aurochs) after;
ᚦ(giant) the third letter;
ᚩ(pagan god) is following it;
ᚱ(riding) write at the end;
ᚲ(ulcer) cleaves next.

ᚼ(hail) has ᚾ(need),
ᛁ(ice), ᛅ(harvest), and ᛌ(sun).

ᛏ(Tiw) [has] ᛒ(birch) and ᛘ(man) in the middle,

ᛚ(water) the clear;
ᛣ(yew) concludes the whole.

5

10

THE NORWEGIAN *RUNE POEM*

(based on the edition by Ludvig Wimmer, *Die Runenschrift*, pp 276ff, with a few italicized emendations suggested by Bruce Dickins, *Runic Poems*, pp 24ff)

Text

I

ᚠ(fé) vældr frǽnda róge;

     fǿðesk ulfr í skóge.

Translation

I

ᚠ(wealth) causes trouble among
                          relatives;
     the wolf lives in the forest.

II
ᚢ (úr) er af illu jarne;
opt løypr ræinn á hjarne.

II
ᚢ(slag) comes from poor iron;
often the reindeer runs over the
hard-frozen snow.

III
ᚦ (þurs) vældr kvenna kvillu;
kátr værðr fár af illu.

III
ᚦ(giant) causes illness in women;   5
few rejoice at bad luck.

IV
ᚬ (óss) er flestra færða

fǫr, en skalpr er sværða.

IV
ᚬ(river mouth) is the way of most
                          journeys;
but a scabbard is of swords.

V
ᚱ (ræið) kvæða rossom væsta;
Reginn sló sværðet bæzta.

V
ᚱ(riding) is said to be worst for horses;
Regin forged the best sword.   1c

VI
ᚲ (kaun) er barna bǫlvan;
bǫl gørver nán fǫlvan.

VI
ᚲ(ulcer) is fatal to children;
death makes a corpse pale.

VII
ᚼ (hagall) er kaldastr korna;
Kristr skóp hæimenn forna.

VII
ᚼ(hail) is the coldest of grains;
Christ created the primaeval wórld.

VIII
ᚾ (nauðr) gerer næppa koste;
nøktan kælr í froste.

VIII
ᚾ(need) leaves little choice;   15
the naked man is chilled by the frost.

IX
ᛁ (ís) kǫllum brú bræiða;
blindan þarf at læiða.

IX
ᛁ (ice) we call the broad bridge;
the blind man must be led.

X
ᛅ (ár) er gumna góðe;
get ek at ǫrr var Fróðe.

X
ᛅ(harvest) is a boon to men;
I say that Frothi was liberal.   20

XI
ᛋ (sól) er landa ljóme;
lúti ek helgum dóme.

XI
ᛋ (sun) is the light of the world;
I bow before the divine judgement.

<table>
<tr><td>

XII
ᛏ(Týr) er æinendr ása;

opt værðr smiðr at blása.

</td><td>

XII
ᛏ(Tiw) is the one-handed member of
        the Æsir;
often has the smith to blow.

</td></tr>
</table>

XIII ᛒ(bjarkan) er laufgrønstr líma; Loki bar *flærða* tíma.	XIII ᛒ(birch) is the greenest-leaved of 25 branches; Loki was lucky in his deception.
XIV ᛉ(maðr) er moldar auki; mikil er græip á hauki.	XIV ᛉ(man) is an augmentation of the dust; great is the claw of the hawk.
XV ᛚ(lǫgr) er, er fællr ór fjalle foss; en gull ero nosser.	XV ᛚ(water) is where a cascade falls from a mountain-side; but ornaments are made of gold. 30
XVI ᛦ(ýr) er vetrgrønstr víða; vant er, er brennr, at svíða.	XVI ᛦ(yew) is the greenest of trees in winter; when it burns, it sputters.

THE ICELANDIC RUNE POEM
(based on the edition by Ludvig Wimmer, *Die Runenschrift*, pp 282ff, with an
italicized emendation in line 17 suggested by Bruce Dickins, *Runic Poems*,
pp 28ff.)

Text	*Translation*
	I

ᚠ(fé) er frænda róg
ok flæðar viti
ok grafseiðs gata.
 	
  arum. fylkir.
	ᚠ(wealth) is trouble among relatives
	and fire of the sea
	and path of the serpent.
	
	  'gold.' king (beginning with *f*).

II

ᚢ(úr) er skýja grátr
ok skara þverrir
ok hirðis hatr.

umbre [for imbre]. vísi.

II

ᚢ(drizzle) is weeping of the clouds
and destruction of the hay-harvest   5
and abhorrence of the herdsman.

'shower.' king (beginning with u).

III

Þ(þurs) er kvenna kvöl
ok kletta búi
ok varðrúnar verr.

saturnus. þengill.

III

Þ(giant) is illness of women
and cliff-dweller
and husband of Varthrun
                        (a giantess).

'Saturn.' king (beginning with th).

IV

ᚬ(óss) er aldingautr
ok ásgarðs jöfurr
ok valhallar vísi.

jupiter. oddviti.

IV

ᚬ(god) is ancient creator   10
and king of Asgard
and lord of Valhalla.

'Jupiter.' king (beginning with o).

V

ᚱ(reið) er sitjandi sæla
ok snúðig ferð
ok jórs erfiði.

iter. ræsir.

V

ᚱ(riding) is joy of the rider
and speedy journey
and labouring of the horse.   15

'journey.' king (beginning with r).

VI

ᚴ(kaun) er barna böl
ok bardaga för
ok holdfúa hús.

flagella. konungr.

VI

ᚴ(ulcer) is fatal to children
and painful spot
and dwelling of putrefaction.

'ulcer.' king (beginning with k).

VII

ᚼ(hagall) er kaldakorn
ok krapadrífa
ok snáka sótt.

grando. hildingr.

VII

ᚼ(hail) is cold grain
and driving sleet   20
and sickness of serpents.

'hail.' king (beginning with h).

VIII

ᚾ (nauð) er þýjar þrá
ok þungr kostr
ok vássamlig verk.

opera. niflungr.

VIII

ᚾ (need) is distress of bond-woman
and state of oppression
and hard labour.

'service.' king (beginning with *n*).

IX

ᛁ (íss) er árbörkr
ok unnar þak
ok feigra manna fár.

glacies. jöfurr.

IX

ᛁ (ice) is bark of rivers   25
and roof of the wave
and destruction for doomed men.

'ice.' king (beginning with *i*).

X

ᚼ (ár) er gumna góði
ok gott sumar
ok algróinn akr.

annus. allvaldr.

X

ᚼ (harvest) is a blessing to men
and good summer
and fully ripe crops.   30

'year.' king (beginning with *a*).

XI

ᛋ (sól) er skýja skjöldr
ok skínandi röðull
ok ísa aldrtregi.

rota. siklingr.

XI

ᛋ (sun) is shield of the sky
and shining ray
and destroyer of the ice.

'sun.' king (beginning with *s*).

XII

ᛏ (Týr) er einhendr áss

ok úlfs leifar
ok hofa hilmir.

mars. tiggi.

XII

ᛏ (Tiw) is the one-handed member of
                              the Æsir
and leavings of the wolf   35
and king of temples.

'Mars.' king (beginning with *t*).

XIII

ᛒ (bjarkan) er laufgat lim
ok lítit tré
ok ungsamligr viðr.

abies. buðlungr.

XIII

ᛒ (birch) is leafy branch
and little tree
and youthful shrub.

'fir-tree.' king (beginning with *b*).

XIV
ᚢ(maðr) er manns gaman
ok moldar auki
ok skipa skreytir.

   homo.   mildingr.

XV
ᛚ(lögr) er vellanda vatn
ok víðr ketill
ok glömmunga grund.

   lacus.   lofðungr.

XVI
ᛦ(ýr) er bendr bogi
ok brotgjarnt járn
ok fífu fárbauti.

   arcus.   ynglingr.

XIV
ᚢ(man) is the joy of man   40
and augmentation of the dust
and adorner of ships.

   'man.'   king (beginning with *m*).

XV
ᛚ(water) is welling stream
and broad geyser
and land of the fish.   45

   'lake.'   king (beginning with *l*).

XVI
ᛦ(yew) is bent bow
and brittle iron
and Farbauti (giant) of the arrow.

   'bow.'   king (beginning with *y*).

Bibliography

EDITIONS OF THE OLD ENGLISH *RUNE POEM*
CITED IN THE TEXT

Arntz, Helmut *Handbuch der Runenkunde* (Halle, 1935) 114–16
Botkine, Leon *La Chanson des Runes* (Havre, 1879)
Dickins, Bruce *Runic and Heroic Poems of the Old Teutonic Peoples* (Cambridge, 1915) 12–23
Dobbie, Elliott Van Kirk *The Anglo Saxon Minor Poems* The Anglo-Saxon Poetic Records VI (New York, 1942)
Ettmüller, L. *Engla and Seaxna Scopas and Boceras* (Leipzig, 1850) 286–9
Grein, C.W.M. and R.P. Wülker *Bibliothek der angelsächsischen Poesie* I (Kassel, 1883) 331–7
Grimm, Wilhelm *Ueber deutsche Runen* (Göttingen, 1821) 217–45
Jones, Frederick George, Jr 'The Old English *Rune Poem*, an Edition' (University of Florida, PhD dissertation, 1967)
Kemble, J.M. 'On Anglo-Saxon Runes' *Archaeologia* 28 (1840) 327–72 (339–45)
Kluge, F. *Angelsächsisches Lesebuch der deutschen Sprache* (Halle, 1888) 38–40
Rieger, M. *Alt-und angelsächsisches Lesebuch* (Giessen, 1861) 136–9
Wülker, R.P. *Kleinere angelsächsische Dichtungen* (Halle, 1882) 37–40

OTHER WORKS CITED IN THE TEXT

Adams, Eleanor N. *Old English Scholarship in England from 1566 to 1800* (New Haven, 1917)
Ælfric see Thorpe
Agrell, Sigurd *Runornas talmystik och dess antika förebild* Skrifter utgivna av Vetenskaps Societeten i Lund VI (Lund, 1927)
– 'Der Ursprung der Runenschrift und die Magie' *Arkiv för nordisk filologi* 43 (1927) 97–109

Aldhelm See Giles, Pitman, and Hamilton

Aristotle See Freese

Arntz, Helmut 'Das Ogom' *Beiträge zur Geschichte der deutschen Sprache und Literatur* 59 (1935) 321–413

– *Handbuch der Runenkunde* Sammlung kurzer Grammatiken germanischer Dialekte B. Ergänzungsreihe Nr. 3 Zweite Auflage (Halle/Saale, 1944) [*Handbuch²*]

– 'Runen und Runennamen' *Anglia* 67/68 (1944) 172–250

Arntz, Helmut and Hans Zeiss *Die einheimischen Runendenkmäler des Festlandes* Gesamtausgabe der älteren Runendenkmäler I (Leipzig, 1939)

ASPR (The Anglo-Saxon Poetic Records) See Krapp and Dobbie

Augustine *Sancti Aurelii Augustini Opera Omnia* PL XXXII–XLVII (see Migne)

Ausonius See Schulze or White

Baehrens, Aemilius *Poetae Latini Minores* V Bibliotheca Scriptorum Graecorum et Romanorum (Leipzig, 1879–83)

Baeksted, Anders 'Begravede Runestene' *Aarbøger för nordisk Oldkyndighed og Historie* (1951), 63–95

– *Islands Runeindskrifter* Bibliotheca Arnamagnaeana II (Copenhagen, 1942)

–*Målrunar og Troldrunar, Runemagiske Studier* Nationalmuseets Skrifter, Arkaeologisk-Historisk Raekke IV (Copenhagen, 1952)

Baesecke, Georg 'Das Abecedarium Nordmannicum' *Runenberichte* I Heft 2–3 (1941) 76–90

– *Vorgeschichte des deutschen Schrifttums* Vor- und Frühgeschichte des deutschen Schrifttums I (Halle/Saale, 1940)

Bald's Leech-Book See under Wright

Balzer, L. *Hällristningar fran Bohuslän* (Göteborg, 1881–1908)

Baugh, Albert C., Kemp Malone, Tucker Brooke, George Sherburn, and Samuel C. Chew *A Literary History of England* (New York, 1948)

Bede's Ecclesiastical History For the original Latin version see Colgrave and Giles; for the Old English translation see Thomas Miller.

Benson, Larry D. 'The Literary Character of Anglo-Saxon Formulaic Poetry' *Publications of the Modern Language Association of America* 81 (1966) 334–41

Bernard, J.H. and R. Atkinson *The Irish Liber Hymnorum* Publications of the Henry Bradshaw Society XIII and XIV (London, 1898)

Bischoff, B. 'Eine Sammelhandschrift Walahfrid Strabos (Cod. Sangall. 878)' Zentralblatt für Bibliothekswesen, Beiheft LXXV: *Aus der Welt des Buches. Festgabe für G. Leyh* (Leipzig, 1950) 30–48

Bliss, A.J. *The Metre of Beowulf* (Oxford, 1967)

Blomfield, Joan 'Runes and the Gothic Alphabet' *Saga-Book of the Viking Society for Northern Research* 12 (1941–2) 177–94, 209–31

Boer, R.C. 'Wanderer und Seefahrer' *Zeitschrift für deutsche Philologie* 35 1–28

Bosworth, Joseph and T. Northcote Toller *An Anglo-Saxon Dictionary* (Oxford, 1898); supplement by T.N. Toller 1921

Brate, E. *Östergötlands runinskrifter* Sveriges runinskrifter II (Stockholm, 1911–15)

Brate, E. and E. Wessén *Södermanlands runinskrifter* Sveriges runinskrifter III (Stockholm, 1924–36)

British Museum, Department of Manuscripts *A Catalogue of the Manuscripts in the Cottonian Library deposited in the British Museum* (Hildesheim; New York: G. Olms, 1974). Reprint of the edition published in London in 1802.

Brodeur, A.G. (trans) *The Prose Edda by Snorri Sturluson* American Scandinavian Foundation, Scandinavian Classics v (New York, 1916)

Brøndsted, Johannes 'Thors fiskeri' *Fra Nationalmuseets Arbejdsmark* (Copenhagen, 1955) 92–104

Bruce-Mitford, R.L.S. *The Sutton Hoo Ship Burial: a Handbook* rev ed (London, 1972)

Bugge, Sophus and Magnus Olsen *Norges Indskrifter med de aeldre Runer. Norges Indeskrifter indtil Reformationen* I (Christiania, 1891–1924) 4 vols. I: *Indledning: Runeskriftens Oprindelse og aeldste Historie*; II–IV: *Textbande*

Caesar See Edwards

Calder, G. *Auraicept na n'éces* The Scholars' Primer (Edinburgh, 1917)

Campbell, Alistair *An Old English Grammar* (Oxford, 1959)

Chadwick, H.M. *The Origin of the English Nation* Archaeological and Ethnographical Series (Cambridge, 1907)

Chambers, R.W., Max Forster, and Robin Flower *The Exeter Book of Old English Poetry* facsimile edition (London, 1933)

Chronicle See Flower

Cicero See Peace

Clarke, D.E.M. (ed) *Hávamál* (Cambridge, 1923)

Cockayne, T.O. *Leechdoms, Wortcunning and Starcraft of Early England* 3 vols (London, 1864–66)

Colgrave, B. and R.A.B. Mynors *Bede's Ecclesiastical History of the English People* (Oxford, 1967)

Columba See Bernard

Commodian See Raby

Cox, R.S. 'The Old English Dicts of Cato: a critical edition' *Anglia* 90 (1972) 1–42

Creed, Robert P. 'A New Approach to the Rhythm of *Beowulf*' *Publications of the Modern Language Association of America* 81 (1966) 23–33

Curtius, Ernst Robert *European Literature and the Latin Middle Ages* Willard Trask (trans) (New York, 1953)

Derolez, René *Runica Manuscripta: The English Tradition* Rijksuniversiteit te Gent Werken uitgegeven door de Faculteit van de Wijsbegeerte en Letteren, Aflevering 118 (Bruges, 1954)

Dickins, Bruce 'Runic Rings and Old English Charms' *Archiv für das Studium der neueren Sprachen* 16 (1935) 252

– 'A System of Transliteration for Old English Runic Inscriptions' *Leeds Studies in English* (1932) 15–19.

Dickins, B. and A.S.C. Ross *The Dream of the Rood* 4th ed (London, 1954)

Diringer, David *The Alphabet* (London, 1948)

Dobbie, Elliott Van Kirk *The Anglo-Saxon Minor Poems* The Anglo-Saxon Poetic Records VI (New York, 1942)

Dreves, Guido M., C. Blume, and H.M. Bannister *Analecta Hymnica Medii Aevi* 55 vols (Leipzig, 1888–1922)

Dumézil, Georges *Les Dieux des Germains* Mythes et Religions XXXVIII (Paris, 1969)

Edda For the *Poetic Edda* see Neckel; for *Hávamál* only see Clarke. For the *Prose Edda* see Holtsmark and the English translation by Brodeur.

Edwards, H.J. (ed and trans) *Julius Caesar's Gallic Wars* Loeb Classical Library (London, 1926)

Egils Saga Skalla-grimmssonar Íslensk fornrit II (Reykjavik, 1933)

Elliott, R.W.V. 'Cynewulf's Runes in *Christ II* and *Elene*' *English Studies* 34 (1953) 49–57

– 'Cynewulf's Runes in *Juliana* and *Fates of the Apostles*' *English Studies* 34 (1953) 193–204

– *Runes, an Introduction* (Manchester, 1959)

– 'The Runes in *The Husband's Message*' *Journal of English and Germanic Philology* 54 (1955) 1–8

– 'Runes, Yews and Magic' *Speculum* 32 (1957) 250–61

Erhardt-Siebold, Erika von *Die lateinischen Rätsel der Angelsachsen* (Heidelberg, 1925)

Eusebius See Hahn

Exeter Book See Chambers and Krapp

Finch, R.G. *The Saga of the Volsungs* Icelandic Texts (London, 1965)

Flower, Robin and Hugh Smith *The Parker Chronicle and Laws* facsimile edition (London, 1941)

Fortunatus See Leo

Freese, J.H. *Aristotle's Rhetorica* (London, 1926)

Friesen, Otto von 'Om runskriftens härkömst' *Språkvet. sällsk. í Uppsala förhandl.* (Uppsala, 1904–6)

– *Rökstenen, runstenen vid Röks kyrka, Lysings härad, Östergötland, läst och tydd* (Stockholm, 1920)

- 'Runes' *The Encyclopaedia Britannica* 14th ed (London, 1929)
Friesen, Otto von, Magnus Olsen, and J. Brøndum-Nielsen *Runorna* Nordisk Kultur vi (Stockholm, 1933)
Giles, J.A. (ed) *Sancti Aldhelmi ex Abbate Malmesburiensi Episcopi Schireburnensis Opera quae extant omnia. Patres Ecclesiae Anglicanae* i (Oxford, 1844)
- *The Complete Works of Venerable Bede* 12 vols (London, 1843–4)
Goldsmith, Margaret 'The Enigma of *The Husband's Message*' *Anglo-Saxon Poetry: Essays in Appreciation for John C. McGalliard* Lewis E. Nicholson and Dolores Warwick Frese (eds) (Notre Dame, 1975) 242–63
Gollancz, Sir Israel (ed) *The Caedmon Manuscript of Anglo-Saxon Biblical Poetry* facsimile edition (Oxford, 1927)
Greenfield, Stanley B. *A Critical History of Old English Literature* (New York, 1965)
Grein, C.W.M. 'Zur Textkritik der angelsächsischen Dichter' *Germania* 10 (1865) 416–29
Grein, C.W.M. and J.J. Köhler *Sprachschatz der angelsächsischen Dichter* Germanische Bibliothek, Abt. i, Reihe iv, Band 4 (Heidelberg, 1912)
Grettis Saga Asmundarsonar Íslensk fornrit vii (Reykjavik, 1936)
Grienberger, Theodor von 'Das angelsächsisches Runengedicht' *Anglia* 45 (1921) 201–20 (N.F. 33)
- 'Die angelsächsischen Runenreihen und die sogenannten Hrabanischen Alphabete' *Arkiv för nordisk filologi* 15 (1899) 1–40
- 'Die germanischen Runennamen i: Die gothischen Buchstabennamen' *Beiträge zur Geschichte der deutschen Sprache und Literatur* 21 (1896) 185–224
Grierson, Philip 'The Purpose of the Sutton Hoo Coins' *Antiquity* 44 (March, 1970) 14–18
Grønbech, Vilhelm *The Culture of the Teutons* 2 vols W. Worster (trans) (London, 1931)
Guinn, Lawrence E. *English Runes and Runic Writing: the Development of the Runes and their Employment* (Ann Arbor, Michigan, 1965)
Hahn, H. 'Die Rätseldichter Tatwin und Eusebius' *Forschungen zur deutschen Geschichte* 26 (Göttingen, 1886) 601–32
Hall, J.R. 'Perspective and Wordplay in the Old English *Rune Poem*' *Neophilologus* 61 (1977) 453–60
Hamilton, N.E.S.A. (ed) *William of Malmesbury's De Gestis Pontificum Anglorum* v Rerum Britannicarum Medii Aevi Scriptores or Chronicles and Memorials of Great Britain and Ireland in the Middle Ages lii (London, 1870)
Hammarström, Magnus 'Om runskriftens härkömst' *Studier i nordisk filologi* xx (Helsingfors, 1930) 1–67
Hauck, Karl Georg 'Herrschaftszeichen eines Wodanistischen Königtums' *Jahrbuch für fränkische Landesforschung* 14 (1954) 9–66

Hávamál See Clarke

Hempl, George 'Hickes's Additions to the Runic Poem' *Modern Philology* 1 (1903) 135–41

– 'The Old English Runes for *a* and *o'* *Modern Language Notes* 11 (1896) 347–52

– 'The Origin of the Runes' *Journal of English and Germanic Philology* 2 (1898) 370–4

Hickes, George *Linguarum Veterum Septentrionalium Thesaurus Grammatico-Criticus et Archaeologicus* (Oxford, 1705)

Hilary of Poitiers See Dreves

Holthausen, F. *Altenglisches etymologisches Wörterbuch* Germanische Bibliotek I, iv, 7 (Heidelberg, 1934)

– 'Zu den altenglischen Rätseln' *Anglia* 35 (1912) 165–77

Holtsmark, Anne and John Helgasen (eds) *Snorri Sturluson's Prose Edda: Gylfaginning og prosa fortellingene av Skalskaparmal* (Copenhagen, 1950)

Horace See Plaistowe

Hwætberht (Eusebius) See Hahn

Jacobsen, Lis 'Rökstudier' *Arkiv för nordisk filologi* 76 (1961) 1–50

Jacobsen, Lis and Erik Moltke *Danmarks Runeindskrifter* 3 vols (Copenhagen, 1941–2)

Jansson, Sven B.F. *The Runes of Sweden* Peter Foote (trans) (Stockholm, 1962)

– *Västermanlands Runinskrifter* Sveriges Runinskrifter XIII (Stockholm, 1964)

Jansson, Sven B.F. and Elias Wessén *Götlands Runinskrifter* Sveriges Runinskrifter XI (Stockholm, 1961)

Jente, R. *Die mythologischen Ausdrücke im altenglischen Wortschatz* Anglistische Forschungen LVI (Heidelberg, 1921)

Jungandreas, W. 'Die germanische Runenreihe und ihre Bedeutung' *Zeitschrift für deutsche Philologie* 60 (1935) 105–21

– 'Zur Runenreihe' *Zeitschrift für deutsche Philologie* 61 (1936) 227–32

Jungner, Hugo and E. Svärdström *Västergötlands Runinskrifter* Sveriges Runinskrifter V (Stockholm, 1940–58)

Junius Manuscript See Gollancz and Krapp

Keller, May Lansfield *The Anglo-Saxon Weapon Names* (Heidelberg, 1906)

Keller, Wolfgang *Angelsächsische Palaeographie. Die Schrift der Angelsachsen mit besonderer Rücksicht auf die Denkmäler in der Volkssprache* 2 vols (Berlin, 1906)

– 'Zum altenglischen Runengedicht' *Anglia* 60 (1936) 141–9 (N.F. 48)

– 'Zur Chronologie der altenglischen Runen' *Anglia* 62 (1938) 24–32 (N.F. 40)

Ker, Neil *Catalogue of Manuscripts Containing Anglo-Saxon* (Oxford, 1957)

Kershaw, Nora *Anglo-Saxon and Norse Poems* (Cambridge, 1922)

Kinander, Ragnar *Smålands Runinskrifter* Sveriges Runinskrifter IV (Stockholm, 1935–61)

Klaeber, F. (ed) *Beowulf and the Fight at Finnsburg* 3rd ed (Boston, 1950)

– 'Die Ing-Verse im angelsächsischen Runengedicht' *Archiv für das Studium der neuren Sprachen und Literatur* 142 (1921) 250–3

– Review of M. Trautmann's *Die altenglischen Rätsel* in *Modern Language Notes* 31 (1916) 426–30

Kock, Ernst A. 'Interpretations and Emendations of Early Old English Texts' *Anglia* 43 (1919) 298–312

Krapp, George Philip (ed) *The Junius Manuscript* The Anglo-Saxon Poetic Records I (New York, 1931)

– *The Vercelli Book* The Anglo-Saxon Poetic Records II (New York, 1932)

Krapp, George Philip and Elliott Van Kirk Dobbie (eds) *The Exeter Book* The Anglo-Saxon Poetic Records III (New York, 1936)

Krappe, A.H. 'Le Char d'Ing' *Revue Germanique* 24 (1933) 23–5

Krause, Wolfgang *Beiträge zur Runenforschung* I–II Schriften der Königsberger Gelehrten Gesellschaft (Halle/Saale, 1932–4)

– 'Die Runen als Begriffszeichen' *Beiträge zur Runenkunde und nordischen Sprachwissenschaft: Festschrift für G. Neckel* Helmut Schlottig (ed) (Leipzig, 1938) 35–53

– *Runeninschriften im älteren Futhark* Schriften der Königsberger Gelehrten Gesellschaft XIII, 4 (Halle/Saale, 1937)

Krause, Wolfgang and H. Jankuhn *Die Runeninschriften im älteren Futhark* Abhandlungen der Akademie der Wissenschaften in Göttingen, Philologische-Historische Klasse Folge III, no. 65 (Göttingen, 1966)

Laistner, L. *Das Rätsel der Sphynx* (Berlin, 1889)

Leo, F. *Monumenta Germaniae Historica, Auctorum Antiquissimorum* IV (Berlin, 1881)

Leyen, F. von der 'Die germanische Runenreihe und ihre Namen' *Zeitschrift des Vereins für Volkskunde* (N.F.) 2 (1930) 170–82

Liestøl, Aslak 'Correspondence in Runes' *Mediaeval Scandinavia* 1 (1968) 17–27

– 'Jeg rister bodruner, jeg rister bjærgruner' *Skalk* (Århus, 1964) no. 5, 18–27

– 'Runer frå Bryggen' *Viking: Tidsskrift for nørron arkeologi* 27 (Oslo, 1964) 5–53

– 'The Literate Vikings' *Proceedings of the Sixth Viking Congress* (Uppsala, 1971) 69–78

Lindquist, Ivar *Religiösa runtexter* II: *Sparlösastenen* Skrifter utgivna av Veterenskaps Societeten i Lund XXIV (Lund, 1940)

Lydekker, Richard *The Ox and its Kindred* (London, 1912)

Magoun, Francis Peabody, Jr 'Bede's Story of Caedmon: the Case-History of an Anglo-Saxon Oral Singer' *Speculum* 30 (1955) 49–63

– 'The Oral Formulaic Character of Anglo-Saxon Narrative Poetry'
   Speculum 28 (1953) 446–67
Malmer, Brita 'A Contribution to the Numismatic History of Norway in the
   Eleventh Century' *Commentationes de nummis saeculorum IX–XI in*
   Suecia repertis I (Stockholm, 1961) 354–6
Mannhardt, W. *Der Baumkultus der Germanen und ihrer Nachbarstämme.*
   Wald- und Feldkulte I (Berlin, 1875)
Marquardt, Hertha *Die altenglischen Kenningar* Schriften der Königsberger
   Gelehrten Gesellschaft XIV, 3 (Halle/Saale, 1938) 103–340
– *Die Runeninschriften der Britischen Inseln. Bibliographie der*
   Runeninschriften nach Fundorten I Abhandlungen der Akademie der Wis-
   senschaften in Göttingen Philologisch-Historische Klasse Folge III, no. 48
   (Göttingen, 1961)
Marstrander, C.J.M. 'De nordiske runeinnskrifter i eldre alfabet' *Viking* 16
   (Oslo, 1953) 1–277
– 'Om runene og runenavnenes oprindelse' *Norsk tidsskrift för sprog-*
   videnskap I (1928) 85–188
Meaney, A.L. 'Woden in England: a Reconsideration of the Evidence'
   Folklore 77 (Summer, 1966) 105–15
Menner, R.J. *The Poetical Dialogues of Solomon and Saturn* The Modern
   Language Association of America Monograph Series XIII (New York, 1941)
Meroney, H. 'Early Irish Letter-Names' *Speculum* 24 (1949) 19–43
Migne, Jacques Paul *Patrologia cursus completus: Patrologia Latina* (Paris,
   1841–9)
Miller, E.J. *That Noble Cabinet: a History of the British Museum* (London,
   1973)
Miller, Thomas *The Old English Version of Bede's Ecclesiastical History of*
   the English People Early English Text Society OS XCV–XCVI (London, 1890)
Moltke, Erik 'De danske Runemønter og deres Praegere' *Nordisk numas-*
   matisk årsskrift (1950) 1–56
Musset, Lucien and F. Mossé *Introduction à la Runologie* Bibliothèque de
   Philologie Germanique XX (Paris, 1965)
Napier, A.S. *Wulfstan* Sammlung englischer Denkmäler in kritischen
   Ausgaben IV (Berlin, 1880)
Neckel, G. and H. Kuhn (eds) *Edda* 3rd ed (Heidelberg, 1962)
Ogilvy, J.D.A. *Books Known to the English, 597–1066* Mediaeval Academy
   of America Publications LXXVI (Cambridge, Mass., 1967)
Olsen, Magnus *Norges Innskrifter med de yngre Runer* 5 vols Norges Indskrif-
   ter indtil Reformationen Afd. II, 35, etc (Oslo, 1941–60)
– 'Runic Inscriptions in Great Britain, Ireland and the Isle of Man' *Viking*
   Antiquities in Great Britain and Ireland VI H. Shetelig (ed) (Oslo, 1954)
   153–233

Omont, Henri Poème anonyme sur les lettres de l'alphabet' *Bibliothèque de l'École des Chartes* 42 (Paris, 1881) 429–41

Owen, W.J.B. and J.W. Smyser (eds) *The Prose Works of William Wordsworth* (Oxford, 1974)

Page, R.I. 'The Inscriptions' Appendix A in D.M. Wilson *Anglo-Saxon Ornamental Metalwork 700–1100 in the British Museum* (London, 1964)

– *An Introduction to English Runes* (London, 1973)

– 'Language and Dating in Old English Inscriptions' *Anglia* 77 (1959) 385–406 (N.F. 65)

– 'The Old English Rune *ear*' *Medium Ævum* 30 (1961) 65–79

– 'The Old English Rune *ēoh, īh,* "yew tree"' *Medium Ævum* 37 (1968) 125–36

Page, T.E. (ed) *Tacitus' Dialogus, Agricola and Germania* Wm. Peterson (trans) Loeb Classical Library (London, 1932)

Paues, Anna 'The Name of the Letter 3' *Modern Language Review* 6 (1911) 441–54

Peace, A.S. *Cicero's De Divinatione* (Urbana, Illinois, 1920)

Philippson, Ernst Alfred *Germanisches Heidentum bei den Angelsachsen* Kölner Anglistische Arbeiten IV (Leipzig, 1929)

– 'Runenforschung und germanische Religionsgeschichte' *Publications of the Modern Language Association of America* 53 (1938) 321–32

Pitman, James Hall *The Riddles of Aldhelm* Yale Studies in English LXVII (New Haven, 1925)

Plaistowe, F.G. and A.F. Watt (eds) *Horace's Epistles and Ars Poetica* (London, [nd])

Pope, John Collins 'Palaeography and poetry: some solved and unsolved problems of the Exeter Book' *Mediaeval Scribes, Manuscripts and Libraries: Essays presented to N.R. Ker* M.B. Parkes and Andrew G. Watson (eds) (London, 1978) 25–65

– *The Rhythm of Beowulf* (New Haven, 1942)

Quintilian See Radermacher

Raby, Frederick J.E. *A History of Christian-Latin Poetry from the Beginnings to the Close of the Middle Ages* (Oxford, 1953)

Radermacher, Ludwig (ed) *Quintilian's Institutiones Oratiae* (Leipzig, 1971)

Redbond, W.J. 'Notes on the Word "eolhx"' *Modern Language Review* 31 (1936) 55–7

Ryan, J.S. 'Othin in England' *Folklore* 14 (Autumn, 1963) 460–80

Schneider, Karl *Die Germanischen Runennamen: Versuch einer Gesamtdeutung* (Meisenheim am Glan, 1956)

Schulze, Wilhelm *Kleine Schriften* (Göttingen, 1934)

Scotus See Baehrens and Omont

Searle, W.G. *Onomasticon Anglo-Saxonicum* (Cambridge, 1897)

Sechnall (Secundus) See Bernard and Dreves

Sedulius See Dreves

Shetelig, H. and H. Falk *Scandinavian Archaeology* E.V. Gordon (trans) (Oxford, 1937)

Sievers, Eduard *Altgermanische Metrik* (Halle, 1893)

– 'Zur Rhythmik des germanischen Alliterationsverses II' *Beiträge zur Geschichte der deutschen Sprache und Literatur* 10 (1885) 451–545

Sisam, Celia *The Vercelli Book* Early English Manuscripts in Facsimile XIX (Copenhagen, 1976)

Sisam, Kenneth 'Cynewulf and his Poetry' *Studies in the History of Old English Literature* (Oxford, 1953) 1–28

– 'Humphrey Wanley' *Studies in the History of Old English Literature* (Oxford, 1953) 259–77

– Review of R.J. Menner's *The Poetical Dialogues of Solomon and Saturn* in *Medium Ævum* 13 (1944) 28–36

Skeat, T.C. *The Catalogues of the Manuscript Collections* rev ed (Trustees of the British Museum, 1962)

Skeat, W.W. 'The Order of Letters in the Runic Futhork' *The Academy* 38 (London, 1890) 477

Smith, Thomas *Catalogus Librorum Manuscriptorum Bibliothecae Cottonianae* (Oxford, 1696)

Snorri Sturluson *Edda* See Brodeur and Holtsmark

– *Ynglingasaga* See Wessén

Söderberg, Sven and Erik Brate *Ölands Runinskrifter* Sveriges Runinskrifter I (Stockholm, 1900–6)

Söderberg, Sven, Erik Brate, Elias Wessén, and others *Sveriges Runinskrifter utgivna av Kungl. Veterhets Historie och Antikvitets Akademien* I–XIII (Stockholm, 1900–). (For individual volumes, see under Brate, Jansson, Jungner, Kinander, Söderberg, Wessén)

Stanley, E.G. 'Old English Poetic Diction and the Interpretation of *The Wanderer, The Seafarer* and *The Penitent's Prayer*' *Anglia* 78 (1955) 413–66

Stephens, George *The Old Northern Runic Monuments of Scandinavia and England* 4 vols (London, Copenhagen, and Lund, 1866–1901)

Storms, Gottfried *Anglo-Saxon Magic* (The Hague, 1948)

Sweet, Henry *The Oldest English Texts* Early English Text Society OS LXXXIII (London, 1885)

Tacitus See T.E. Page

Tatwine See Hahn

Thorpe, Benjamin *Homilies of the Anglo-Saxon Church* (London, 1843–6)

Thurneysen, R. 'Zum Ogom' *Beiträge zur Geschichte der deutschen Sprache und Literatur* 61 (1937) 188–208

Tolkien, J.R.R. 'Sigelwara Land' *Medium Ævum* 3 (1934) 95–106

Vietor, Wilhelm *Die Northumbrischen Runensteine* Beiträge zur Textkritik, Grammatik und Glossar (Marburg, 1895)

Vigfusson, Gudbrand and F. York Powell *Corpus Poeticum Boreale* 2 vols (New York, 1965)

Volsungasaga See Finch

Wanley, Humphrey *Antiquae Literaturae Septentrionalis Liber Alter seu Humphredi Wanleii Librorum Veterum Septentrionalium, qui in Angliae Bibliothecis extant, nec non multorum Veterum Codicum Septentrionalium alibi extantium Catalogus Historico Criticus* (Oxford, 1705)

Wessén, Elias *Runstenen vid Röks kyrka* (Stockholm, 1958)

– *Snorri Sturluson's Ynglingasaga* Nordisk filologi Ser. A, no. 6 (Stockholm and Copenhagen, 1952)

Wessén, E. and Sven B.F. Jansson *Upplands Runinskrifter* Sveriges Runinskrifter VI–IX (Stockholm, 1940–58)

White, H.G.E. (ed) *Ausonius* Loeb Classical Library (London, 1919)

Wilbur, Terence H. 'The Word "rune"' *Scandinavian Studies* 29 (1957) 12–18

William of Malmesbury See Hamilton

Wilson, D.M. *The Archaeology of Anglo-Saxon England* (London, 1976)

– 'A Group of Anglo-Saxon Amulet Rings' *The Anglo-Saxons* Peter Clemoes (ed) (Cambridge, 1959) 159–70

Wimmer, Ludwig F.A. *Runeskriftens Oprindelse og Udvekling i Norden* (Copenhagen, 1874)

– *Die Runenschrift* Revised and enlarged edition of *Runeskriftens* (above), translated out of the original Danish into German by F. Holthausen (Berlin, 1887)

Wordsworth, William See Owen

Wrenn, C.L. 'Late Old English Rune-Names' *Medium Ævum* 1 (1932) 24–34

Wright, Cyril Edward *Bald's Leech Book* Early English Manuscripts in Facsimile V (Copenhagen, 1955)

Wright, T. and R.P. Wülker *Anglo-Saxon and Old English Vocabularies* 2 vols (London, 1884)

Wulfstan See Napier

Ynglingasaga See Wessén

McMaster Old English Studies and Texts

CPSIA information can be obtained
at www.ICGtesting.com
Printed in the USA
BVHW082349270822
645598BV00007B/929

9 781487 592684